THE CREATIVE BLACK BOOK® 1989

PRINT · PHOTOGRAPHY · ILLUSTRATION · TV

Copyright © The Creative Black Book 1989
We are not responsible for errors or omissions.
All rights reserved.
The Creative Black Book, 401 Park Avenue South, New York, NY 10016
(212) 684-4255 Facsimile (212) 481-4296
Telex 230199 SWIFT UR Attn: CBB
President: James J. Pfister
Director of Finance and Administration: John Frenville
Creative Director: Joseph S. Napolitano
Advertising Sales Director: Joy Baker
Marketing Director: Maria Reveley
Sales:
Sales Administration Manager: Maria Ragusa
Sales Representatives: Caroline Hauser, Janie Celeste Hewson, Sandy Jaffe,
Linda Kaufman, Linda Levy, Allegra Wilde, Juliette Wolf
Sales Administrative Staff: Alice Bilodeau, Julia Fisher,
Deborah Lynn Haley, Stacey Hunter, Lynn Hyzer,
Juliette Robbins, Mara Roldan
Production:
Production Director: Meggin Chinkel Siefert
Production Staff: Cathy Citarella, Lynn Feinberg, Carol Schultheiss
Studio:
Studio Manager: Celia Brayley
Studio Artists: Patricia McShea, Cynthia Rhett
Administrative:
Controller: Chet D. Krinsky
Accounting Manager: Lea Pavlides
Project Coordinator: Lecia Wood
Administrative Staff: Russell Brown, Judy Chin, Florence Johnson, Karen Price,
Kirk Oliphant, Maureen Simmons, Donnell White

The Creative Black Book is distributed worldwide by:
The Creative Black Book
401 Park Avenue South, New York, NY 10016
(212) 684-4255
Telex 230199 SWIFT UR Attn: CBB
Facsimile: (212) 481-4296

The Creative Black Book
is a trademark of The Creative Black Book
which is registered in the U.S. Patent and Trademark Office

THE CREATIVE BLACK BOOK® 1989

The Creative Black Book
is a trademark of The Creative Black Book
which is registered in the U.S. Patent and Trademark Office
ISBN (Portfolio Edition) 0-916098-38-9
ISSN (Portfolio Edition) 0740-283X
Much of the art work contained in this publication
is protected by prior copyright in the name of the artist,
and is reproduced here with permission.
No art shown in this publication may be reproduced in any form
without first obtaining the permission of the artist.

Printed in Italy by Arnoldo Mondadori Editore Verona.

CONTENTS

GRAPHICS
DESIGN PAGE **3**
ILLUSTRATION PAGE **17**
STUDIO SERVICES PAGE **129**

PHOTOGRAPHY
ORIGINAL PAGE **141**
STOCK PAGE **957**

PRINTS
RETOUCHERS PAGE **973**
PRINTERS PAGE **989**
LOCATION & **CASTING** PAGE **999**
BACKDROPS PAGE **1,005**
PROPS PAGE **1,013**

TELEVISION
LIVE ACTION PAGE **1,027**
ANIMATION PAGE **1,067**
MUSIC & **SOUND** PAGE **1,085**

INDEX

2H Studio, 54-55
Affatato, Tom, 372-373
Aguanno, Tony, 960-961
Ahlberg, Ron, 442-443
Aiko, 1069
Albert, Jade, 194-195
Alexander Photography, 593
Alsop, Mark E., 24
Altamore, Bob, 456-457
Altman, Ben SPG, 640-641
Altman, Elizabeth Associates, 638-641
Altoriso, Cynthia, 1006-1007
Ameijide, Raymond, 112-113
American Artists, 56
Ammirati, Robert, 324-325
Anderson, Kathryn, 668, 795
Anderson, Richard, 38-39
André, Bruce Photography, Inc., 700-701
Anton, Jerry, 524-525
Appleoff, Sandy, 42
Arciero, Tony, 220-221
Aresu, Paul, 372-373
Aresu/Goldring Studio, 372-373
Aristo, Donna, 536-537
Arndt, Jim, 594-597
Art Farm, The, 140
Ash, Michael, 590-591, 622-623, 718-721, 748-749
Astrow, Dana, 1033-1036
Aubry, Daniel, 320
Avis, Paul, 260-261
Backes, Nick, 34-35
Baker, Chuck, 446-447
Baldwin, Joel, 172-173
Baraban, Joe, 928-929
Barasa, Mary Ann, 642-643
Bartels, Ceci Associates, Inc., 56, 61-74, 86, 376-377, 1024, 1056-1075
Barton, Paul, 386-387
Baseman, Gary, 93
Bassinson Productions, 754-755
Bate, Brad, 1046
Bates, Harry, 82
Bean, John, 296-297
Beautiful People Unlimited, Inc., 1001
Beebower Brothers, 886-889
Belk, Michael, 358-359
Bell, Tony, 864-865
Benson, Hank, 858-859
Benson, Robin, 1047
Berman, David Films, Inc., 1055
Berman, Howard, 242-245

Bernstein & Andriulli, Inc., 262-267
Bernstein, Steve, 996
Bethe, Lori, 1087
Bevan, Paul, 156-159
Bibikow, Walter, 546-547
Bieber, Tim, 622-623
Biernat, Anna, 691
Big City Films, 1058-1063
Big City Productions, 238-255
Big Deahl Productions, 1028-1031
Bishop, David, 426-427
Björkman, Steve, 100-101
Blachut, Dennis, 196-197
Blackman, Barry, 414-415
Blackman, Jeffrey E., 332-333
Blakeley, Jim, 812-813
Blaustein, John, 870-873
Bliss, Jan, 644-647
Block Film Group, The, 1069
Bloncourt, Nelson, 500-501
Bobbé, Leland, 176-177
Boehm, Roger, 50
Bohm, Linda, 492-493
Boies, Alex, 18
Bole, Cliff, 1045
Borow, Mark, 1021
Bosch, Peter, 204-205
Bowles, Douglas A., 53
Boyer, Susan, 272-273
Bradley Printing Company, The, 989-992
Brady, Steve, 190-191
Bramhall, William, 108
Breitrose, Howard, 484-485
Brello, Ron Jr., 364-365
Brenckman, Rick, 1087
Bright, James Backgrounds, 1008
Bringham, Jerry, 21
Broderson, Charles, 1006-1007
Brody, Richard, 366-369
Bronstein, Steve, 238-241
Brock Model Works, 1022-1023
Brou Productions, Inc., 48
Brown, Doug, 196-203, 926-927
Brown, Helena, 1033-1036
Brown, Michael David, 112-113
Brown, Nancy, 592
Brown, Peter, 103
Bruml, Kathy, 568-569
Bruning, Bill, 72
Bruno Photography, Inc., 342-343
Budnik, Victor, 726-729
Burchill, Linda, 626-629
Burlingham, Tricia, 748-755
Burnett, David, 218-219
Busacca, Mary, 744-747

Busch, Lon, 112-113
Bush, Charles William, 818-819
Buzzco Associates, Inc., 1072
Byrnes, Charles, 1058-1063
Cadd, Ray, 44-45
Cadge, Jeff,.308-309
Cafarelli, Vincent, 1072
Cahill, Joe, 540-541
Cailor, Jerry, 456-457
Cailor/Resnick Studio, 456-457
Caldwell, Jordan, 1079
Campbell, Barbara, 294-295
Caplan, Skip, 454-455
Caputo, Elise, 184-191
Carmel, 410-411
Carney Film, 636-637
Carney, Joann, 636-637
Carp, Stan, 868-869
Carpenter, Brent, 1013
Carr, Robb, 974-975
Cary & Co., 75
Casalini, Tom, 612-613
Casey, Marge Associates, 502-513
Cassandra, Agency, 1002
CatPak Studio, 70-71
Cecchini, Roberto, 1038-1039
Celluloid Animation Studios, 1077
Chalfant, Flip, 894-895
Chalkin, Dennis Studio, 286-287
Charles, Lisa, 502-503
Chase-Lalanne, Millicent, 814-815
Chechik, Jeremiah, 1038-1039
Chelnik, Marc, 1070
Chilvers, Colin, 1047
Christensen, Paul, 316-317
Christine, 856-857
Chrynwski, Walt, 330-331
Chung, Ken-Lei, 856-857
Ciccarelli, Gary, 56
City Limit Productions, 536-537
Clark, Marty, 920
Clemens, Clint, 476-479
Clifford, Geoffrey, 504-505
CoCo, 314-319
Cobb & Friend, 1058-1063
Cobb, Jan, 259
Cochran, Bobbye & Assoc., 46-47
Cody, Dennie, 955
Cohen, Bruce, 398-399
Cohen, James, 390-391
Cohen, Stewart Charles, 946-947
Cohn, Ric, 480-481
Coleman, Woody Presents, Inc., 58
Colen, Corinne, 146-147
Collier, Jan, 30-32
Collignon, Daniele, 17

Collins, Chris, 336-337
Comp Art Plus, 132-133
Comp Factory, The, 130
Considine, Carol, 398-399
Constantinos, 877
Continuity Graphic Assocs., Inc.,
    87, 138-139
Contoräkes, George, 926-927
Contrino, Tom, 340-341
Cook, Kathleen Norris, 778-779
Cook, Warren, 778-779
Coppock, Ron, 840-841
Corcoran, Arlene, 23, 622-623
Corey, Carl Film, Inc., 680-683
Corey, Carl Photography, Inc.,
    680-683
Cosgrove, Dan, 17
Cowan, Frank Studio, Inc., 512-513
Creative Advantage, The, Inc., 76
Crecco, Michael, 182-183
Crockett, David, 131
Crofton, Bill, 669
Crum, Lee, 924-925
Csicsko, David Lee, 22
Culberson, Earl, 246-249
Cummins, Jim, 828-829
D'Orio, Tony, 616-617
Dai Nippon, 993
Dakota Productions, 904-905
Dakota, Irene, 904-905
Dakota, Michael, 904-905
Dale, Robert, 27
Dallison, Ken, 112-113
Datoli, Michael, 558-559
Davis, Jack, 112-113
De Leon, Katrina, 318-319
de Wys, Leo Inc., 962-963
DeMuth, Michelle, 484-485,
    546-547
Debold, Bill, 634-635
Debold, Cindy.& Associates,
    634-635
Demarest, Chris, 108
Derhacopian, Ron, 837
Deschamps, Bob, 112-113
Design Photography, 668, 795
Devlin, Bill, 112-113
Devlin, Jeff, 1047
DiComo, Charles, 132-133
Diamond Art Studio, 12-13
Diaz, Rick, 912-913
Dickens, Holly Design, 4-5
Dictenberg, Robin, 146-155
Diez, Fernando, 902
Directing Artists, 1028-1031
Domingo, Ray, 112-113

Dorr, Chuck, 428-429
Doty, Eldon, 44-45
Douglass, Dirk, 788-789
Douglass, Karen, 1053
Drew, Terry David, 624
Driving Incorporated, USA, 1016
DuBroff, Don SPG, 638-641
Dublin, Rick, 625
Ducoté, Kim, 487
Duggan, Lee, 112-113
Duka, Lonnie, 756-757
Duke, Dana, 526-527
Durrance, Dick II, 560-561
Dwiggins, Gene, 498-499
Dynamic Duo Studio, Inc., The, 105
Eastman, George, 1074
Easy-Writer Music, Inc., 1087
Eaton & Iwen, Inc., 986-987
Ebel Productions Inc., 1056-1057
Edahl, Ed, 360-361
Edson, Steven, 362-363
Eldridge, 120-125
Ella, 516-519
Elledge, Paul, 692-693
Energy Productions, 1078
Engel, Mary, 256-257, 364-365
Englert, Michael, 468
Englert, Timothy, 468
Epstein, Rhoni, 818-819
Erickson, Jim, 922-923
Errico, Jerry, 536-537
Evans, Marty, 817
Ewert, Steve, 706-707
Exit Productions, Inc., 434-435
FPG International, 971
Farber, Robert, 532-535
FeBland, David, 116-117
Feldman, Ken, 698-699, 776-777
Feldman, Robert, 344-345
Fellerman, Stan, 404-405
Felt, Jim, 620-621
Fennimore, Linda, 90-91
Fernsell, Robin, 420-423
Fiat, Randi & Associates, 22-23, 586-589, 608-613, 900-901
Film Search/The Image Bank, 1027
Finneran, Kathy & Bill, 1014-1015
Fione, Dan, 59
Fischer, Carl, 430-431
Fishman, Chuck, 538-539
Fleder, Gary, 1046
Focus on Sports, Inc., 957
Forastieri, Marili, 520-521
Forbes, Patti, 1089
Forelli, Chip, 542-543
Forrest, David, 1089

Foster, Richard, 1040-1043
Foster, Stephen, 6-7
Foster, Susan, 110
Foulke, Douglas, 352-353
Fowler, Carl, 668, 795
France, Jeff, 1062-1063
Fraser, Doug, 30-31
Fraser, Renée, 141
Fredrickson, Mark, 65
Freidman, Eric, 442-443
Friedlander, Ernie, 736-737
Friedman, Harold Consortium, Ltd., 1081
Friedman, Rufus D., 1081
Froomer, Brett, 272-273
Fruzyna, Frank, 74
Funk, Mitchell, 346-347
Funny Farm, 44-45
G.M.S., 1047
GFI Graphics for Industry, 129
Galante, Dennis, 552-553
Galton, Beth, 402-403
Galvin, Kevin, 370-371
Garcia, Elma, 860-863
Gardner, Derek, 216-217
Gardner, Jean, 740-741
Gebbia, Doreen, 412-413
Geiger, Michael, 514-515
Gelberg, Bob, 930-931
Gem Studio, Inc., 136-137
Gemignani, Joe, 941
Gerczynski, Tom, 794
Getsug, Don Studios, 684-685
Giddens, Jim, 1047
Girvin, Tim, 96-97
Glass, Leora, 1033-1036
Glass, Randy, 78
Glenn, C.W. & Associates, 624
Glenn, Eileen, 686-687
Glick, Ivy, 812-813
Globus Brothers Studios, 395
Gold, Charles, 474-475
Goldring, Barry, 372-373
Goldsmith, Lynn, 310-311
Gomberg, Susan, 27
Gomez, Rick, 952-953
Goodwin, Phyllis, 516-519
Gorman, Greg, 750-751
Gottlieb, Dennis, 393-394
Graber, Jack, 76
Graham, Corey, 776-777
Graham, Mariah Studio, 81
Graham, Stephen, 690
Gray, Dennis, 868-869
Gray, Mitchel Ltd., 262-263
Gray, Walter, 658-659

Green, Richard, 1087
Greka-Walter, Kiki, 398-399
Greller, Fred, 976-977
Grigg, Robert L., 748-749
Grohe, Stephen F., 376-377
Gross, Cy, 488-489
Grubaugh, Kurt, 23, 866-867
Gunne, Jack, 1047
H.S.I., 1033-1036
Haefner, James, 660-661
Hagio, Kunio, 120-121
Haiman, Todd Merritt, 490-491
Hainey, Dan, 1047
Halbert, Michael, 26
Hall, Marni & Associates, 79, 820-821, 868-869
Hallstein, 956
Hamilton, Mark, 469
Hamilton, Susan, 418-419
Hampton, Laurie, 770-771
Hankin, Jamie, 496-497
Hansen, Wendy, 392
Hanson, Jim and Talent, 432-433 802-803, 808-809
Hanson, Wendy, 680-683
Hardiman, Miles, 49
Harlib, Joel & Assoc., 33-40, 78, 606-607, 748-749, 817
Harmon, Rodd, 212-213
Harrington, Lois, 842-843
Harrington, Marshall, 842-843
Harris, Matthew, 1033-1036
Harris, Michael, 234-235
Hashi Studio, Inc., 268-269
Haskins, Sam, 437
Hathon, Elizabeth, 482-483
Hauser, Marc, 610-611
Hausman, George, 442-443
Havlicek, Karel, 33
Hawker, Christopher, 626-629
Heath, Peter, 1047
Heath, R. Mark, 28, 130
Heffernan Films, 722-725, 1048-1051
Heffernan, Terry, 722-725, 1048-1051
Heisler, Gregory, 590-591
Henderson, Chip, 948-949
Henderson, Eric, 934
Henderson/Muir Photography, 948-949
Hernandez, Raymond, 3
Heuberger, William, 554-555
Heyert, Elizabeth, 300-301
Hill, Jim, 648-649, 1045
Hine, Skip, 550-551
Hing, Edward, 562-563

Hing/Norton Photography, 562-563
Hoff, Terry, 20
Hoffman, Paul, 744-747
Hofmann, Ginnie, 112-113
Holden, Andrew, 854-855
Holland, Mary, 836
Holland, Robert, 940
Holt, Rita, 216-223
Holtzman Stavros, Inc., 1033-1036
Holtzman, Henry, 1033-1036
Holzemer, Buck, 688-689
Hood, Robin, 916-917
Hooper, Thomas, 506-507
Hopson, Melissa, 776-777
Horikawa, Michael D., 808-809
Huber, Vic, 792-793
Hudson, Bill & Associates, 1038-1039
Huerta, Gerard, 54-55
Huet, John, 326-327
Hughes, April & Assocs., 736-737
Hughes, Judy, 458-459
Huibregtse, Jim, 500-501
Hulsey, Kevin, 75
Hurewitz, Gary, 238-255
Huyssen, Roger, 54-55
Hyatt, Nadine, 817-819
Hylén, Bo, 762-763
Ikeda, Shig, 540-541
Image Bank, The, 224-225, 592, 776-777, 1027
Ink Tank, The, 1067
Innervision Productions, Inc., 1054
Iooss, Walter, 170-171
Izui Photography, Inc., 656-657
Izui, Richard, 656-657
Jedell, Joan, 817-823, 918-919
Jenkins, Bill, 70-71, 1024
Jimison, Tom, 903
Johnson, Arlene, 586-587
Johnson, Forest, 910-911
Jones, Aaron, 202-203
Jones, Harrison, 642-643
Jones, Lou, 304-305
Jordano, Dave, 672-673
Joy Art Music, Ltd., 1090
Judd, 280-281
KCMP Productions, Ltd., 1079
Kahan, Eric, 312-313
Kahn, Harvey, 476-479
Kalish, Lionel, 112-113
Kamin, Vincent & Assocs., 100-101, 104, 322-323, 408, 560-561, 672-673 866-867, 904-905
Kamper, George, 406-407
Kan Photography, Inc., 416-417

Kaplan, Alan, 264-265
Kaplan, Carol, 420-423
Kaplan, Holly, 342-343
Kaplan, Peter B., 256-257
Kasnot, Keith, 68
Katrina, 318-319
Kawachi, Yutaka, 494-495
Kazu Studio, Ltd., 632-633
Kearney, Mitchell, 936-937
Keith, Kelly, 826-827
Keith, Ken, 620-621
Kelley, Barbara, 57
Kelly/Mooney, 466-467
Kemper, Bud, 124-125
Kendrick, Robb, 900-901
Kenney, John & Associates, 928-929
Kerr, Ralph, 298-299
Killeen, Tom, 124-125
Kimball, Ron, 760-761
Kimmelman, Dotty, 1079
Kimmelman, Phil, 1079
Kinast, Susan, 650-651
Kinetics, 1074
King, Jennifer Susan, 717
Kjollesdal, Hallstein A., 956
Klanderman, Leland, 73
Kleber, John, 23
Klein, Matthew, 182-183
Klem, Tom The Modelmaker, 1017
Kloc, Howard, 691
Klocworks, 691
Knable, Ellen & Associates, 78, 822-824
Knight, Harrison, 294-295
Knudson, Kent, 796-797
Koeffler, Ann, 776-777
Kohler, Chris, 920
Kojima, Tak, 180-181
Kolansky, Palma, 428-429
Konishi, Angie, 656-657
Korman, Alison, 426-427
Koster, Aaron, 118
Kozan, Dan, 258
Kozyra, James, 188-189
Kramer, Joan & Associates, 970
Krantz, Jim Studios, Inc., 666-667
Krasner, Carin, 752-753
Kraus, Brian, 384-385
Kreis, Ursula, 406-407
Kriegshauser, Shannon, 66-67
Krongard, Paula, 352-355
Krongard, Steve, 432-433
Kubinyi, Laszlo, 112-113
Kufner, Gary, 878-881
Kugel, Candy, 1072

Kuhn, Chuck, 776-777, 1045
Kuhn, Peter, 1016
Kulp, Curtis, 1046
Kuntzsch, John, 1022-1023
Kurtz & Friends, 1069
La Ferla, Sandro, 1009
Lackow, Andy, 84-85
Laidman, Allan, 758-759
Lambert, Mary, 1033-1036
Lamotte, Michael, 814-815
Landecker, Tom, 784-785
Langley, David, 522-523
Lanker, Brian, 152-155
Lanpher, Keith, 938-939
Larkin, Mary, 462-465
Lashua, Sonia, 424-425
Latorre, Robert, 954
Laurance, Bruce, 436
Lawder, John & Assoc., 770-771
Lawfer, Larry, 448-449
Lawlor on Location, Inc., 754-755
Lawlor, John, 754-755
Lawson, Jim, 668, 795
Le-Tan, Pierre, 108
LeBon, David, 846-847
Leach, David, 586-589
Lee, Jared D., 126
Lee, Rhea, 1033-1036
Leff, Jerry Assocs., Inc., 114
Lemkowitz, Laura, 336-337
Lemmon, John Films, 1068
Lerman, Gary, 259
Lester, Mike, 51
Levy, Franck, 444-445
Levy, Richard, 284-285
Lewin, Elyse, 820-821
Leyser, Ron, 1060-1061
Lieberman, Jerry Productions, 1073
Lindgren & Smith, 30-31
Locations Extrordinaire, 1000
Logan, Kevin, 378-379
Look & Company, 1091
Loonan, Dennis, 1053
Lorenz, Lee, 112-113
Loumakis, Constantinos, 877
Loven, Paul, 836
Lukmann, Geri, 1013
Luppino, Michael, 508-509
Luria, Dick Photography, Inc., 270-271
Lynch, Larry & Andrea, 818-819
Lyons, Roger, 1033-1036
M&M Productions, 898-899
MZH&F, 1089
Madris, Stephen, 570-571
Main Street Productions, Inc., 1052

Maisel, Jay, 178-179, 958-959
Major League Productions, Inc., 1046
Maloney, Tom & Associates, 684-685
Malyszko, Mike, 458-459
Manhattan Model Shop, 1014-1015
Maniatis, Michael, 1018-1019
Mann, Ken, 146-155
Manno, John, 208-211
Marí, Victoria, 1090
Marathon Recording, 1089
Mardon, Allan, 112-113
Maresca, Frank, 544-545
Marie, Barbara, 75
Markow, Paul, 838-839
Marsden, Dominic, 740-741
Martel, Maureen, 160-175
Martha Productions, 23
Martin, Bard, 382-383
Martinez, Oskar, 307
Masters, Charles, 462-463
Maurizio, Cynthia, 1070
McBain/Sharpe, 758-759
McCallum, John, 708-709
McCarthy, Tom, 918-919
McConnell & Borow, Inc., 1021
McCormick, Ned, 226-227
McDermott, John, 798-799
McDonnell, Patrick, 19
McGrath, Judy, 674-679
McGuire, Gary, 852-853
McKay, Colleen, 520-521
McMasters, Deborah, 1040-1043
McNaughton, Toni, 806-807
McWilliams, Clyde Studio, 982-983
McWilliams/Welbeck Associates, Inc., 982-983
Mead, Joyce, 960-961
MediChrome, 968-969
Mehlman, Elwyn, 112-113
Meisel, Paul, 108
Melillo, Nicholas, 580-581
Menda, George, 418-419
Mendheim, Michael, 104
Menken, Howard, 516-517
Mennemeyer, Ralph & Associates, 314-319
Meo, Frank, 324-325
Meola, Eric, 168-169
Merjos, Stavros, 1033-1036
Meyerson, Arthur, 882-883
Michal, Marie, 112-113
Michelson, Eric, 564-565
Midnight Oil Studios, 14
Miller, Peter Darley, 851

Miller, Randy, 892-893
Miller, Richard, 710-711
Miller, Scott, 1047
Miller, Susan, 398-399
Milroy/McAleer, 768-769
Mimms, Melissa, 899
Minh Studio, 392
Mitchell, Dean, 124-125
Mizono, Robert, 772-775
Mondadori, 994-995
Morawski, Mike, 748-749
Morello, Joe, 566-567
Morgan, Jay P., 826-827
Morgan, Jeff, 302-303
Morris, Leonard, 460-461
Morrison, Rick, 254-255
Morrison, Ted, 314-315
Morrow, Skip, 77
Moss, Peter, 1038-1039
Mougin, Claude, 166-167
Mucchi, Fabio, 572-573
Muir, Steve, 948-949
Mulligan, Joseph, 298-299
Muna, R.J., 730-733
Munk, David, 758-759
Murawski, Alex, 112-113
Murphy, Dennis, 932-933
Murphy, Sally, 706-707
Myers, Lou, 112-113
Nadler, Jeff, 822-823
Nahoum, Ken, 470-473
Nathan, Eunice, 366-371
Neary, Jeanne, 1091
Neaves, Ed, 942-943
Neleman, Hans, 156-159
Nichols, Chet, 1076
Nichols, Garry, 124-125
Nicolini, Sandra, 670-671
Niefield, Terry, 344-345
Nienkirchen, Red, 1087
No Soap Productions, 1085
Noble, Richard, 718-721
Noonan, Julia, 102
Norton, Janine, 562-563
Norwood, Nick, 944-945
Nozicka, Steve, 606-607
O'Neill, Michael, 160-161
O'Rourke Page Associates, 808-809
O'Rourke, Gene, 808-809
Officer, Hollis, 602-603
Oliphant Backdrops, 1005
Oliphant Backdrops (BCPS), 1005
Oliphant Backdrops (Pan Pacific), 1005
Olive Jar Animation, 1075

Olof Wahlund Photography, Inc., 214-215
Opus III, 1092
Ores, Kathy, 716
Ovation Films, Inc., 1080
Padys, Diane, 162-165
Page Associates, 437, 452-453
Page, Jackie, 437
Pahmer, Hal-GFI, 129
Papadopolous, Peter, 184-187
Parham, Kevin, 1070
Parsons, John, 114
Paul, Reid, 1046
Pearson, Lee, 804-805
Peck, Everett, 52
Pelosi & Chambers, 906-907
Penny & Stermer Group, The, 80, 102
Pepera, Fred, 36-37
Perier, Jean-Marie, 1038-1039
Perkins, Ray, 678-679
Perno, Jack, 676-677
Perweiler, Gary, 434-435
Petöe, Dénes, 228-233
Peters, Bob, 112-113
Peterson, Grant, 568-569
Peterson, Vicki, 516-519, 820-821
Petricone, Art, 1080
Petroff Photography, 670-671
Petrucelli, Tony, 236-237, 780-783
Photo Researchers, Inc., 964-965
Photocom, 802-803
Picture Perfect/RV Rental, 1000
Pierce, Richard, 440-441
Pilossof, Judd, 280-281
Pinkney, Jerry, 112-113
Pitts, Ellyn, 278-279
Plotkin, Bruce, 412-413
Pool, Linda, 604-605
Pope, Kevin, 64
Poplis, Paul, 702-703
Porto, James, 578-579
Potts, Carolyn, 708-709
Powers, Guy, 410-411
Pribble, Laurie, 100-101
Probert, Jean, 62
Prop Art, 1021
Prop Shop, The, 1020
Pruzan, Michael, 174-175
Puro, Norina, 89
Quon, Mike, 10-11
Raab, Michael, 282-283
Rabin, Bill & Associates, 636-637, 818-819, 928-929
Radencich, Michael, 604-605
Rajs, Jake, 290-291

Randall, Bob Photography, 816
Raphaele/Digital Transparencies, Inc, 978-979
Rapp, Gerald & Cullen, Inc., 111-113, 119
Rascona Studio, 742-743
Ravenhill, Helen, 92
Ravon, Jean-Michel, 1038-1039
Rawi·Sherman (U.S.A.) Inc., 1037
Rawi·Sherman Films Inc., 1037
Raycroft, Jim, 452-453
Red Circle Studios, 321-323
Reid, Ken, 698-699
Renard Represents, 94-101
Resnick, Elliot, 456-457
Rezny, Aaron, 524-525
Rhythm & Hues, Inc., 1076
Riccio, Kathryn, 1076
Richmond, Jack, 548-549
Rickles, Tom, 921
Riley, Edward T., Inc., 108
Ritter, Robin, 278-283
Robb, Steve, 338-339
Robbins, Bill, 738-739
Robinson, James, 570-571
Robinson, Madeleine, 776-777
Rodriguez, Robert, 95
Romero, Javier, 8-9
Rose, Uli, 396-397
Rosenberg, Arlene, 390-391
Rosenman, Marjorie, 838-839
Rosenthal, Barry Studio, 438-439
Rosner, Eric H., Inc., 556-557
Ross, Larry, 109
Rotundo, Tony, 764-767
Rubin, Al, 212-213
Rubin, Kathy, 1047
Rubin, Laurie, 608-609
Rush, Michael, 704-705
Rusing Photography, 866-867
Russell, John, 864-865
Russo, Karen, 474-475, 560-561
Rutherford, Mike, 942-943
Ryan & Friends, 1071
Ryan, Steve, 540-541
Rysinski, Edward, 306
Sacco, Kevin, 131
Sacramone, Dario, 334-335
Sadin Photo Group, Ltd., 638-641
Sadin, Abby SPG, 638-639
Sahaida, Michael, 321
Salinas, Bruno, 108
Salzman, Richard W., 52-53
Samerjan, Peter, 844-845
Samuels, Rosemary, 402-403
Sanchez, Kevin, 786-787

Sander, Vicki, 208-211
Sanders, Kathy, 716
Sanders, Paul, 824
Sandwick, Bill, 1033-1036
Santa-Donato Studios, Paul, Inc., 134-135
Santore, Charles, 112-113
Sartan, Edward, 258
Sato, Susumu, 350-351
Savage, Clinton, 321-323
Saxon, Robert, 558-559
Scarlett, Nora, 288-289
Schackmann, Shirley, 1076
Scharf, Linda, 83
Schelling, Susan, 734-735
Schewe, Jeff, 654-655
Schiavone, George, 884-885
Schofield, Glen A., 115
Schumer, Arlen, 105
Schwab, Michael, 98-99
Schwartzberg, Louis, 1078
Scott, Denis, 648-649
Scott, Freda, 20-21, 726-735
Secunda, Shel, 348-349
Sedelmaier, J.J., 1067
Segerstrom, Rebecca, 350-351
Sehven, August, 326-327
Seidman, Barry, 276-277
Seidman, Billy & Co., 1089
Seltzer, Abe Studios, Inc., 198-201
Shadow Light Productions, 1070
Shanahan, Nancy, 802-803
Shapiro, Bonnie, 238-255
SharpShooters, 788-789, 878-881, 898, 908-909, 912-913, 941, 950-953, 966-967
Shepherd, Judith, 393-394
Shooting Star Productions, Inc., 1053
Short, Skip, 1047
Shotwell, Charles, 598-601
Siciliano, Ric, 1070
Siegel Photographic, Inc., 832-835
Siegel, David, 832-833
Silverman Productions, 1044
Silverman, Jay Productions, 764-767
Simon, Debra, 396-397
Simpson, Jerry, 576-577
Sirrell, Terry, 86
Skillicorn Associates, 616-619, 754-755, 828-829
Skogsbergh, Ulf, 356-357
Skott, Michael, 450-451
Small, David, 108
Smith, Emily, 206-207

Smith, Jeff, 206-207
Smith, Ralph, 890-891
Smith, Richard Hamilton, 644-647
Smith, Sean, 374-375
Snowberger, Ann, 622-623, 692-693
Snyder, Celia S., 790-793
Soldat, Rick, 700-701
Solomon, Adele, 1070
Solomon, Debra, 60
Soluri, Tony, 674-675
Somekh, Ric, 408
Sorensen, Dickson, 1038-1039
Source Force, The, 258
Spano/Roccanova Retouching, Inc., 973
Spelman, Steve, 278-279
Spierman, Shelley, 488-489
Sports Chrome, 960-961
Sprouls, Kevin, 106-107
St. John Associates, 462-465
St. John, Lynn, 464-465
Standart, Joe, 322-323
StatCat, 1024
Steele, Robert G., 32
Steigman, Steve, 1058-1059
Stephens, Nancy, 398-399
Stern, Laszlo, 486
Stewart, Tom, 620-621
Stieber, Doug, 658-659
Stillman, Whit, 108
Stock Broker, The, 972
Stock Shop, The, 968-969
Stockland, Bill, 160-175
Stoecklein, David, 848-849
Stogo, Don, 848-849
Streano, Vince, 825
Streano/Havens, 825
Stricker, Alexander, 834-835
Stroster, Maria, 43
Studio 3, Inc., 620-621
Sumichrast, Jösef, 94
Summer, Bill, 437
Sumpter, Will, 894-895
Sund, Carol, 776-777
Supley, Walter, 76
Sutcliffe, Doug, 1001
Sutton, Jane A., 260-261
Sweet Represents, 78
Sweet, Ron, 806-807
Tabu Studios, Inc., 999
Tanenbaum, Robert, 112-113, 119
Tannenbaum, Dennis, 314-319
Tao, Yoko, 800-801
Tartaro Color Labs, 980-981
Taylor, Cynthia, 1076

Team Russell, 864-865
Tepke, Janice, 632-633
Teske, Kurt, 1081
Thomas, Mark, 292-293
Tiani, Alex, 41
Tobias, Jerry, 908-909
Togashi, Eileen C., 374-375
Toto, Joe, 222-223
Tracy, Janis, 618-619
Trailer, Martin, 830-831
Tucker, Bill, 710-711
Tucker, Ezra, 58
Tuke, Joni Inc., 630-631, 650-651
Tullio & Rans, 1086
Turgeon, Jim, 80
Turnau, Jeff, 950-951
Turner & deVries, 850
Turner, John Terence, 800-801
Turner, Pete, 224-225
Uher, John, 409
Umans, Marty, 334-335
Umlas, Barbara, 286-289, 292-293
Unangst, Andrew, 148-151
United Lithographing Corporation, 996
Utterback, Michal, 1038-1039
Uzzell, Steve, 530-531
Valen Associates, 88
Valen, Herb, 88
Vallon, Arlene, 284-285
van Ackeren Company, Inc., The, 1045
van Ackeren, Michael, 1045
Van Hamersveld, John, 123
Van Petten, Rob, 388-389
Van Schelt, Perry, 79
Vedros, Nick & Associates, 662-665
Ventola, Giorgio, 614-615
Verougstraete, Randy, 44-45
Villani, Ron, 40
Virnig, Janet, 50
Visages, 851
Voicecasting, a No Soap Co., 1085
von Hoffmann, Gail, 274-275
von Hoffmann, Trip, 274-275
Wagenaar, David, 652-653
Wagner, Gert, 437
Wahlstrom, Richard, 802-803
Wahlund, Olof Photography, Inc., 214-215
Walker, Ken, 92
Wans, Glen, 696-697
Ward, Les, 694-695
Ward, Tony, 528-529
Warren, Ann, 1076
Warren, Todd Productions, Inc., 1000
Warshaw, Andrea, 976-977
Watford, Wayne, 69
Watson, George, 416-417
Watson, Michael, 192-193
Weaks, Dan, 250-253
Weisbrot, Rick, 328-329
Weisner, Kris, 864-865
Weiss, David, 510-511
Weiss, Stacy, 806-807
Welling, Kathy, 274-275
Welzenbach, John, 630-631
Westerman, Charlie, 712-715
Wexler, Ed, 44-45
Whalen, Judy, 954
Wheeler Pictures, 504-505
White, Bill Productions, 1032
White, Bill Studio, 354-355
White, Frank, 896-897
Whyte, Douglas, 400-401
Wickart, Mark, 122
Wiley, David, 100-101
Wilkes, Stephen, 582-585
Williams, Jimmy, 914-915
Willis, Joe, 898
Winter, Jerry Retouching, 984
Witte, Michael, 112-113
Wohrman, Scott, 935
Wolfgang, Sherri, 105
Wolfson Photography, Inc., 266-267
Wolfson, Jeffrey, 380-381
Woloshin, Sid, Inc., 1088
Wood, James B., 806-807
Woodfin Camp & Associates, 560-561
Wright, Ted, 63
Wu, Ron, 574-575
Yarbrough, Carl, 876
Yeates, Stephen, 1038-1039
Yellen, Bert & Associates, 214-215, 754-755
Yesawich & Welsh, 956
Young, Eric, 1033-1036
Young, Rick, 424-425
Zajack, Greg, 810-811
Zak in the West, 874-875
Zan Productions, 328-329
Zanetti, Gerald Assoc., Inc., 142-145
Zanetti, Lucy, 142-145
Zapp, Carl, 518-519
Zazula Electronic Retouching, 985
Zazula, Hy Associates, Inc., 985
Zelman, Elyn, 438-439
Ziering, Bob, 25

Zimmer, Eleanor, 1058-1063
Zimmerman, David, 398-399
Zimmerman, Jerry, 29
Zimmerman, John, 437
Zwart Studios, Inc., 790-793
Zwart, Jeffrey, 790-791

DIALING INTERNATIONALLY

TO (YOU WANT TO CALL)

When dialing a European country, dial the international access code (below), drop the initial "0" of the phone number ("9" for Finland), then dial the remainder of the number.

FROM (YOU ARE IN)

	Austria	Belgium	Canada	Denmark	Finland	France	Germany	Gr. Britain	Greece	Ireland	Italy	Japan	Netherlands	Norway	Portugal	Spain	Sweden	Switzerland	USA
Austria	—	0032	001	0045	00358	0033	06	0044	0030	00353	040	90081	0031	0047	00351	0034	0046	050	001
Belgium	0043	—	001	0045	00358	0033	0049	0044	0030	00353	0039	0081	0031	0047	00351	0034	0046	0041	001
Canada	01143	01132	—	01145	011358	01133	01149	01144	01130	011353	01139	01181	01131	01147	011351	01134	01146	01141	1
Denmark	00943	00932	0091	—	009358	00933	00949	00944	00930	009353	00939	00981	00931	00947	009351	00934	00946	00941	0091
Finland	99043	99032	9901	99045	—	99033	99049	99044	99030	990353	99039	99081	99031	99047	990351	99034	99046	99041	9901
France	1943	1932	191	1945	19358	—	1949	1944	1930	19353	1939	1981	1931	1947	19351	1934	1946	1941	191
Germany	0043	0032	001	0045	00358	0033	—	0044	0030	00353	0039	0081	0031	0047	00351	0034	0046	0041	001
Gr. Britain	01043	01032	0101	01045	010358	01033	01049	—	01030	0001	01039	01081	01031	01047	010351	01034	01046	01041	0101
Greece	0043	0032	001	0045	00358	0033	0049	0044	—	00353	0039	0081	0031	0047	00351	0034	0046	0041	001
Ireland	1643	1632	161	1645	16358	1633	1649	03	1630	—	1639	1681	1631	1647	16351	1634	1646	1641	161
Italy	0043	0032	001	0045	00358	0033	0049	0044	0030	00353	—	0081	0031	0047	00351	0034	0046	0041	001
Japan	00143	00132	0011	00145	001358	00133	00149	00144	00130	001353	00139	—	00131	00147	001351	00134	00146	00141	0011
Netherlands	0943	0932	091	0945	09358	0933	0949	0944	0930	09353	0939	0981	—	0947	09351	0934	0946	0941	091
Norway	09543	09532	0951	09545	095358	09533	09549	09544	09530	095353	09539	09581	09531	—	095351	09534	09546	09541	0951
Portugal	0743	0732	071	0745	07358	0733	0749	0744	0730	07353	0739	09781	0731	0747	—	0734	0746	0741	0971
Spain	0743	0732	071	0745	07358	0733	0749	0744	0730	07353	0739	0781	0731	0747	07351	—	0746	0741	071
Sweden	00943	00932	0091	00945	009358	00933	00949	00944	00930	009353	00939	00981	00931	00947	009351	00934	—	00941	0091
Switzerland	0043	0032	001	0045	00358	0033	0049	0044	0030	00353	0039	0081	0031	0047	00351	0034	0046	—	001
USA	01143	01132	—	01145	011358	01133	01149	01144	01130	011353	01139	01181	01131	01147	011351	01134	01146	01141	—

If your exchange is not equipped to dial direct internationally, dial "0" and give the operator the number.

12 NOON
DUBLIN
LISBON
LONDON

1 PM
AMSTERDAM MILAN
BRUSSELS MUNICH
COPENHAGEN OSLO
DUSSELDORF PARIS
FRANKFURT ROME
HAMBURG STOCKHOLM
MADRID VIENNA

2 PM
ATHENS
HELSINKI

8 PM
HONG KONG

9 PM
TOKYO

2 AM
ANCHORAGE
HONOLULU

4 AM
LOS ANGELES
SAN FRANCISCO
SEATTLE
VANCOUVER

5 AM
DENVER

6 AM
CHICAGO KANSAS CITY
DALLAS MEXICO CITY
DETROIT NASHVILLE
HOUSTON NEW ORLEANS
ST. LOUIS

7 AM
ATLANTA NEW YORK
BOSTON PHILADELPHIA
MIAMI TORONTO
MONTREAL
WASHINGTON D.C.

9 AM
BUENOS AIRES

1989

JANUARY
S	M	T	W	T	F	S
1	2	3	4	5	6	7
8	9	10	11	12	13	14
15	16	17	18	19	20	21
22	23	24	25	26	27	28
29	30	31				

FEBRUARY
S	M	T	W	T	F	S
			1	2	3	4
5	6	7	8	9	10	11
12	13	14	15	16	17	18
19	20	21	22	23	24	25
26	27	28				

MARCH
S	M	T	W	T	F	S
			1	2	3	4
5	6	7	8	9	10	11
12	13	14	15	16	17	18
19	20	21	22	23	24	25
26	27	28	29	30	31	

APRIL
S	M	T	W	T	F	S
						1
2	3	4	5	6	7	8
9	10	11	12	13	14	15
16	17	18	19	20	21	22
23	24	25	26	27	28	29
30						

MAY
S	M	T	W	T	F	S
	1	2	3	4	5	6
7	8	9	10	11	12	13
14	15	16	17	18	19	20
21	22	23	24	25	26	27
28	29	30	31			

JUNE
S	M	T	W	T	F	S
				1	2	3
4	5	6	7	8	9	10
11	12	13	14	15	16	17
18	19	20	21	22	23	24
25	26	27	28	29	30	

JULY
S	M	T	W	T	F	S
						1
2	3	4	5	6	7	8
9	10	11	12	13	14	15
16	17	18	19	20	21	22
23	24	25	26	27	28	29
30	31					

AUGUST
S	M	T	W	T	F	S
		1	2	3	4	5
6	7	8	9	10	11	12
13	14	15	16	17	18	19
20	21	22	23	24	25	26
27	28	29	30	31		

SEPTEMBER
S	M	T	W	T	F	S
					1	2
3	4	5	6	7	8	9
10	11	12	13	14	15	16
17	18	19	20	21	22	23
24	25	26	27	28	29	30

OCTOBER
S	M	T	W	T	F	S
1	2	3	4	5	6	7
8	9	10	11	12	13	14
15	16	17	18	19	20	21
22	23	24	25	26	27	28
29	30	31				

NOVEMBER
S	M	T	W	T	F	S
			1	2	3	4
5	6	7	8	9	10	11
12	13	14	15	16	17	18
19	20	21	22	23	24	25
26	27	28	29	30		

DECEMBER
S	M	T	W	T	F	S
					1	2
3	4	5	6	7	8	9
10	11	12	13	14	15	16
17	18	19	20	21	22	23
24	25	26	27	28	29	30
31						

HOLIDAYS

JAN 1/NEW YEAR'S DAY
JAN 16/MARTIN LUTHER KING JR.'S BIRTHDAY
FEB 12/LINCOLN'S BIRTHDAY
FEB 14/VALENTINE'S DAY
FEB 20/WASHINGTON'S BIRTHDAY—OBSVD
MARCH 17/ST. PATRICK'S DAY
MARCH 19/PALM SUNDAY
MARCH 24/GOOD FRIDAY
MARCH 26/EASTER SUNDAY
APRIL 20/PASSOVER BEGINS
MAY 14/MOTHER'S DAY
MAY 29/MEMORIAL DAY—OBSVD
JUNE 18/FATHER'S DAY
JULY 4/INDEPENDENCE DAY
SEPT 4/LABOR DAY
SEPT 30/ROSH HASHANAH
OCT 9/YOM KIPPUR
OCT 9/COLUMBUS DAY—OBSVD
OCT 31/HALLOWEEN
NOV 7/ELECTION DAY
NOV 23/THANKSGIVING DAY
DEC 23/HANUKKAH
DEC 25/CHRISTMAS DAY
WRITE TO US

GRAPHICS

DESIGN
ILLUSTRATION
STUDIO SERVICES

DESIGN

CONCEPTS, PROMOTIONAL, POINT OF PURCHASE,
PACKAGING, PRODUCT, INDUSTRIAL, SURFACE,
INTERIOR/EXTERIOR DESIGN, ILLUSTRATION/RENDERING,
LETTERING, CONSULTATION SERVICES AVAILABLE

RAYMOND HERNANDEZ DESIGN
718/462 9072

Hyatt Resorts
Waikoloa, Hawaii

WHISTLES

● BLAUPUNKT
the difference is pronounced.

Racing Silks

The Designers

MistletoeMania

Holly Dickens designs lettering for:
ADA, Anheuser Busch, Beatrice Foods, Citicorp, Coca Cola, General Mills, Honda, Kraft, Lorimar, Marshall Field's, McDonald's, Philip Morris, Ralston Purina, 7-UP, Sears, Stouffers and Tropicana

HOLLY DICKENS DESIGN
312.280.0777
FAX 312.280.1725

STEPHEN·FO

SLEIGHT OF HAND

Saying Goodbye at the STATION

Special Touch

AM 1130
WNEW
NEW YORK

TANGLE
WNEW AM 1130

STER·DESIGN

145 WEST 28 ST · NYC
212.967.2533

A UNIQUE BLEND OF DESIGN LETTERING AND ILLUSTRATION FOR AD AGENCIES CORPORATIONS AND PUBLISHERS

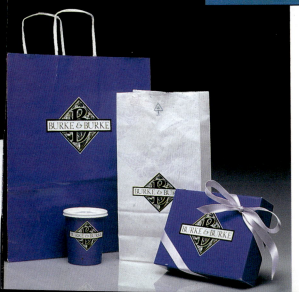

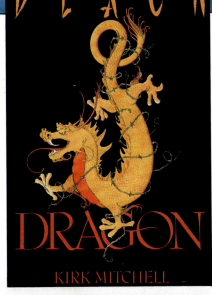

UNUSUAL GRAPHICS

Graphic Design
Illustration
Animation
Advertising
Logotypes
Brochures
Posters
Packaging

JAVIER
D E S

TIME, INC. ANNUAL REPORT

NEW YORK LIFE

PANTHEON BO

ALFRED KNOPF

FORTUNE MAGAZINE

THE NEW YORK TIMES

EMBASSY OF SPAIN

BENETTON

THE BOSTON GLOBE

AMERICAN EXPRESS

ADVERTISING AGE

ROMERO
D E S I G N

529 West 42nd Street, Suite 1H
New York City 10036 (212) 564 3991

THE QUALITY REVIEW

THE NEW YORK TIMES

WHITTLE COMMUNICATIONS, INC.

MIKE QUON DESIGN

568 BROADWAY • NEW YORK CITY 10012 • FAX 212•219•0331

BARRON'S

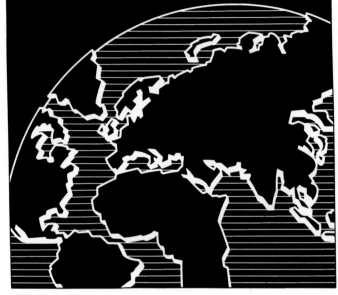
AT&T

CHAMPION

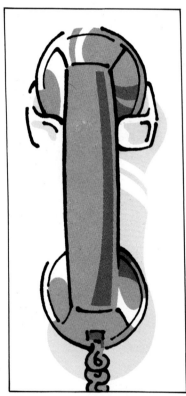
SHOPPER'S AUTOMATIC MONEY

AIRLINE PROMOTION

OFFICE, NYC 212·226·6024
A FULL SERVICE DESIGN STUDIO SPECIALIZING IN ADVERTISING ART

COCA-COLA

THE LEAGUE OF WOMEN VOTERS

W. T. QUINN

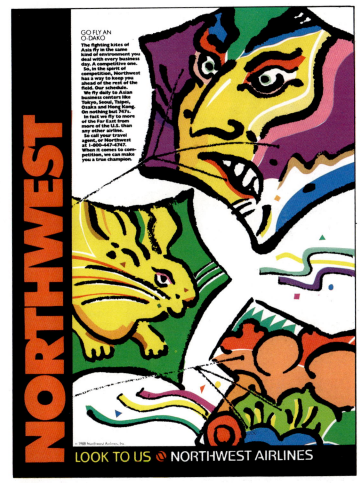
NORTHWEST AIRLINES

BRITISH AIRWAYS

© MIKE QUON DESIGN OFFICE 1989

MATILDA BAY

GETTY

11

DESIGN ILLUSTRATION

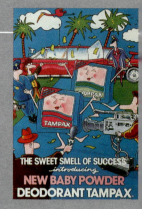

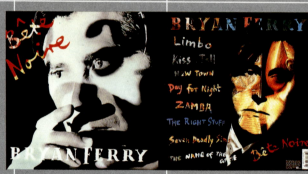

DIAMOND ART STU

STORYBOARDS COMPS

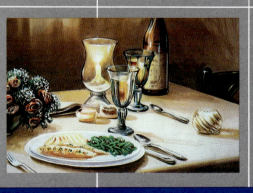

Animatics
Packaging
P.O.P.
Retouching
Mechanicals
Color Correction
Lettering
Photography
Slides
Copywriting
Special Projects

STUDIO 212.685.6622

 At Midnight Oil Studios, we always strive to give our clients the best of both worlds. Combining old world craftsmanship with modern imagination, we create art that has dynamic impact, and stands the test of time. Marketing smart & fashion savvy. Work that sells. Work you can be proud of. In a world of confusion and compromise, there's still a place where clarity and vision are possible – Midnight Oil Studios. Call us today!

DESIGN
ILLUSTRATION
ADVERTISING
POSTERS & P.O.P.
PACKAGING
COPYWRITING
51 MELCHER STREET
BOSTON
MASSACHUSETTS
02210
(617) 350-7970
FAX 350-7971

ILLUSTRATION

DAN COSGROVE

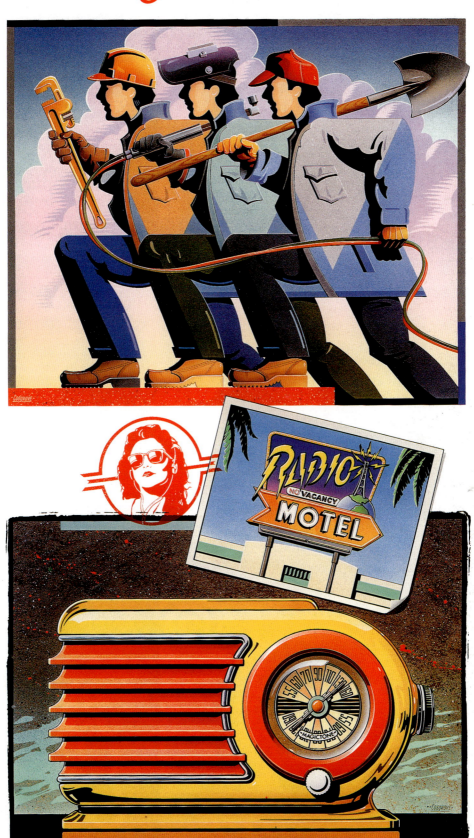

NEW YORK DANIELE COLLIGNON (212) 391-1830   CHICAGO (312) 527-0375

ALEX BOIES
612-333-2418

126 North 3rd Street
Minneapolis, MN 55401

CLIENTS
Benjamin Thompson
 & Associates, Inc.
Carbone Smolan Associates
Carmichael/Lynch
Cross Associates
Esprit
Esquire
Hallmark
H. B. Fuller
Little & Company
McCaffrey & Ratner
Money
Recycled Cards
Rubin Cordaro Design
St. Paul Chamber Orchestra
University of Minnesota
Whittle Communications
World Trade Center

Call:
Patrick McDonnell
201·549·9341
FAX 201·548·4986

FOR A NEW TWIST.

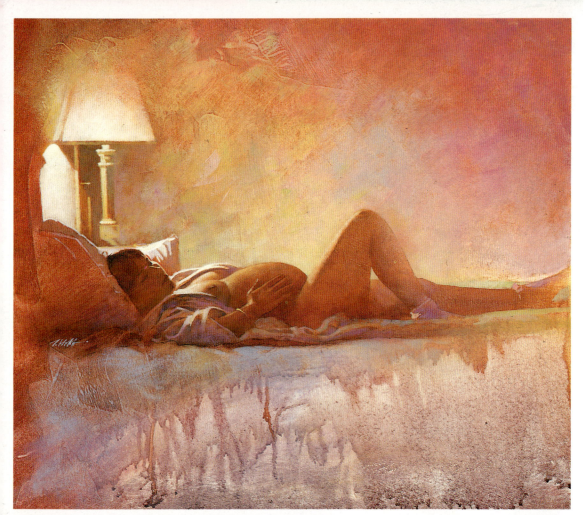

T. Hoff

TERRY HOFF ILLUSTRATION
1525 Grand Ave.
Pacifica, CA 94404
(415) 359-4081

FREDA SCOTT

Artists Representative
415 621 2992

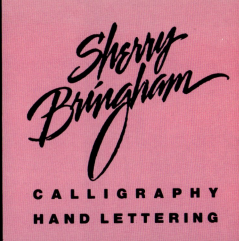

Sherry Bringham
CALLIGRAPHY HAND LETTERING

Cheno

Birthday Bubbles

Americana

Ohsawa

It's more exciting

The Natural Snack

Panache

Make it a Memory

Celebrate!

FREDA SCOTT
Artists Representative
415 621 2992

DAVID CSICSKO

David Csicsko   Represented by Randi Fiat   312.784.2343

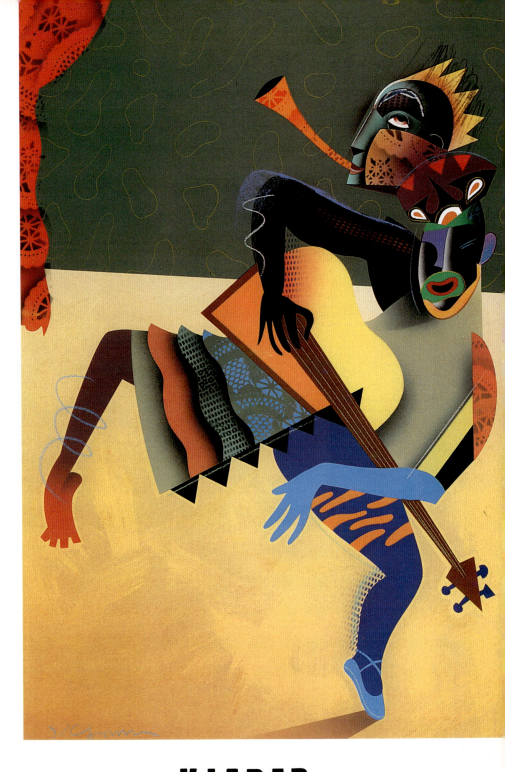

J o H n KLEBER

REPRESENTED BY RANDI FIAT IN CHICAGO 312 784 2343, KURT GRUBAUGH IN SAN FRANCISCO 415 381 3038, MARTHA PRODUCTIONS IN LOS ANGELES 213 204 1771 AND ARLENE CORCORAN IN MINNEAPOLIS 612 823 4821. CLIENTS INCLUDE ARMOUR DIAL, PLAYBOY, 3M, CONTROL DATA, WINNEBAGO, PILLSBURY, HARLEY DAVIDSON, YMCA INTERNATIONAL, MARSHALL FIELDS, DAYTON HUDSON, XEROX, MCA RECORDS, PIZZA HUT, DOW CORNING, AND ADAGE.

ALSOP

Technical & Scientific Illustration
(617) 527-7862

I'll show you how it works.

Give your technical projects to an artist who *understands* all that stuff. Using advanced computer-aided design tools, I'll produce not just the best view but the *ten* best views. Fast. And with all the detail you want. Then I'll turn the concept sketch into a vivid airbrush rendering that explains as well as illustrates.

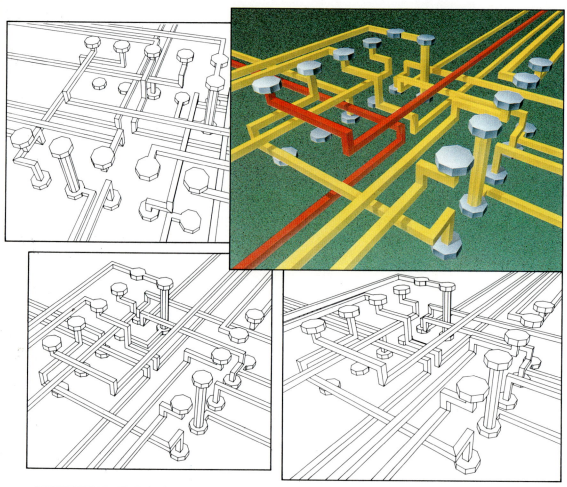

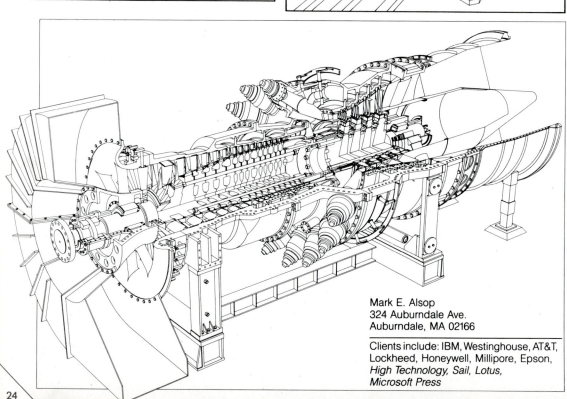

Mark E. Alsop
324 Auburndale Ave.
Auburndale, MA 02166

Clients include: IBM, Westinghouse, AT&T, Lockheed, Honeywell, Millipore, Epson, *High Technology, Sail, Lotus, Microsoft Press*

Bob Ziering represents Bob Ziering (212) 873-0034

MICHAEL HALBERT
ILLUSTRATOR

2419 Big Bend • St. Louis, MO 63143
(314) 645-6480

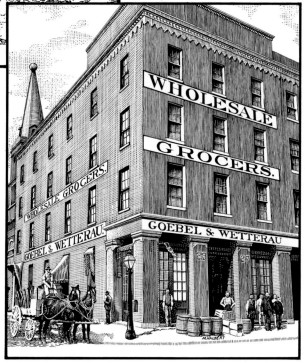

· R · M · HEATH ·

301 · 366 · 4633   FAX # 301 · 727 · 5250
TELEX # 197599 RMHINC

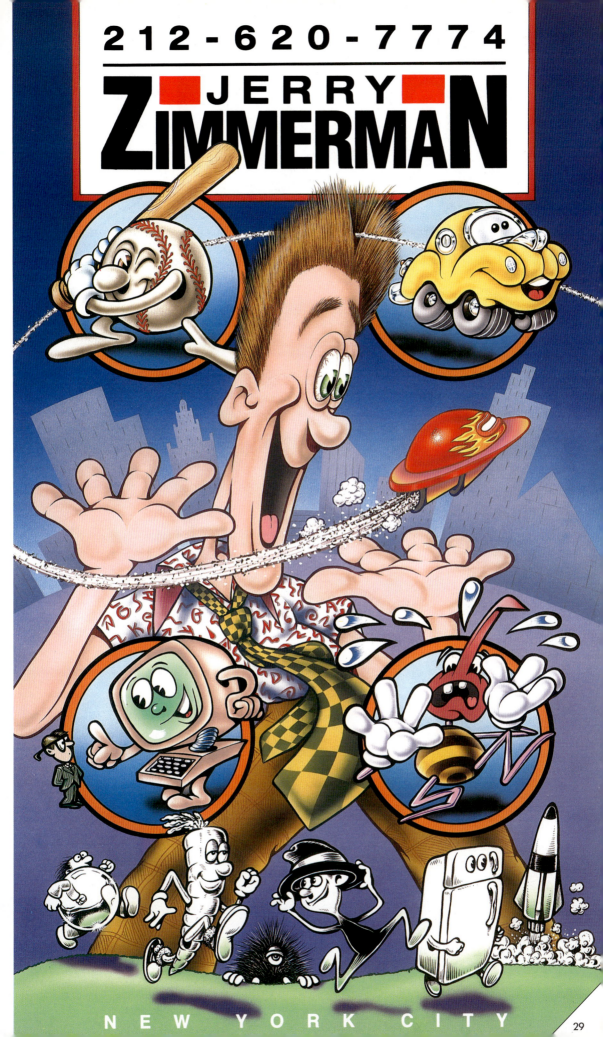

Douglas

NORTHEAST STATES · (212) 929-5590 · Lindgren & Smith
WEST & MIDWEST STATES · (415) 552-4252 · Jan Collier
EUROPE - LONDON · 267-6862 · Europe Unlimited

Fraser

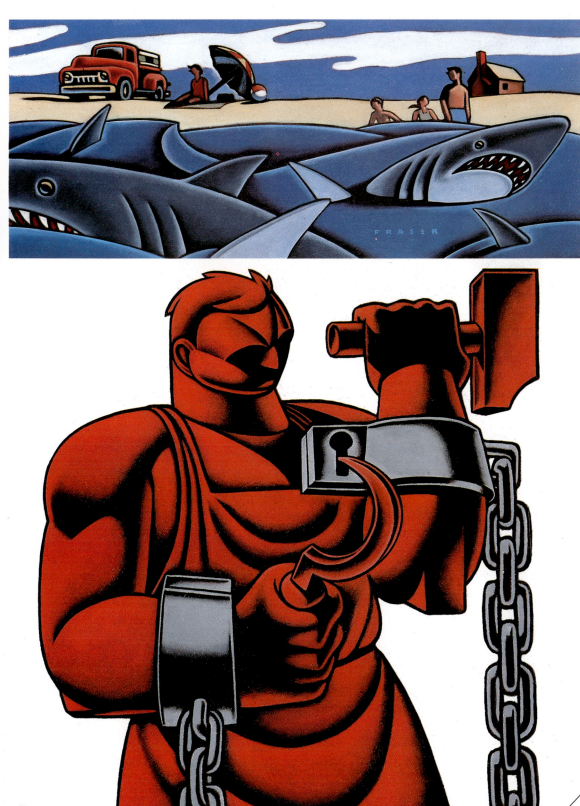

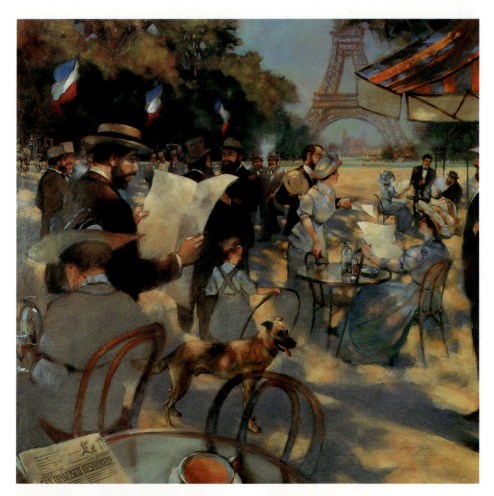

CLIENT: AUSTIN ROVER CARS

Robert Gantt Steele

Agent: Jan Collier (415) 552-4252   *Artist's Studio (415) 923-0741*

Clients Include: American Express, Pan American, Ogilvy & Mather New York, Rockwell International, Motorola, Colony Vineyards, Beverly Hills Hotel, AT&T, GTE Sprint, Bank of America

KAREL HAVLICEK

**REPRESENTED BY
JOEL HARLIB ASSOCIATES
312.329.1370**

405 N. WABASH AVE., CHICAGO 60611   FAX US 24 HOURS: 312.329.1397
TO RECEIVE OUR MAILINGS CALL, WRITE OR FAX US

REALISTIC ANIMALS,
INSECTS, FRUITS
AND VEGETABLES

NICK BACKES

REPRESENTED BY JOEL HARLIB ASSOCIATES

TO RECEIVE OUR MAILINGS CALL, WRITE OR FAX US

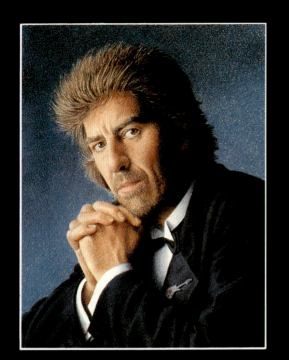

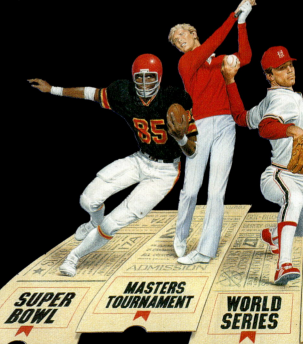

312.329.1370 405 N. WABASH AVE., CHICAGO 60611   FAX US 24 HOURS: 312.329.1397

HARLIB

PEOPLE & PEOPLE IN ENVIRONMENTS

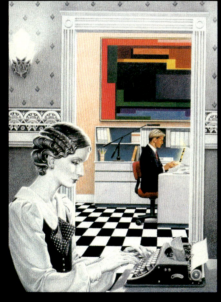

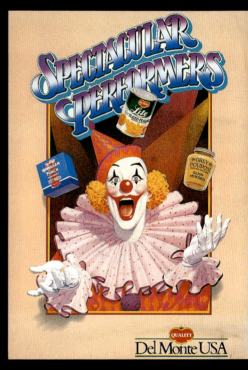

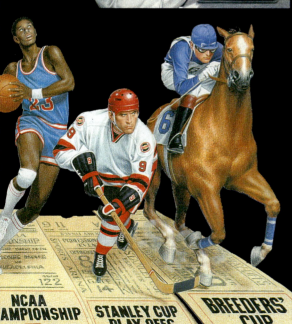

35

FRED PEPERA

REPRESENTED BY JOEL HARLIB ASSOCIATES

TO RECEIVE OUR MAILINGS CALL, WRITE OR FAX US

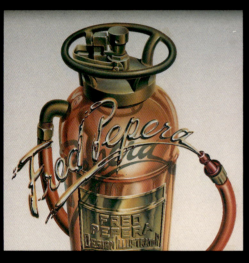

312.329.1370   405 N. WABASH AVE., CHICAGO 60611   FAX US 24 HOURS: 312.329.1397

HARLIB

REALISTIC PRODUCTS AND LETTERING

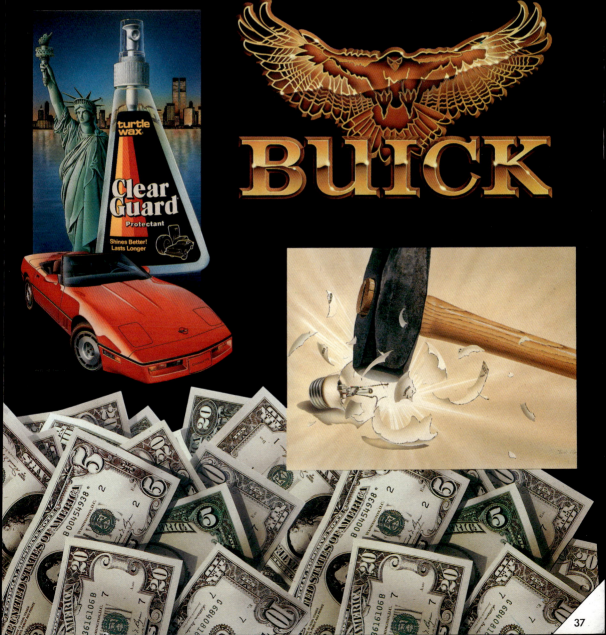

37

RICHARD ANDERSON

REPRESENTED BY JOEL HARLIB ASSOCIATES

TO RECEIVE OUR MAILINGS CALL, WRITE OR FAX US

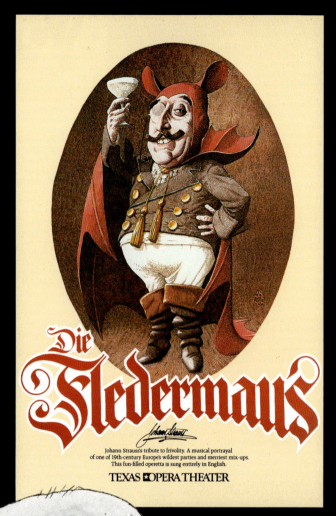
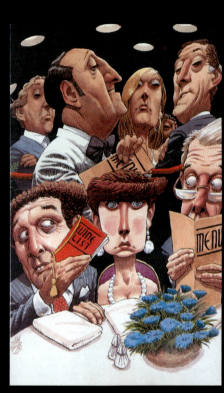

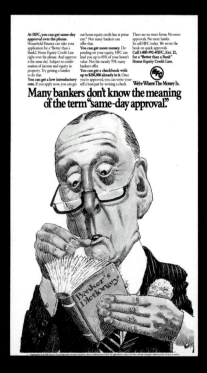

312.329.1370 405 N. WABASH AVE., CHICAGO 60611 FAX US 24 HOURS: 312.329.1397

HARLIB

COLOR AND B&W
CHARACTER AND
CARICATURE
ILLUSTRATIONS

RON VILLANI

405 N. WABASH AVE., CHICAGO 60611   FAX US 24 HOURS: 312.329.1397
TO RECEIVE OUR MAILINGS CALL, WRITE OR FAX US

REPRESENTED BY
JOEL HARLIB ASSOCIATES
312.329.1370

HARLIB

POP ART,
COMIC BOOK
REALISM AND
SILHOUETTES

Alex Tiani (203) 661-3891 Fax: (203) 869-5823
Bright ideas captured on film and paper
European contact (Sweden): Mark Goldsmith (46) 764-65660
Clients include AT&T, American Express, CBS Records,
Chemical Bank, IBM, Long Island Savings Bank, Mass Mutual,
New York Life, Pitney Bowes, Polaroid, SAS, Scott Paper

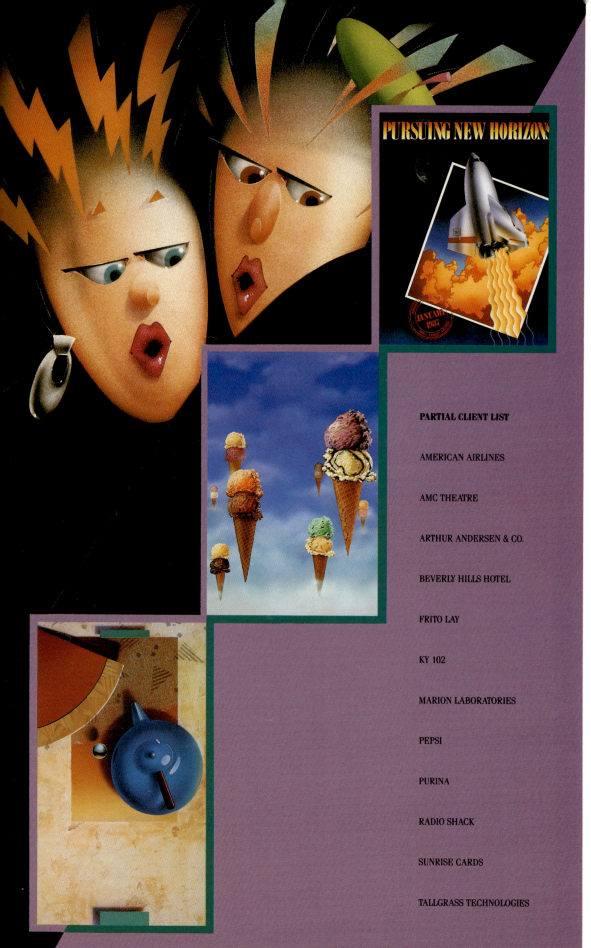

PURSUING NEW HORIZONS

PARTIAL CLIENT LIST

AMERICAN AIRLINES

AMC THEATRE

ARTHUR ANDERSEN & CO.

BEVERLY HILLS HOTEL

FRITO LAY

KY 102

MARION LABORATORIES

PEPSI

PURINA

RADIO SHACK

SUNRISE CARDS

TALLGRASS TECHNOLOGIES

APPLEOFF ILLUSTRATION (816)-753-5421
4931 BELL ST. KANSAS CITY, MO 64112

FUNNY FARM:

ED WEXLER

"That night at the California Cafe, the cuisine was as fresh as expected. And so was Harry."

Don't leave home without it.®

San Francisco • Mill Valley • Walnut Creek • San Ramon • Los Gatos • Palo Alto • San Jose • Yountville
© 1987 American Express Travel Related Services Company, Inc.

Being a Hyundai dealer can be a real trip.

If you're an authorized Hyundai dealer, you could be bound for glory. As the lucky winner of the grand prize in our special dealer drawing® — a trip for two to Korea during the 1988 Olympic Games. Plus a brand new Hyundai Excel automobile to use as a sales promotion tool for your customers. We'll also be giving away two other free trips to Korea for two, five pianos and fifty cordless phones.

It's all part of our 1st Anniversary Celebration, thanking Hyundai dealers for making our first year of operations in the U.S. so successful. And letting you know how much we value your continued partnership.

Complete details about our celebration have been mailed to all authorized Hyundai dealers. For additional information about our drawing or Hyundai dealerships, call 1-800-544-7808

⌁HYUNDAI

ELDON DOTY

The wine trivia quiz. How high is your score?

Today's Gallo. All the best a wine can be.

Clients include: Foote, Cone & Belding, N.W. Ayer, Inc., J. Walter Thompson U.S.A. Inc., A & M Records, McCann-Erickson, Inc., Tracy-Locke, Cochrane Chase, Dentsu/Young & Rubicam, Dyer/Kahn, Inc., Ogilvy & Mather, Inc., Walt Disney, Bozell, Jacobs, Kenyon & Eckhardt, Paramount Pictures, CBS & NBC, Doyle & Partners, Inc., McCaffrey & McCall, Inc., 20th Century Fox.

REPRESENTING TOP HUMOROUS ILLUSTRATORS: RANDY VEROUGSTRAETE NICK PRICE ED "BIG DADDY" ROTH BO

COMMITTED TO HUMOR

RANDY VEROUGSTRAETE

RAY CADD

Los Angeles (213) 451-1910
FAX (213) 451-3955
New York (212) 944-2224

STAAKE ED WEXLER RAY CADD ELDON DOTY AMY BRYANT RON BARRETT ROWLAND WILSON BENTON MAHAN

B O B B Y E

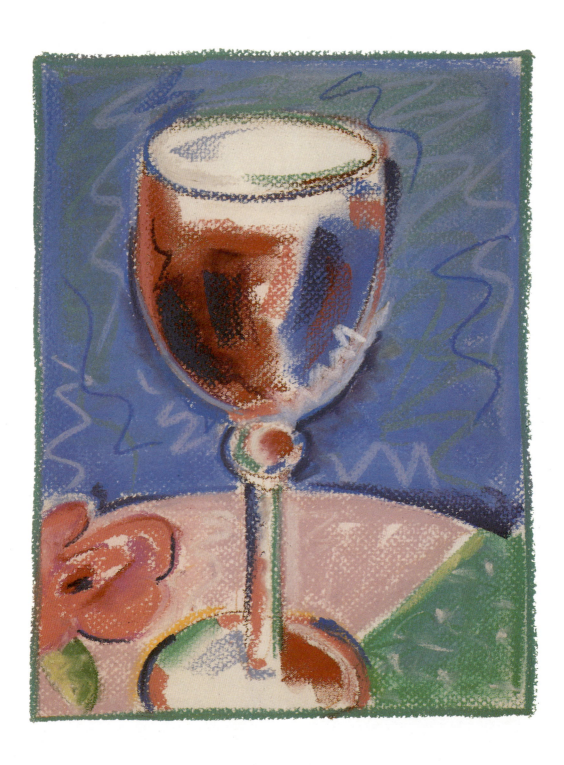

COCHRAN

CHICAGO
312.943.5912
FAX NUMBER
312.943.9669

NEW YORK
212.557.5820

CLIENTELE
AMERICAN EXPRESS
ANHEUSER-BUSCH
AT&T, KRAFT
HERMAN MILLER
PHILLIP MORRIS
SMITHSONIAN INSTITUTE
UNITED AIRLINES

MIKE LESTER

Fax: (404) 447-9559   Phone: (404) 447-5332
Reel On Request

EVERETT PECK

ILLUSTRATION & ANIMATION

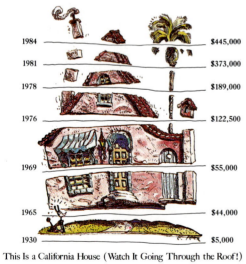

This Is a California House (Watch It Going Through the Roof!)

RICHARD · W · SALZMAN
ARTIST · REPRESENTATIVE

619 · 272 · 8147
FAX / 619 · 272 · 0180
212 · 997 · 0115

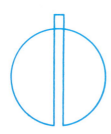

DOUGLAS A. BOWLES

RICHARD · W · SALZMAN
ARTIST · REPRESENTATIVE

619 · 272 · 8147
FAX/619 · 272 · 0180
212 · 997 · 0115

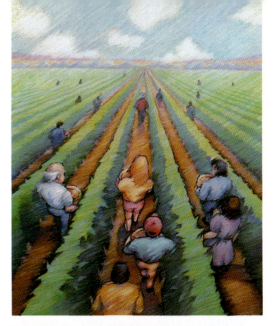

53

ROGER HUYSSEN

(203) 656·0200

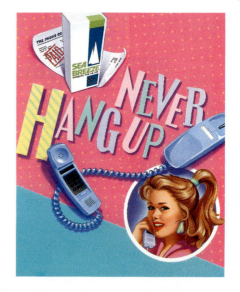

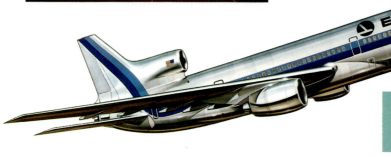
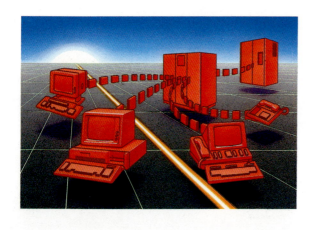

GERARD HUERTA

(203) 656·0505

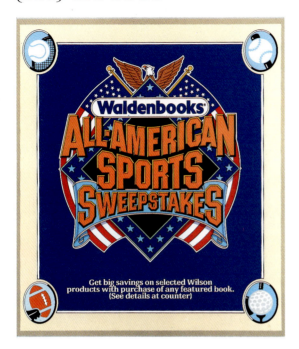

Messenger service to and from NYC

Telecopier in office

ROGER HUYSSEN

GERARD HUERTA

45 Corbin Drive
Darien, CT 06820

GARY CICCARELLI

Gary Ciccarelli/Studio (313) 278-3504
New York/American Artists (212) 682-2462 • St. Louis/Ceci Bartels Assoc. (314) 241-4014

BARBARA
KELLEY
555 10TH STREET, BROOKLYN N.Y., 11215 718-788-2465

· COLOR AND BLACK & WHITE PORTFOLIOS ·

woody Coleman presents inc.

Ezra Tucker
(216) 661-4222

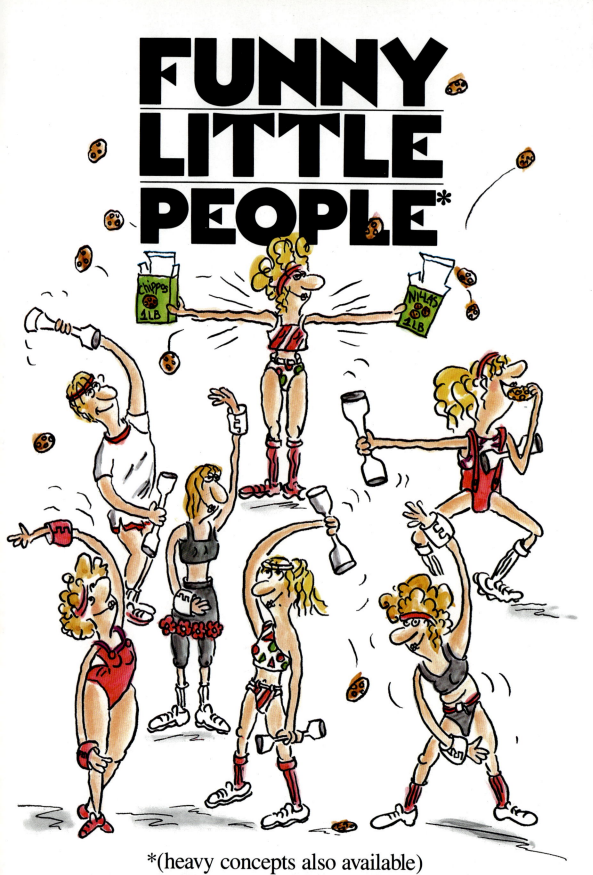

TED WRIGHT

NYC (212) 912-1877　　Chicago (312) 786-1560　　St. Louis (314) 241-4014　　FAX (314) 241-9028

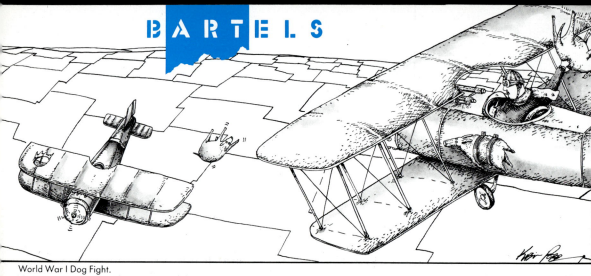

World War I Dog Fight.

Absolutely living too close to the microwave tower.

The Nelsons fall prey to another tourist trap.

No matter how hard she tried, Flo never found any shapes in the clouds.

The Chef's Surprise.

Greetings from the middle of Nowhere.

MARK FREDRICKSON

NYC (212) 912-1877   Chicago (312) 786-1560   St. Louis (314) 241-4014   FAX (314) 241-9028

BARTELS

65

KRIEGSHAUSER

KEITH KASNOT

NYC (212) 912-1877   Chicago (312) 786-1560   St. Louis (314) 241-4014   FAX (314) 241-9028

BARTELS

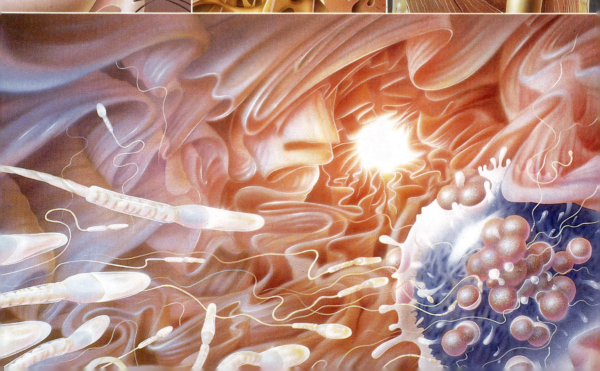

Adapted from *Behold Man* by Albert Bonniers, ©1974.

WAYNE WATFORD

NYC (212) 912-1877 Chicago (312) 786-1560 St. Louis (314) 241-4014 FAX (314) 241-9028

BARTELS

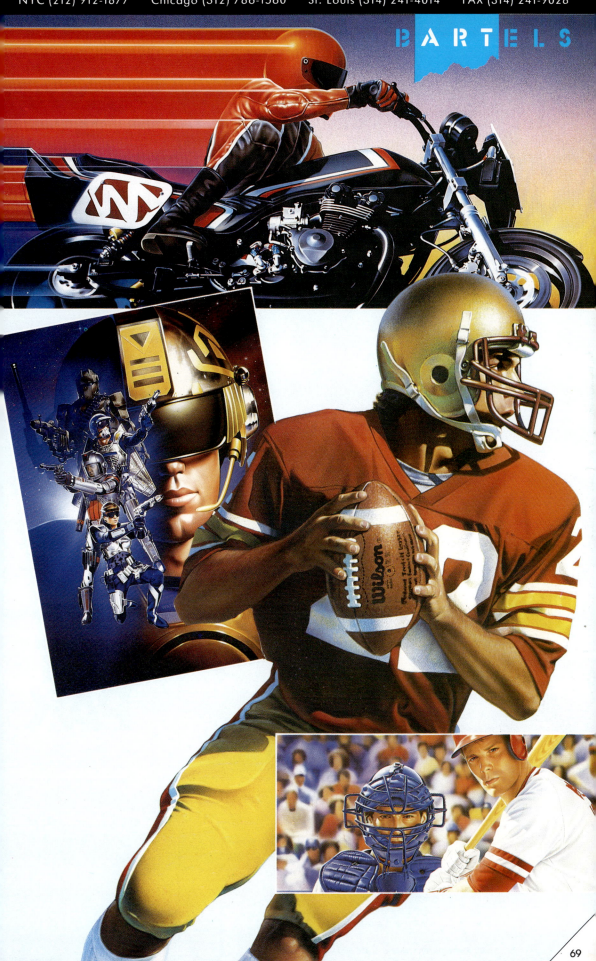

69

CATPAK

NYC (212) 912-1877 Chicago (312) 786-1560 St. Louis (314) 241-4014 FAX (314) 241-9028

BEFORE CATPAK
This is what you'll get when you use a good continuous-tone original in a newspaper ad.

The CatPak, Dallas — your source for newspaper and magazine images that won't turn to mush.

IF you keep sending nice, expensive, re-touched images off to newspapers and magazines and getting back tear-sheets that look like potato prints, cut it out.

Send CatPak stipple drawings instead. You'll like them a lot better because they're a *lot* harder to screw up.

Your clients' ads will look fresh and snappy.

Their competition in the same publications will look flat, gritty and maybe a little out of focus.

You'll be a hero.

We'll make a few hundred bucks.

Everyone will win.

So.

Call in the Cat.

We do a very good business in drawings rendered in a broad range of styles — each designed to compensate for the limitations of the high speed press.

Send us your product, or a sketch of what you want, or a photograph you'd like turned into a nice *print-anywhere* image, and we'll send you back an illustration that won't need intensive care in the middle of the night when the bell rings and the big presses roll.

The **CAT PAK**

Specialists in food and product illustration tough enough to survive in the real world.

In Texas, call 214 744-4421
FAX: 214 720-0080

AFTER CATPAK
This is what you'll get when you send that same publication a CatPak Illustration.

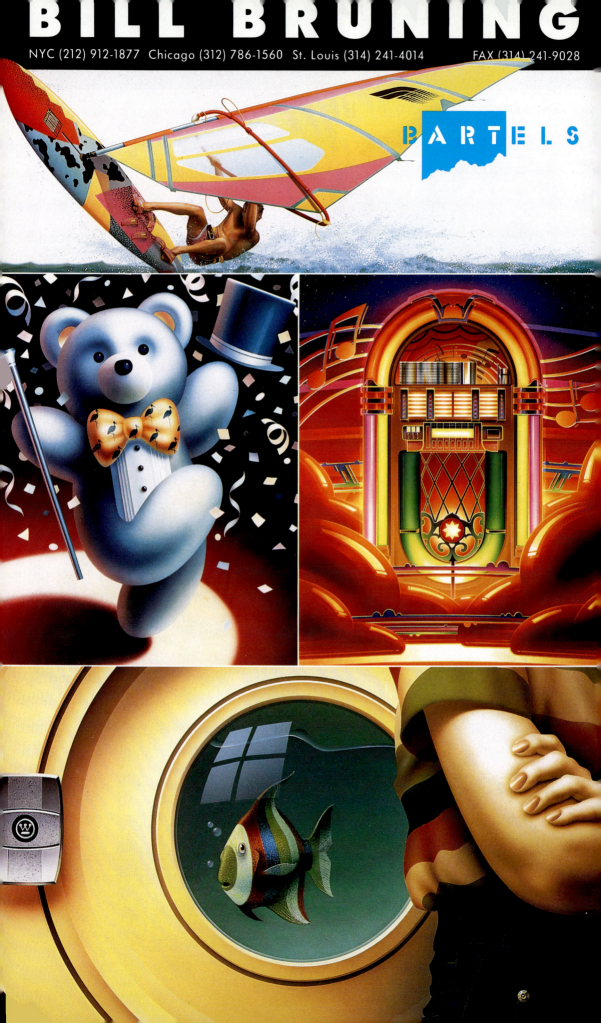

FRANK FRUZYNA

NYC (212) 912-1877   Chicago (312) 786-1560   St. Louis (314) 241-4014   FAX (314) 241-9028

BARTELS

KEVIN HULSEY
ILLUSTRATION INC.

TECHNICAL ILLUSTRATION   213 · 876 7600 FAX IN STUDIO

LOS ANGELES; BARBARA MARIE REPRESENTS 213•874 1444/ATLANTA; CARY & CO. 404•881 0087

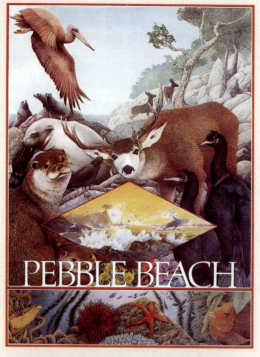

"Pebble Beach"
Gold Medal/Best Illustration
1987 International
Advertising Festival of N.Y.
Client: GE Plastics

"Dog & Cat"
Client: Arm & Hammer'

"Adirondacks"
Self-Promotion Poster

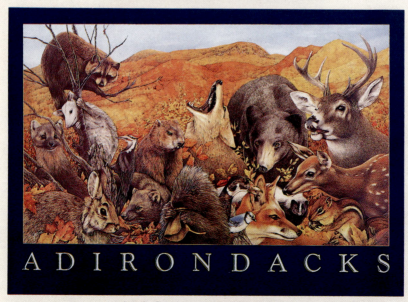

Jack Graber (518) 370-0312
Represented by: Walter Supley
the Creative Advantage, 707 Union St., Schenectady, N.Y. 12305

STUDIO (802) 464-5523 FAX (802) 464-2555
BOX ONE TWO THREE, WILMINGTON, VERMONT 05363

RANDY GLASS/STUDIO (213) 462-2706
LOS ANGELES/ELLEN KNABLE & ASSOCIATES, INC. (213) 855-8855
SAN FRANCISCO/SWEET REPRESENTS (415) 433-1222
CHICAGO/JOEL HARLIB ASSOCIATES, INC. (312) 329-1370

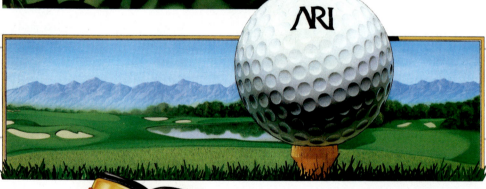

JIM TURGEON

ILLUSTRATION & LETTERING
REPRESENTED BY THE PENNY & STERMER GROUP 212-243-4412
IN CHICAGO 312-861-1039

HARRY BATES

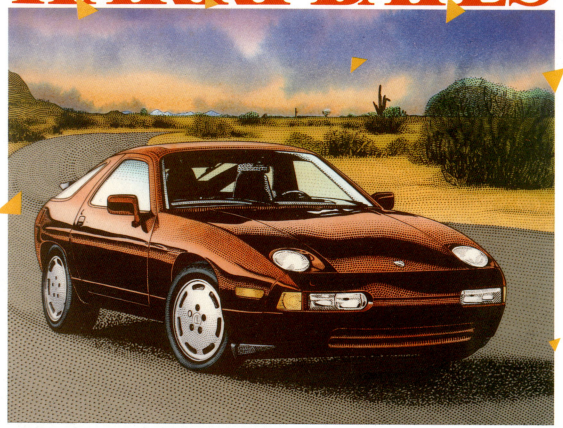

(718) 693-6304

LINDA SCHARF
P.O. BOX 1562, BROOKLINE, MA 02146 USA 617-738-9294

CLIENT LIST UPON REQUEST

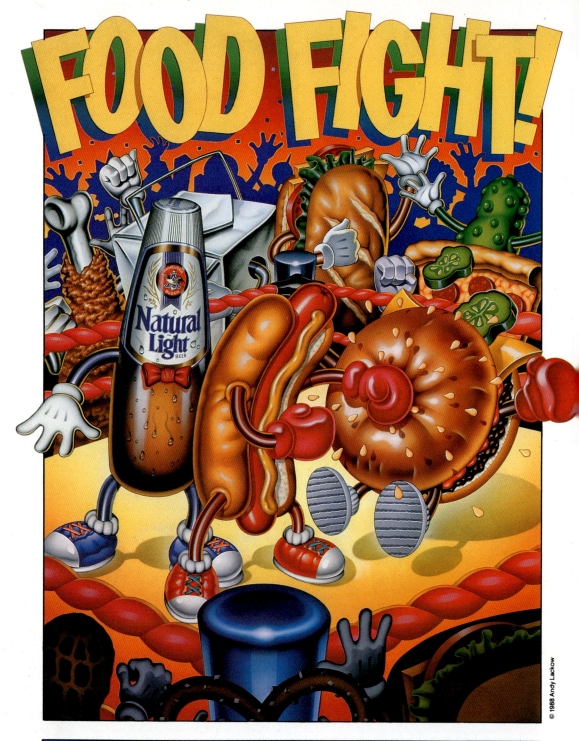

ANDY LACKOW STUDIO

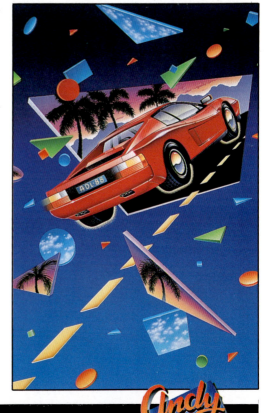

212 · 472 · 8898

Ralston Purina

Terry Sirrell

Campus Life

Olver Dunlop Assoc.

Fax Available

Studio
312-980-7047

Represented in the Midwest, Excluding Chicago, by:
314-241-4014
BARTELS

In Chicago and Elsewhere Call Studio.

International Councils of Shopping Centers

Additional Samples found in the '86, '87, '88 Black Book.

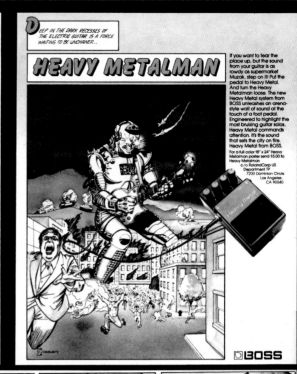

TTJ SAYS COMIC ART... A GOOD IDEA.

CONTINUITY GRAPHIC ASSOC. INC.

62 WEST 45TH STREET • NEW YORK, N.Y. 10036

CALL OUR REPS AT (212) 869-4170. IF WE HAD MORE SPACE, WE'D SPEND IT WRITING ABOUT THEM. THEY'RE THE NICEST IN TOWN.

CHAS ADDAMS · BARSOTTI · BOOTH · WHITNEY DARROW · JOSEPH FARRIS · WM HAMILTON · STAN HUNT · H MARTIN · MODELL · ZIEGLER · WOODMAN · ROWLAND WILSON · GAHAN WILSON · WEBER · SYVERSON · STEVENSON · SAXON · RICHTER

CELEBRATE
with the country's leading cartoonists

Herb Valen
VALEN ASSOCIATES

Box 8, Westport, CT 06881
Box 1011, Del Mar, CA 92014
619-259-5774

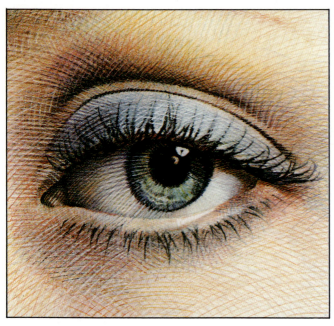

LINDA FENNIMORE

ILLUSTRATION

808 WEST END AVE. #801
NEW YORK, NEW YORK 10025
(212) 866-0279

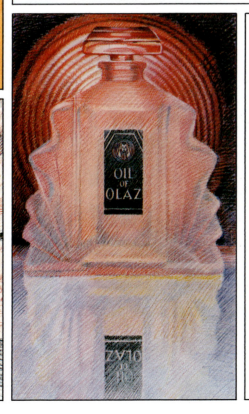

WALKER

ILLUSTRATION

KEN WALKER
816-931-7975

jözef sumichrast

REPRESENTED IN NEW YORK BY MADELINE RENARD (212) 490-2450
STUDIO (312) 295-0255

ROBERT RODRIGUEZ

RENARD
REPRESENTS
212·490·2450
TELECOPIER:
212·697·6828

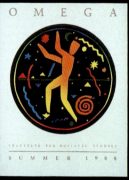
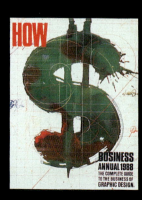

Tim Girvin Design, Inc.
911 Western Avenue
Suite 408
Seattle, WA 98104

206.623.7808
206.623.7918
Fax 206.340.1837

Represented in New York
by Renard Represents
212.490.2450

ALPHABET DESIGN
Custom Typeface Development

Design Solutions For:

ABC, Aldus Corporation, American Express, Bloomingdale's, Burlington, CBS Entertainment, Clairol, Duracell, Estee Lauder, Generra, Herman Miller, Inc., Hoffmann-LaRoche, Inc., IBM Corporation, Levi Strauss, LucasFilm, Ltd., Maybelline, Microsoft Press, Milton Bradley Company, Nordstrom, Paul Masson, Revlon, *Time, Town & Country*, United Airlines, Universal Studios, Walt Disney Productions, and Westin Hotels and Resorts.

M I C H A E L

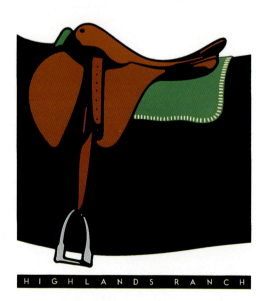

CLIENTS: APPLE, BENETTON, BRITISH PETROLEUM, COCA-COLA
DOYLE DANE BERNBACH (LONDON AND DÜSSELDORF), ESPRIT
GRAPHIS, LEVI STRAUSS, NY TIMES MAGAZINE, PENTAGRAM
SPORTS ILLUSTRATED, TAKENOBU IGARASHI (TOKYO) AND MORE

SCHWAB

STUDIO	**NEW YORK**	**LONDON**
415-546-7559	212-490-2450	267-6862
SAN FRANCISCO	MADELINE RENARD	EUROPE UNLTD

STEVE BJÖRKMAN
Studio: (714) 261-1411 Fax: (714) 261-7528

New York
Renard Represents (212) 490-2450
Fax (212) 697-6828

Chicago
Vincent Kamin & Assoc. (312) 490-2450

Los Angeles
Laurie Pribble (818) 574-0288

San Francisco
David Wiley (415) 441-1623

101

JULIA · NOONAN

REPRESENTED BY THE PENNY & STERMER GROUP
(212) 243-4412

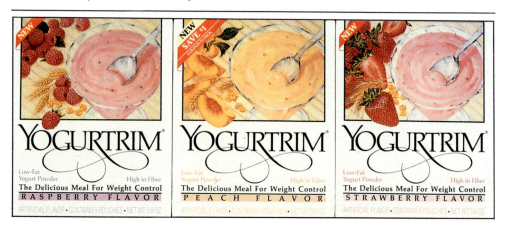

Packaging art a specialty

Clients include:
Mc Donald's
M&M Mars
Fruitcrest Corp.
General Foods
Birdseye
N.Y. Times
Clairol
Colgate Palmolive
San Martin Wines
Lever Bros.
NBC
CBS
Vicks
Mott's
Sunkist

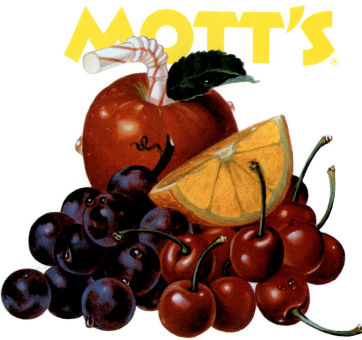

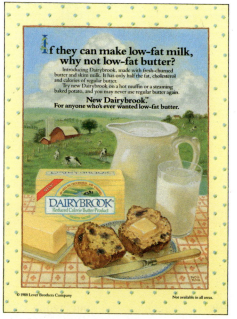

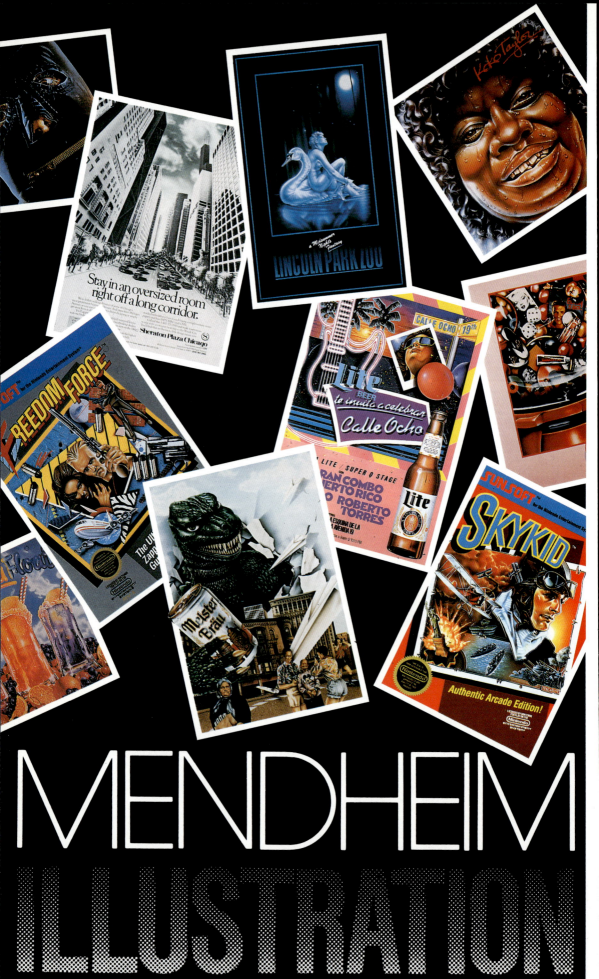

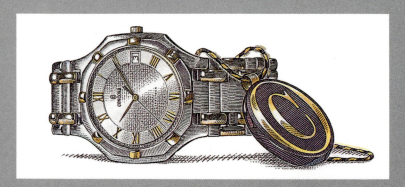

KEVIN SPROULS

STUDIO / FAX:

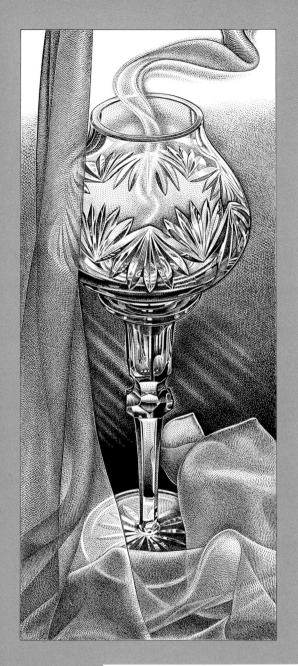

KEVIN SPROULS

201·722-5408

RILEY ILLUSTRATION

PIERRE LE-TAN

DAVID SMALL

WILLIAM BRAMHALL

CHRIS DEMAREST

PAUL MEISEL

Whit Stillman, Director   (212) 925-3053   Bruno Salinas, Associate
Edward T. Riley, Inc.   81 Greene St.   New York, NY 10012

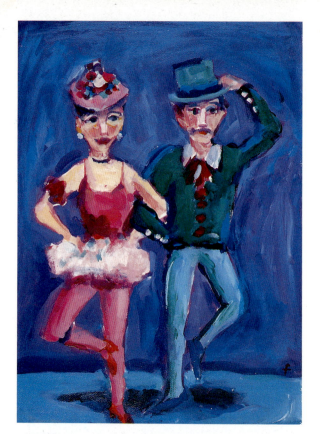

SUSAN FOSTER
301-652-3848
4800 Chevy Chase Drive
Suite #500
Chevy Chase, MD 20815

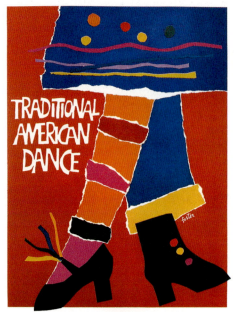

When you need quality illustration and you can't afford to fool around...consult

THE ULTIMATE AUTHORITY

You have enough problems as it is. So give yourself a break.

Spare yourself that familiar sinking feeling when the deadline day comes and the illustration you ordered still isn't quite right or quite ready.

When you need quality illustration and you can't afford to fool around, why not consult The Ultimate Authority? Call Gerald & Cullen Rapp, Inc.

There's got to be a reason why we probably sell more quality illustration than anyone else. And there is.

We not only represent an impressive group of the nation's most talented illustrators and cartoonists.

We offer superb service, based on 41 years of experience, to help you meet expectations and deadlines with minimum fuss and hassle.

When you buy from an unknown illustrator, based on two or three reproduced samples, you really have no way of knowing what you are getting into.

Were those pieces really typical? How long did they take? How many revisions were needed? How much guidance did they require from an A.D.?

But we have been dealing with each of our recognized artists for an average of 15 years. We know exactly what we can expect and what you can expect.

We can give you lightning two-way communication. Call us about your needs. We'll fax you quotes and pencil sketches.

And if we can't help you, we'll suggest who might be able to.

So the next time you need the right illustration at the right time, don't be overwhelmed by the hundreds of possibilities.

Give yourself a break.

Give us a ring.

Meanwhile flip the page for our free file box offer.

Gerald & Cullen Rapp, Inc.
108 East 35 St. (#7), New York, NY 10016 • (212) 889-3337 • Fax (212) 889-3341

© 1988

WE BELIEVE WE SELL MORE ANYONE ELSE IN THE WORLD.

RAY AMEIJIDE

MICHAEL DAVID BROWN

LON BUSCH

KEN DALLISON

LEE DUGGAN

GINNIE HOFMANN

LIONEL KALISH

LASZLO KUBINYI

ALEX MURAWSKI

LOU MYERS

BOB PETERS

JERRY PINKNEY

GERALD & CULLEN RAPP, INC.
108 East 35 St. (#7), New York 10016
Phone: (212) 889-3337 • Fax (212) 889-3341

QUALITY ILLUSTRATION THAN HERE ARE 23 REASONS WHY:

JACK DAVIS

BOB DESCHAMPS

BILL DEVLIN

RAY DOMINGO

LEE LORENZ

ALLAN MARDON

ELWYN MEHLMAN

MARIE MICHAL

CHARLES SANTORE

BOB TANENBAUM

MICHAEL WITTE

FREE FILE BOX

The field's best reference source for contemporary advertising illustration. Write to us on your company letterhead and we will send you our file box. It's packed with miniature color portfolios of our artists' work.

© 1988

JERRY LEFF
ASSOCIATES, INC.
NEW YORK
TEL: (212) 697-8525
FAX: (212) 949-1843

JOHN PARSONS

REPRESENTED BY JERRY & WILMA LEFF
420 LEXINGTON AVE. NEW YORK CITY 10170

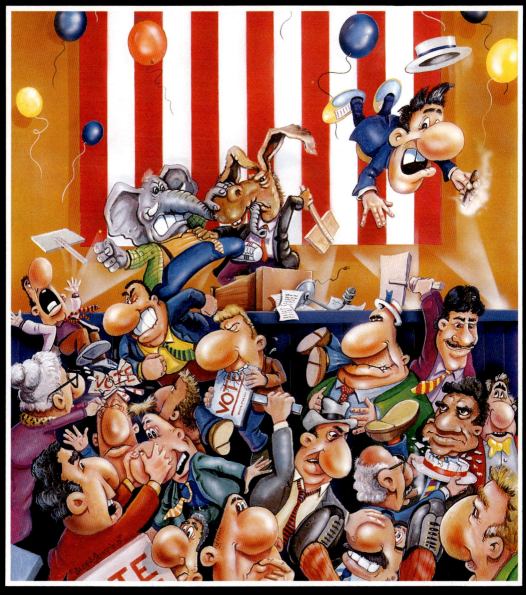

GLEN A. SCHOFIELD 4 HILLSIDE AVENUE
ROSELAND, N.J. 07068 201-226-5597

DAVID FEBLAND

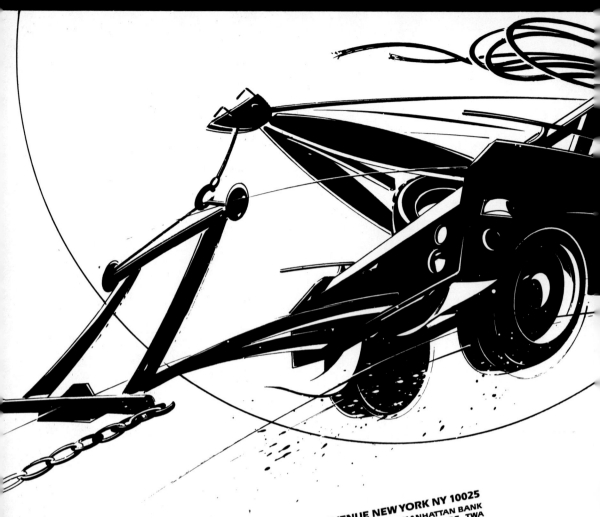

DAVID FEBLAND STUDIO 670 WEST END AVENUE NEW YORK NY 10025
CLIENTS: ABC AMERICAN EXPRESS ATLANTIC RECORDS AVIS CHASE MANHATTAN BANK
DISNEYLAND EXXON GENERAL FOODS IBM MACY'S REVLON SONY T.V. GUIDE TWA
FOR ADDITIONAL WORK SEE ALSO: CREATIVE BLACK BOOK 1986, 7, 8
AMERICAN SHOWCASE 7, 8, 10, 11, 12 CORPORATE SHOWCASE 4, 5, 6, 7
STOCK IMAGES AVAILABLE   DIRECT TELECOPIER SERVICE TO STUDIO

"I don't think Marty is asking for seconds, mother. I think Marty's requesting the Heimlich Maneuver. Aren't you, Marty?"

FUNNY LINES

AARON KOSTER
(201) 536-2815

Cartoons and humorous drawings for ads, brochures, editorials, film, posters, slides, storyboards, billboards, smorgasbords, greeting cards, etc.

Robert Tanenbaum

5505 Corbin Avenue
Tarzana, California 91356
PHONE: 818-345-6741
FAX: 818-346-9015

Represented by:
GERALD &
CULLEN RAPP, Inc.
108 E. 35 St.
NEW YORK, N.Y. 10016
PHONE: 212-889-3337
FAX: 212-889-3341

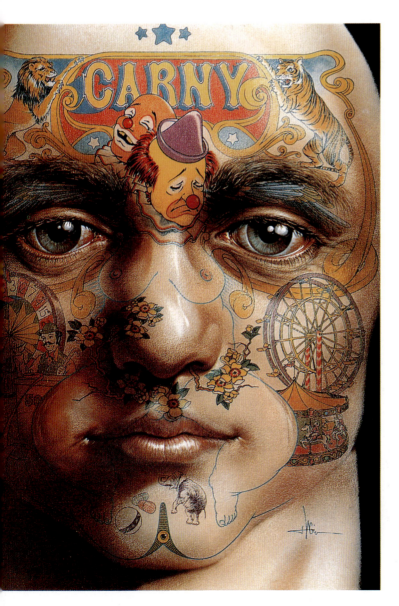

KUNIO HAGIO

ELDRIDGE

916 OLIVE STREET
SAINT LOUIS, MISSOURI 63101-1400
FAX 314.231.3042   314.231.6800
1.800.544-4791

6293 SURREY RIDGE ROAD
LISLE, IL 60532
(312) 369-0164
FAX AVAILABLE

REPRESENTED OUTSIDE
ILLINOIS BY:

ELDRIDGE

916 OLIVE STREET
SAINT LOUIS, MISSOURI 63101-1400
FAX 314.231.3042   314.231.6800

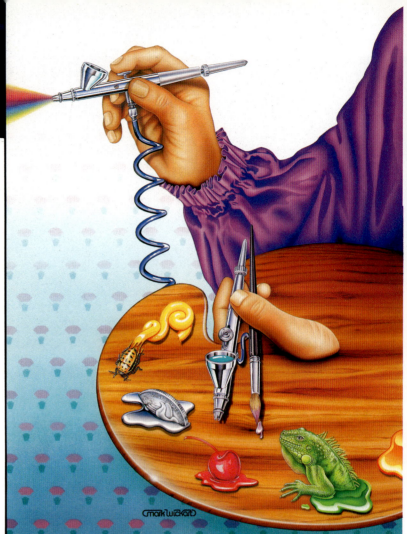

VAN HAMERSVELD

"THE QUINTESSENTIAL CALIFORNIA DESIGNER"
—ART CENTER REVIEW, WALTER BERNARD

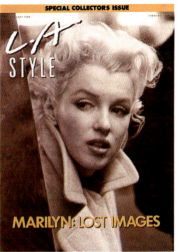

"I don't think we're designing so much for readers or non-readers as much as we are for a demographic profile of a consumer...The magazine system is one of free enterprise more than it is one of free press...Magazines have a certain credibility and integrity. In fact they define and criticize the credibility of information distributed in all other packages."–Art Center Review, John Van Hamersveld

"CREATOR OF THE FAMOUS 1965 'ENDLESS SUMMER' POSTER"
—KIRK JACKSON, TIMES STAFF WRITER

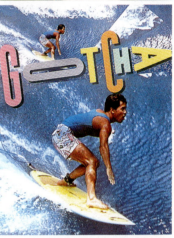

The "Endless Summer" movie campaign poster for 1966 published and printed then by Personality Poster, recently entered the collection of The New York Museum of Modern Art.

"This Warner Communication Annual Report is the best thing I have ever seen, you can quote me on that..."
—ROBERT MILES RUNYAN, L.A. DESIGNER

Designed by Pentagram, illustrated by John Van Hamersveld in his painterly, collage style. Art Director, Peter Harrison & Harold Birch.

"The evolution of art in many ways reflects the evolution of the artists themselves as similar themes are recycled with a new twist," he said.

A one hundred fifty foot stainless steel sign for the KATE MANTELINI Restaurant. Architecture by Morphosis.

916 OLIVE STREET
SAINT LOUIS, MISSOURI 63101-1400
FAX 314.231.3042
314.231.6800

ELDRIDGE

GARRY NICHOLS

BUD KEMPER

TOM KILLEEN

DEAN MITCHELL

ELDRIDGE

916 OLIVE STREET
SAINT LOUIS, MISSOURI 63101-1400
FAX 314.231.3042   314.231.6800

JARED D. LEE
(513) 932-2154
2942 Hamilton Rd., Lebanon, Ohio 45036

Meeting Manager

ANIMATION REEL ON REQUEST

FAX MACHINE
(513) 932-9389

©Jared D. Lee Studio, Inc. 1989

W.B. Doner & Co.

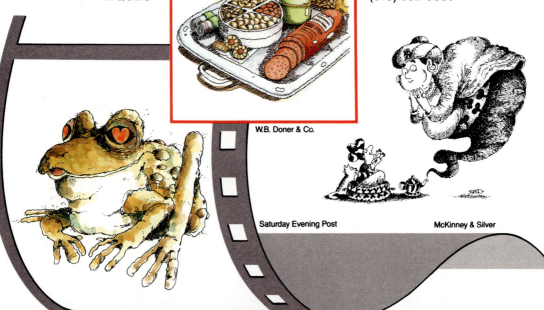

Saturday Evening Post

McKinney & Silver

TV Credits:
New York Telephone, U.S. Postal Service, Kraft Foods, Illinois Lottery, Viewmaster, Taco Johns, Reflex

STUDIO SERVICES

TOTAL CONTROL

Graphics for Industry, Inc. puts you in total control. From model making to retouching, we have everything it takes to bring your ideas to life in full, graphic detail.

Manning the controls at Graphics for Industry are some of the best designers in the business. Their knowledge and experience will make your job seem easy. Our capabilities include letterers, paste-up and mechanical artists, retouchers, illustrators and silkscreening. And Graphics for Industry has it all in-house—backed by more than twenty years worth of experience.

We're experts in color correcting. Special effects. And we're skilled in the art of model making, (creating containers and mechanical devices out of almost any material).

Call Graphics for Industry today. And put your imagination behind the controls.

GRAPHICS FOR INDUSTRY INC.

GRAPHICS FOR
INDUSTRY INC.
8 W 30TH ST.
NYC 10001

CALL
HAL PAHMER
212-889-6202

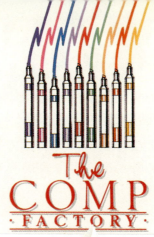

Manufacturer of story boards, comprehensives, layout, design and animatics.
The Comp Factory is a division of R. Mark Heath Illustrations, Inc.

301 • 366 • 4633   FAX # 301 • 727 • 5250
TELEX # 197599 RMHINC

COMPS STORYBOARDS

DAVID CROCKETT
212-889-6754

KEVIN SACCO • STORYBOARDS • 212-779-9290

At *Comp* Art Plus, we're not *comp*lacent about quality. That's why we've *comp*iled the best artists in the business. In every sense, we make sure that our work *comp*lements exactly what you had in mind. Whether it's storyboards, *comp*s, or animatics, we *comp*lete the job on time. What's more, we think you'll appreciate our *comp*osure under pressure. And should there be any changes, no matter how *comp*lex, we're always there to give you the service you deserve. From *comp*uters to *comp*act make-up, at *Comp* Art Plus, we have the *comp*etence you're looking for.

 There's no *comparison*.

212·689·8670 or 1·800·243·*COMP*
120 East 34th Street, NY 10016

Two steps to advertising immortality.

One:
Think up the world's greatest campaign.

Two:
Get Santa-Donato to comp it up.

ANIMATICS · COMPS · STORYBOARDS
(212) 921-1550

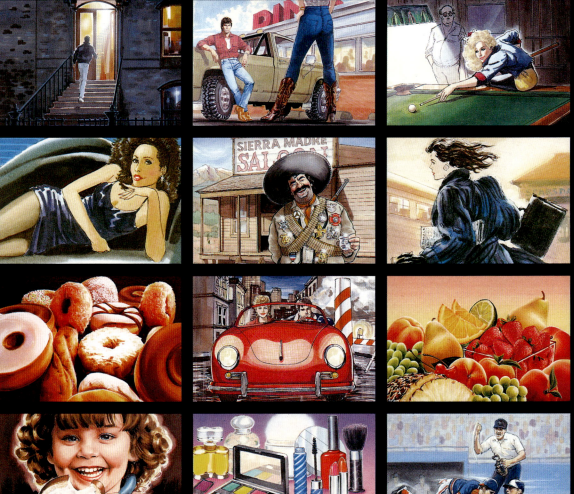

**STORYBOARDS • COMPS • CAMPAIGNS • ANIMATICS
MECHANICALS • TYPE • CUSTOM TRANSFERS**

420 Lexington Avenue • New York, N.Y. 10170 • (212) 687-3460

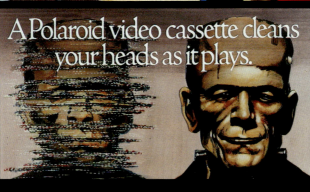

CONTINUITY GRAPHIC ASSOC. INC.

62 WEST 45TH STREET NEW YORK, N.Y. 10036

CALL OUR REPS AT (212) 869-4170. IF WE HAD MORE SPACE, WE'D SPEND IT WRITING ABOUT THEM. THEY'RE THE NICEST IN TOWN.

ANIMATICS • COMPS • STORYBOARDS
(212) 688-4555
420 LEXINGTON AVE., NEW YORK, N.Y. 10170

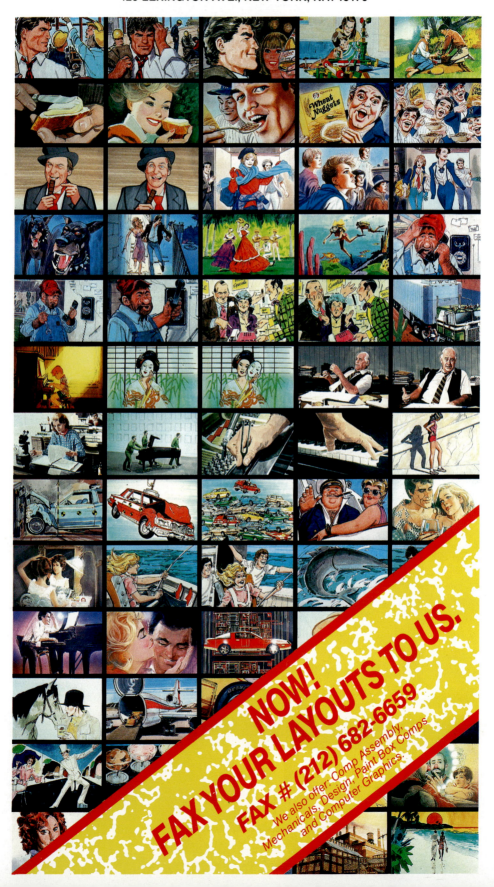

140

PHOTOGRAPHY

ASSIGNMENT & STOCK

zanetti

GERALD ZANETTI ASSOCIATES INC.
REPRESENTED BY LUCY ZANETTI
212-473-4999

Earth • Fire • Air • Water

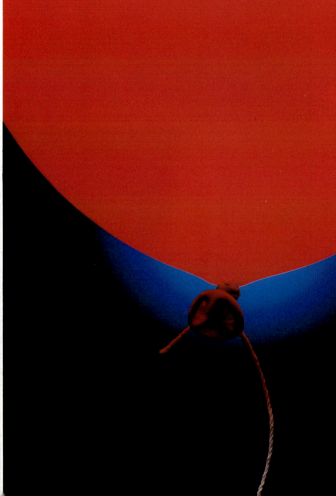

ANDREW UNANGST
(212) 889-4888

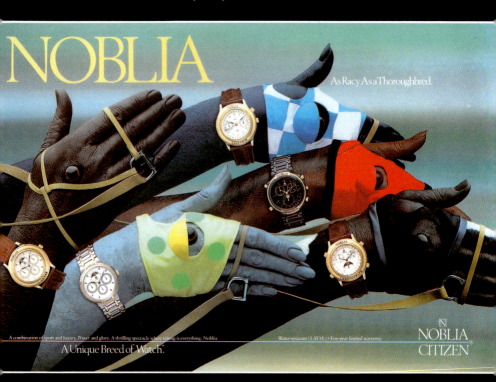

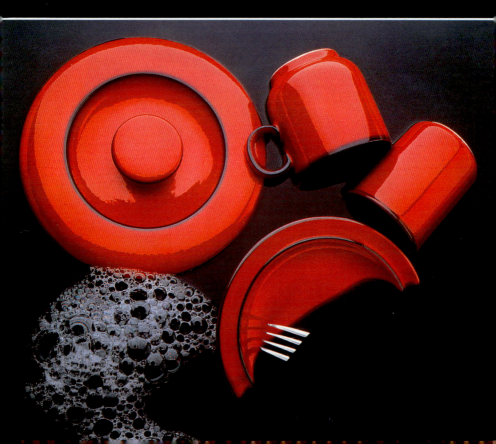

REPRESENTED BY
KEN MANN AND ROBIN DICTENBERG
(212) 944-2853
PRINT AND TELEVISION

ANDREW UNANGST
(212) 889-4888

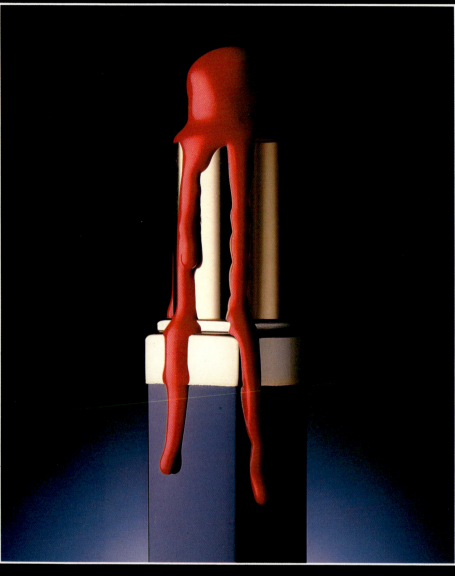

KEN MANN AND ROBIN DICTENBERG
(212) 944-2853
PRINT AND TELEVISION

Judith Leiber

Handbags/Accessories

B R I A N

represented by ken man
20 west 46th street, n. y.,

L A N K E R

n and robin dictenberg.
n. y. 10036 · 212 · 944 · 2853

B R I A N

represented by ken man
20 west 46th street, n.y.,

L A N K E R

© BRIAN LANKER 1989

n and robin dictenberg.
n. y. 10036 · 212 · 944 · 2853

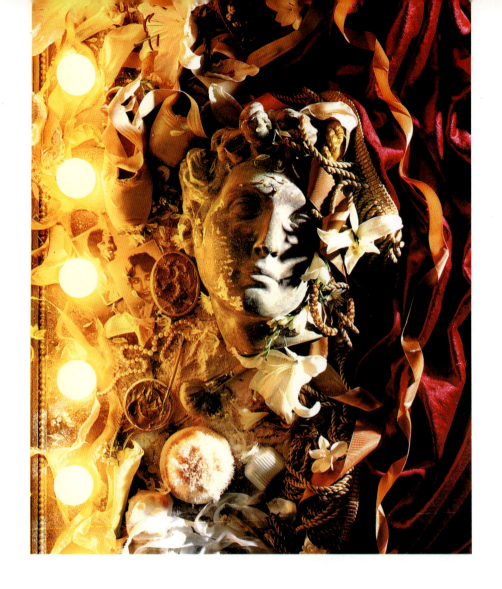

NELEMAN

HANS NELEMAN
NEW YORK
PAUL BEVAN
212.645.5832
LONDON
ANNA TAIT
01.743.3171

NELEMAN

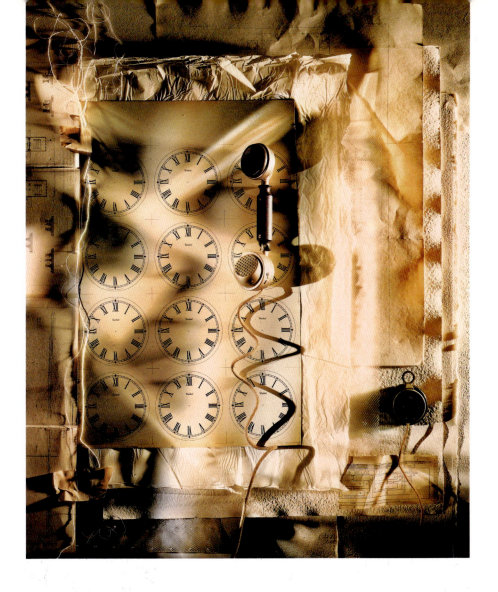

HANS NELEMAN
NEW YORK
PAUL BEVAN
212.645.5832
LONDON
ANNA TAIT
01.743.3171

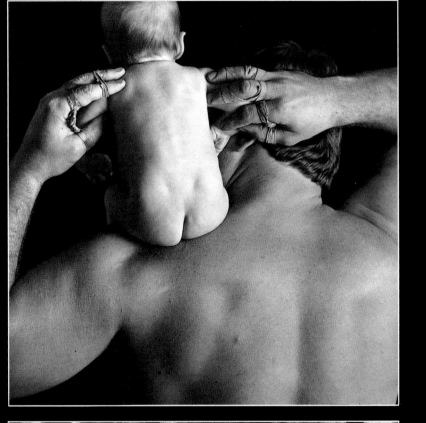
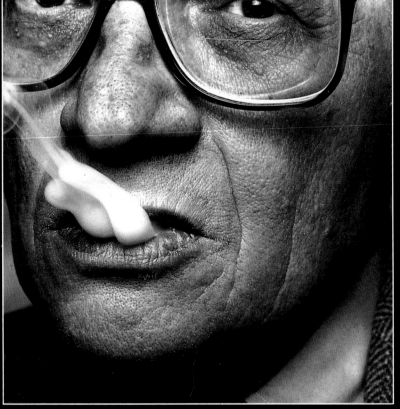

MICHAEL

Studio 212-807-8777

© MICHAEL O'NEILL 1989

L O'NEILL

Represented by Stockland & Martel 212-972-4747

DIANE
PADYS
STUDIO

New York, New York

Representation:

Stockland • Martel

212.972.4747

DIANE
PADYS
STUDIO

New York, New York

Representation:

Stockland • Martel

212.972.4747

CATHY HARDWICK
Y.E.S. at Bloomingdale's

ERIC ME[G]

535 GREENWICH STREET NYC 10013 212-255-5150

OLA

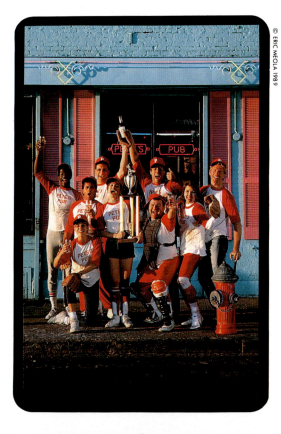

© ERIC MEOLA 1989

IN NYC CALL STOCKLAND & MARTEL 212-972-4747

WALTER IOOSS

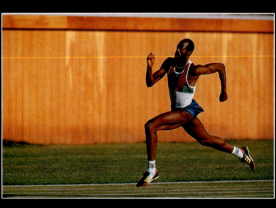

Represented by
Bill Stockland & Maureen Martel
212-972-4747

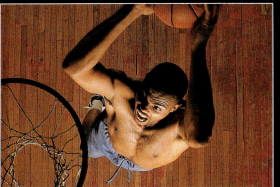

© WALTER IOOSS

JOEL
REPRESENTED BY

Sanka
Kronenbourg
M&M's
Corning
Michelob
Meridian Hotels
Amtrak
Camel
Fuji Film
Bass Shoes
American Express
Lorillard
Bloomingdales
L'Oreal
Martell
Schoeneman
Benson & Hedges
Irving Trust
Kodak
Chevrolet
Scope
Playtex
Avon
Kool-Aid
Johnnie Walker
U.S. Tobacco
Coca-Cola
Nikon
Buccellati
Distiller's Company
Pepsi
Levolor
Anheuser Busch
Procter & Gamble
Lever Brothers
Maxwell House
JC Penny
Money
Esquire
Bank Of America
Warner Lambert
Smirnoff
Vantage
Eastern Airlines
Spiegel
Coors
Prince Matchabelli
Bacardi
Dewars
Barclay

BALDWIN

BILL STOCKLAND & MAUREEN MARTEL   212.972.4747

Town & Country
U.S. Trust
Seagrams
Liggett & Meyers
Ron Rico
Adidas
Merit
General Foods
Jell-O
Crest
Colombian Coffee
Navy
Budget Rent-A-Car
N.Y. Telephone
Minute Maid
Waldorf Astoria
Inc. Magazine
AT&T
Johnson & Johnson
Warner-Lambert
Paco Rabanne
Courvoisier
Sheraton Hotels
Optima
First Republic Bank
Gucci
Freddie Mac
Citibank
Hyatt Hotels
Saint Gillian
Carolina Herrera
Manufacturers Hanover
New York Times
American Airlines
International Coffee
Visa
Saga Furs
Schick
Newsweek
Land 'O Lakes
Hallmark
Martex
Delta Airlines
Bristol Meyers
Metropolitan Home
Cheseborough Ponds
Milton Bradley
Congoleum
Commodore
Holiday Inns
CBS Records

© JOEL BALDWIN 1989

51 W. 28TH ST.
N.Y.C. 10001
212 685 5238

LELAND BOBBÉ

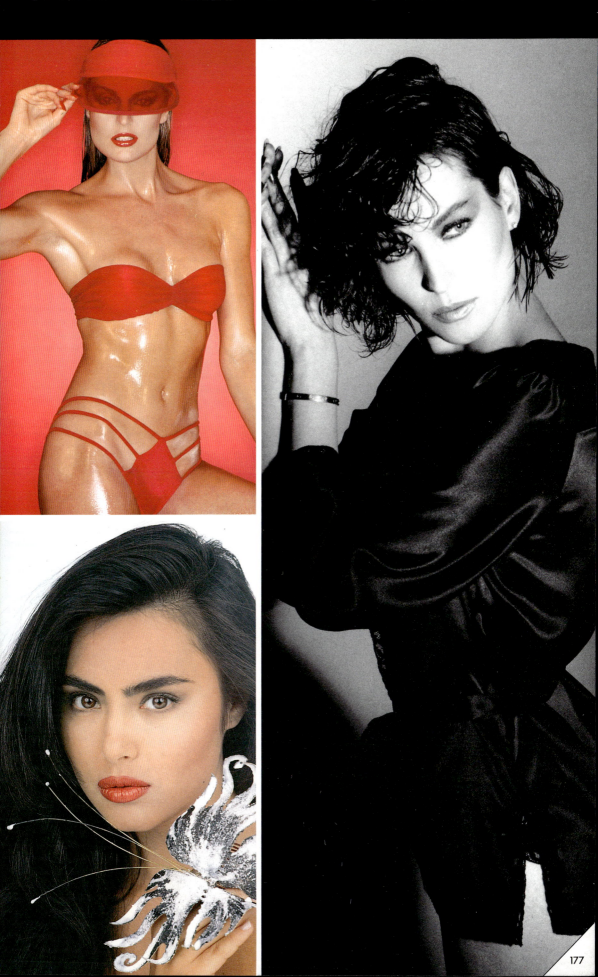

TOM SIMONS, RIZZO, SIMONS, COHN, INC. FOR THE NEW ENGLAND

RICH SILVERSTEIN, GOODBY BERLIN & SILVERSTEIN FOR ROYAL VIKING LINE

MARK FENNIMORE, OGILVY & MATHER FO

JAY MAISEL ON

Great clients allow you to do your best;
We'd like to do our best for you.

JAN KOBLITZ, MC CANN ERICKSON FOR AMERICAN EXPRESS

MICHAEL WINSLOW, MC KINNEY & SILVER FOR NORTH CAROLINA

UNITED TECHNOLOGIES

SCOTT TAYLOR, TAYLOR AND BROWNING FOR AMERICAN BARRICK

ASSIGNMENT.

For assignment or stock, call **212-431-5157** and ask for Emily.
For our Maxifolio, write on your letterhead.
JAY MAISEL, 190 BOWERY, NY, NY 10012.

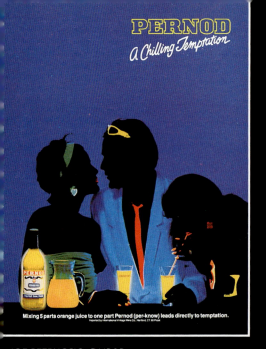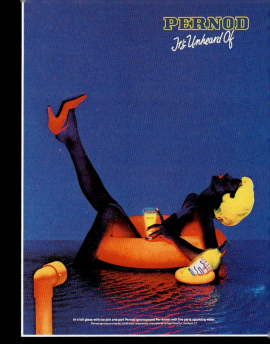

JOE PETRUCCIO DMB&B

TAK KOJIMA
PHOTOGRAPHY

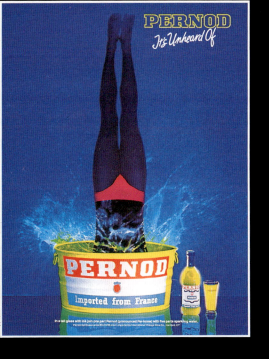

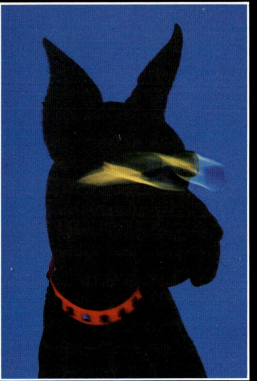
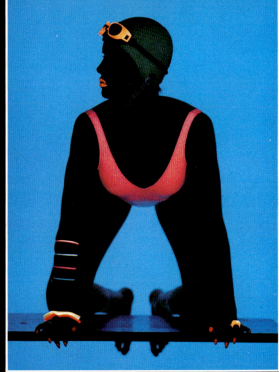

TAK KOJIMA

PHOTOGRAPHY

25 WEST 23RD STREET, NEW YORK, N.Y. 10010 PHONE 212 243-2243 FAX 212 674-1106

Matthew Klein 104 W.17th St., N.Y., N.Y. 10011 (212) 255-6400

Represented by Michael Crecco (212) 682-3422

"*Matthew Klein has done virtually every food photograph I've needed for the past 17 years. Perfectly.*"

—*Milton Glaser*

Peter Papadopolous, 78 Fifth Avenue, New York, New York 10011. 212-675-8830

PAPADO

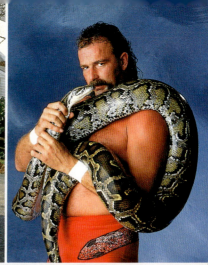

Representative: Elise Caputo, 212-725-0503.

POLOUS

Fax: 212-691-5667
Ask for our traveling mini-portfolio.

Peter Papadopolous, 78 Fifth Avenue, New York, New York 10011. 212-675-8830

PAPADO

Representative: Elise Caputo, 212-725-0503.

POLOUS

Fax: 212-691-5667
Ask for our traveling mini-portfolio.

REPRESENTED BY ELISE CAPUTO (212) 725-0503

BRADY

BRADY THRIVES IN ALL KINDS OF LIGHT
STEVE BRADY PHOTOGRAPHY, INC. 1 BOND STREET, #3B N.Y.C. 10012   NY STUDIO 212-979-6322
REPRESENTED BY ELISE CAPUTO 212-725-0503   TX STUDIO 713-660-6663

MICHAEL WATSON STUDIO   PRINT+TELEVISION

133 WEST 19th   NY, NY 10011   212 620 3125

DENNIS

REPRESENTED BY DOUG BROWN

BLACHUT

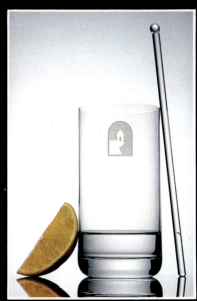

(212) 953-0088 PRINT AND TELEVISION

SELTZER

443 W. 18 St., New York, N.Y. 10011, (212) 807-0660 FAX (212) 691-3357

STUDIOS

Represented by **Doug Brown** (212) 953-0088

SELTZER

443 W. 18 St., New York, N.Y. 10011, (212) 807-0660 FAX (212) 691-3357

STUDIOS

Represented by **Doug Brown** (212) 953-0088

Represented
In New York By
Doug Brown
212 953 0088

aaron jones

800 448 9939

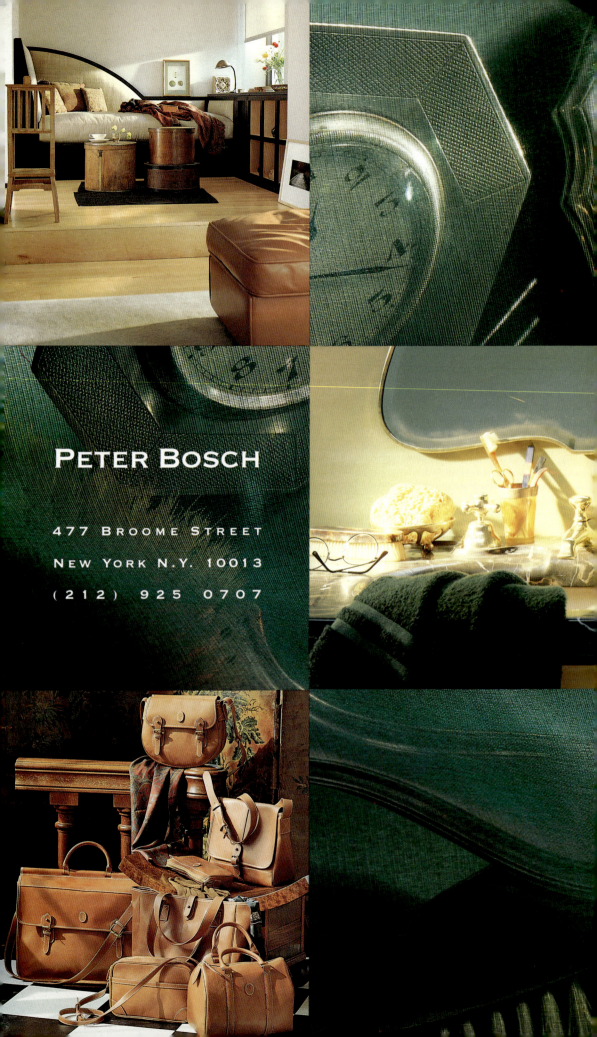

205

JEFF SMITH

30 East 21st Street,
New York, New York 10010
Representative: Emily Smith
(212) 674-8383

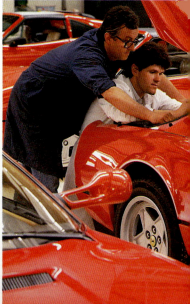

MANNO

© 1989 JOHN MANNO

JOHN MANNO PHOTOGRAPHY
20 WEST 22ND STREET
NEW YORK NEW YORK 10010
212 243 7353

REPRESENTED BY VICKI SANDER
212 683 7835

MANNO

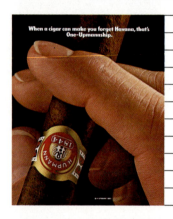

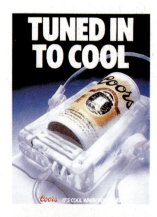

© 1989 JOHN MANNO

REPRESENTED BY VICKI SANDER 212 683 7835

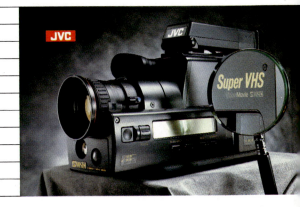

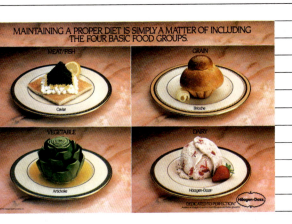

ADIDAS
AMERICAN EXPRESS
ARAMIS
BAZAAR
BERGDORF GOODMAN
BOTANY 500
CHRISTIAN DIOR
CUTTY SARK
ESQUIRE
HATHAWAY
HENRY GRETHEL
J C PENNEY
KOOL
L'EGGS
LEE JEANS
McGREGOR
MEN'S GUIDE TO FASHION
MICHELOB
NEW WOMAN
PACO RABANNE
PAUL HARRIS
RUSSELL
SMIRNOFF
YVES SAINT LAURENT

AL

250 MERCER STREET NEW YORK CITY 10012 212 674 4535

RUBIN

REPRESENTED BY RODD HARMON 212 245 8935

OLOF

Olof Wahlund Photography Inc. 7 East 17th Street, New York 10003 (212) 929 9067

Represented by Bert Yellen Associates, Inc. 420 East 54th Street, New York 10022 (212) 838 3170

Olof Wahlund Photography Inc. 7 East 17th Street, New York 10003 (212) 929 9067

Represented by Bert Yellen Associates, Inc. 420 East 54th Street, New York 10022 (212) 838 3170

Derek Gardner

RITA HOLT, & ASSOCIATES, INC.
(212) 683-2002   FAX: (201) 738-5499

David Burnett

RITA HOLT & ASSOCIATES, INC.
(212) 683-2002   FAX: (201) 738-5499

Arciero

TONY ARCIERO IN DETROIT (313) 477-9944.
IN PARIS CONTACT CHRISTIAN 331-45-06-1880.

RITA HOLT & ASSOCIATES, INC.
(212) 683-2002   FAX: (201) 738-5499

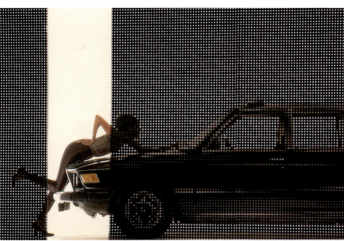

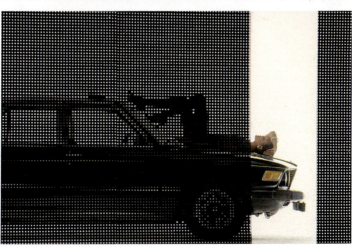

JOE TOTO LOVES

13-17 LAIGHT STREET, NEW YORK,
NEW YORK 10013 (212) 966-7626

SHOOT PEOPLE.

RITA HOLT & ASSOCIATES, INC.
(212) 683-2002   FAX: (201) 738-5499

223

PETE TURNER

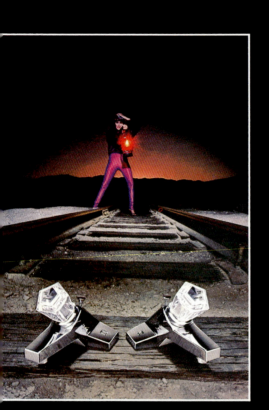

212-765-1733 FAX 212-765-5817
154 W. 57 ST., NYC 10019 – STOCK: IMAGE BANK

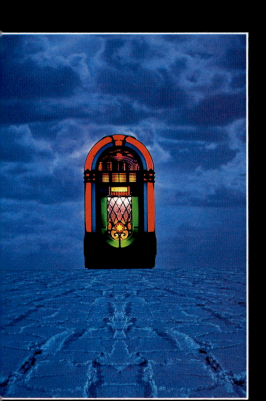

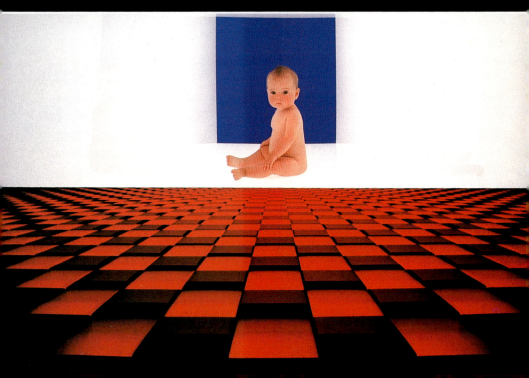

DÉNES PETÖE 22 WEST 27TH STREET

Dénes Petöe

NEW YORK, NY 10001 (212) 213-3311

© 1989, Dénes Petöe

Dénes Petöe

DÉNES PETÖE 22 WEST 27TH STREET

Dénes Petöe

NEW YORK, NY 10001   (212) 213-3311

© 1989, Dénes Petoe

Dénes Petöe

DÉNES PETÖE 22 WEST 27TH STREET

Dénes Petöe

NEW YORK, NY 10001 (212) 213-3311

© 1989, Dénes Petoe

Dénes Petöe

MICHAEL HARRIS
Print and Television

18 West 21 Street New York City 10010 (212) 255-3377

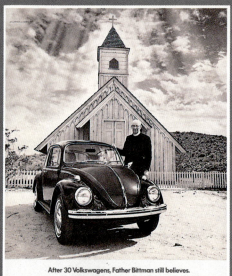
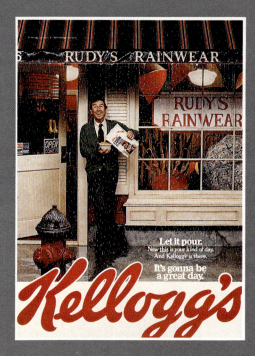

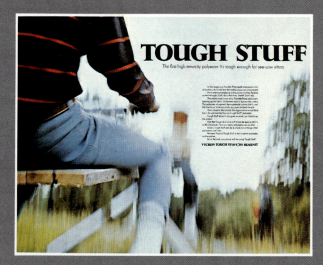

PETRUCELLI ASSOCIATES INC.
TONY PETRUCELLI   212-490-9269

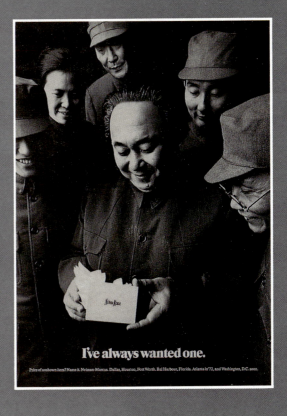

TO SEE MORE OF THE PORTFOLIO SEE CALIFORNIA WORKBOOK AND BLACK BOOK PAGES 708-711 WEST SECTION.

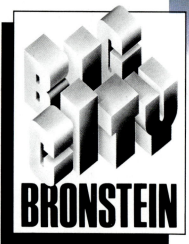

STEVE BRONSTEIN
5 E. 19TH ST. NYC 10003
(212) 473-3366
REPRESENTED BY
GARY HUREWITZ
BONNIE SHAPIRO

MINIATURE SET

MINIATURE SET

STEVE BRONSTEIN
5 E. 19TH ST. NYC 10003
(212) 473-3366
REPRESENTED BY
GARY HUREWITZ,
BONNIE SHAPIRO

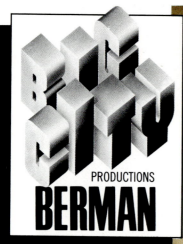

HOWARD BERMAN
5 E. 19TH ST. NYC 10003
(212) 473-3366
REPRESENTED BY
GARY HUREWITZ
BONNIE SHAPIRO

HOWARD BERMAN
5 E. 19TH ST. NYC 10003
(212) 473-3366
REPRESENTED BY
GARY HUREWITZ
BONNIE SHAPIRO

BIG CITY PRODUCTIONS
CULBERSON

EARL CULBERSON
5 E. 19TH ST. NYC 10003
(212) 473-3366
REPRESENTED BY
GARY HUREWITZ
BONNIE SHAPIRO

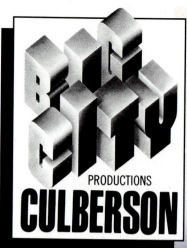

EARL CULBERSON
5 E. 19TH ST. NYC 10003
(212) 473-3366
REPRESENTED BY
GARY HUREWITZ
BONNIE SHAPIRO

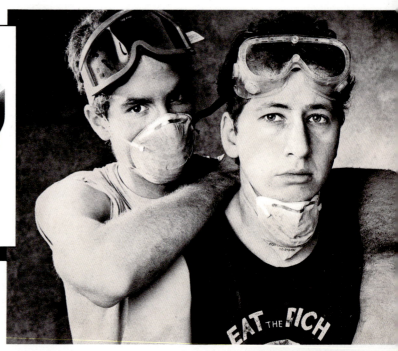

DAN WEAKS
5 E. 19TH ST. NYC 10003
(212) 473-3366
REPRESENTED BY
GARY HUREWITZ
BONNIE SHAPIRO

BIG CITY PRODUCTIONS
WEAKS

DAN WEAKS
5 E. 19TH ST. NYC 10003
(212) 473-3366
REPRESENTED BY
GARY HUREWITZ
BONNIE SHAPIRO

BIG CITY PRODUCTIONS
MORRISON

RICK MORRISON
5 E. 19TH ST. NYC 10003
(212) 473-3366
REPRESENTED BY
GARY HUREWITZ
BONNIE SHAPIRO

ON TOP

STATUE OF LIBERTY / ELLIS ISLAND FOUNDATION INC.

HELMSLEY SPEAR / DOUGLAS LIEGH ORGANIZATION

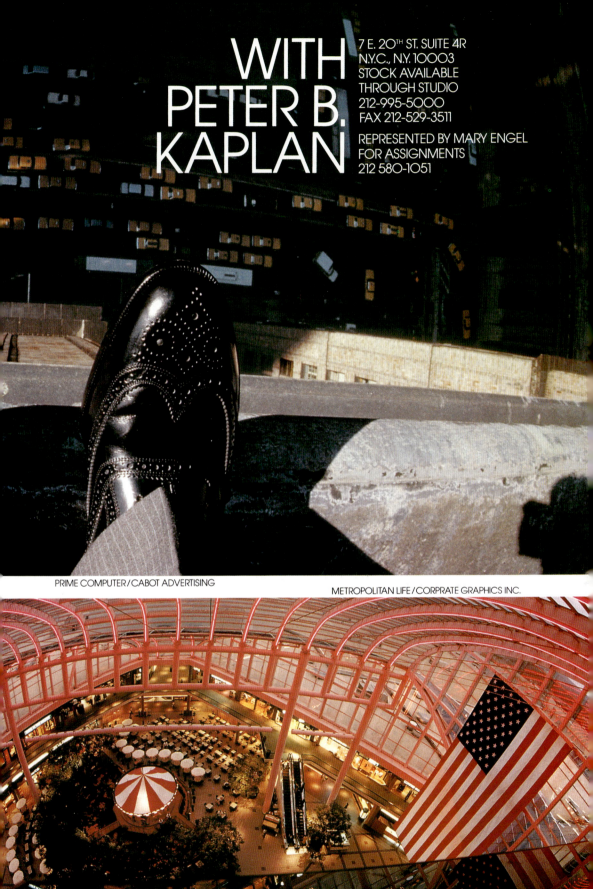

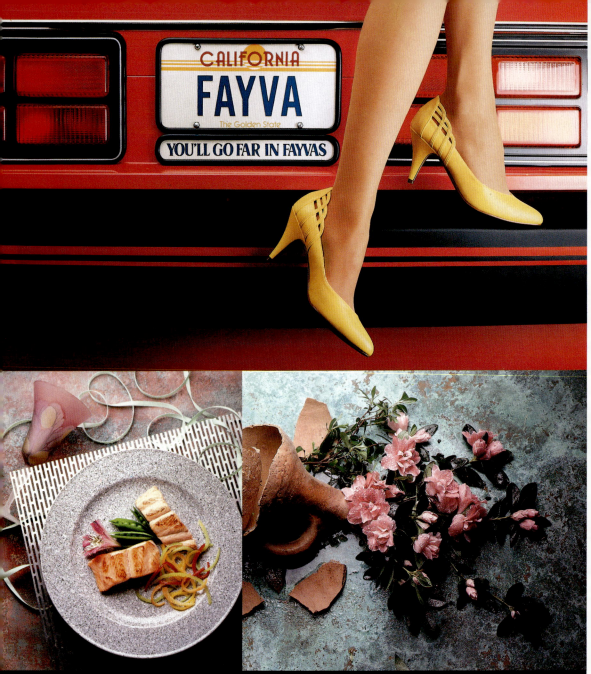

DAN KOZAN

DAN KOZAN STUDIO 32 W. 22ST. N·Y·C· 212·691·2288
REPRESENTED BY: THE SOURCE FORCE, EDWARD SARTAN (212) 643·3100

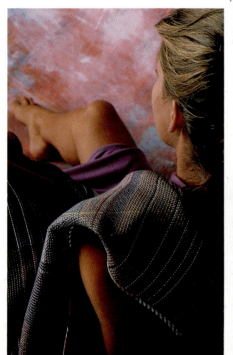

To see our Portfolio,
contact Jane A. Sutton
603/627-2659   Fax 603/627-4854
Out of town accounts welcome
Paul Avis Photographer, Inc.

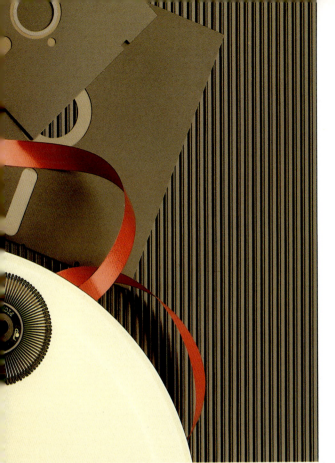

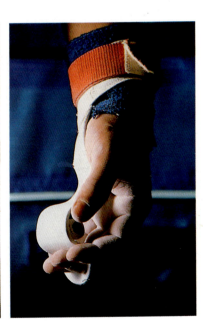

MITCHEL GRAY

145 HUDSON STREET, NEW YORK CITY 10013   212-226-0223
REPRESENTED BY BERNSTEIN & ANDRIULLI, INC. • 212/682-1490

WOLFSON

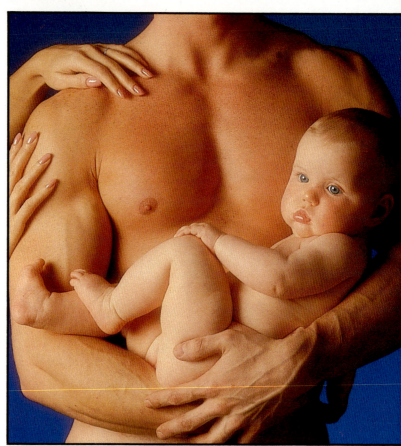

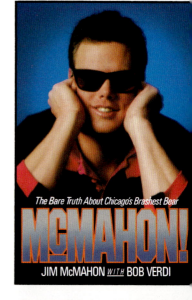

The Bare Truth About Chicago's Brashest Bear

McMAHON!

JIM McMAHON WITH BOB VERDI

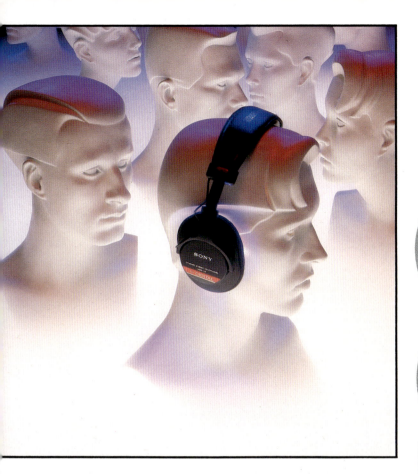

WOLFSON PHOTOGRAPHY INC.
133 WEST 19TH STREET
NEW YORK, N.Y. 10011
212-924-1510

REPRESENTED BY BERNSTEIN & ANDRIULLI
212-682-1490
FAX: 212-286-1890

Shoot with the wrong photographer and a bad picture isn't the only thing you'll get.

HASHI STUDIO INC.
TEL. (212) 675-6902
FAX. (212) 633-0163
николай NEW YORK

Ever wonder what it's like to work with Hashi?

HASHI STUDIO INC.
TEL. (212) 675-6902
FAX. (212) 633-0163
NEW YORK

Heartbeat

*F*or two years Dick Luria has been creating a series titled "Artists and Craftsmen in America"—intimate portraits of this country's most exciting and unique artists and craftspeople in their environments including: a ninth degree black belt, a Broadway costumer, a Navajo sculptor, a Maine lobsterman and many more.

In this personal odyssey, as well as in over 300 advertising assignments, Dick Luria shoots to capture the heart.

Call Dick Luria and experience the heartbeat.

DICK LURIA
212-929-7575

© BRETT FROOMER 1989

BRETT FROOMER

REPRESENTED BY
SUSAN BOYER

7 EAST 20TH STREET
NEW YORK, NY 10003

212/533-3113

VON HOFFMANN TRIP *Presents* **100 WAYS TO BE MEAN & ORNERY**

#5 ENROLL YOUR FRIEND IN THE "PET OF THE MONTH CLUB."

VON

ASSOCIATE KATHY WELLING

HOFFMANN TRIP

Represented by Gail von Hoffmann   (212) 575-1041 • (201) 377-0317

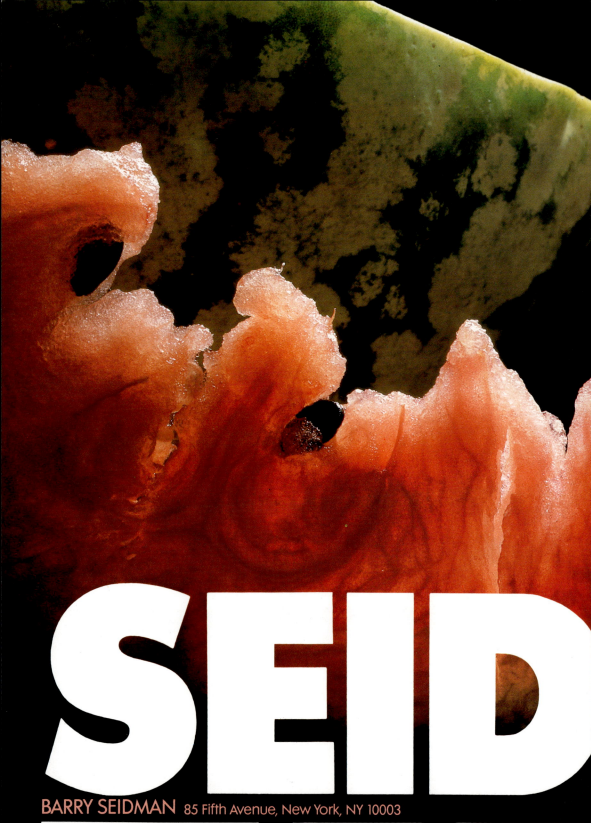

SEID

BARRY SEIDMAN 85 Fifth Avenue, New York, NY 10003

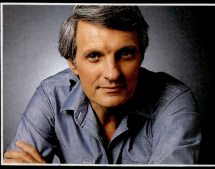

Wells, Rich, Greene

Ally Gargano

Backer Spielvogel Bates

TV REEL AVAILABLE

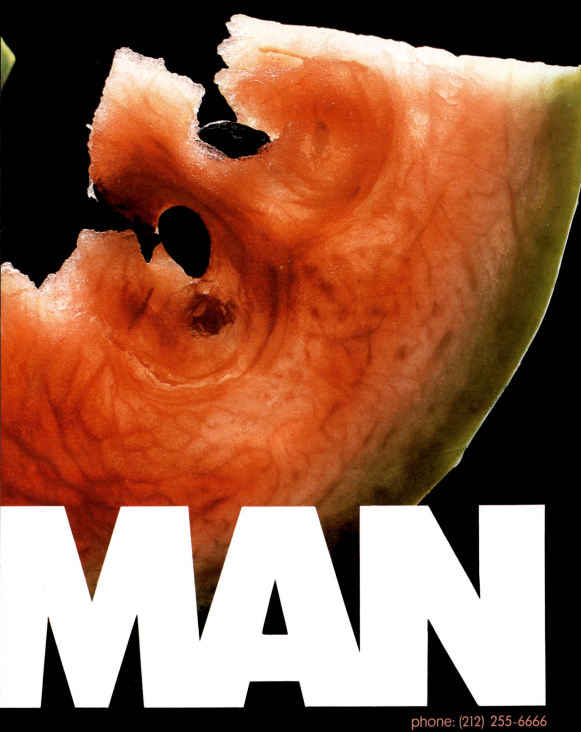

MAN

phone: (212) 255-6666

Tatham Laird & Kudner

Backer Spielvogel Bates

Grey

SPEL·MAN

Steve Spelman • 260 West 10th Street   New York   New York 10014 • 212 242 9381
Represented by Robin Ritter & Ellyn Pitts • 212 645 1177

© 1988 Steve Spelman

SPEL·MAN

Steve Spelman • 260 West 10th Street   New York   New York 10014 • 212 242 9381
Represented by Robin Ritter & Ellyn Pitts • 212 645 1177

© 1988 Steve Spelman

Judd Pilossof 142 West 26 Street NYC 10001
Represented by Robin Ritter (212) 645-1177

MICHAEL RAAB represented

by robin ritter 212·645·1177

Raab.

831 broadway, new york, n.y. 10003
212 533 0030

Joel Avirom – Harper & Row

Patrick Flaherty – HHCC

Bob Cooney – R.A. Cooney, Inc.

Gwenne Wilcox – Donovan & Green

Toshi – RGP Ltd.

RICHARD LEVY

5 West 19th Street

New York City 10011

212 243 4220

FAX: 212 243 6247

Represented by Arlene Vallon

718 706 8112

Nik Ives – Ogilvy & Mather

DENNIS CHALKIN STUDIO INC

5 East 16th Street
New York, New York 10003
212·929·1036

Represented by Barbara Umlas
212·534·4008

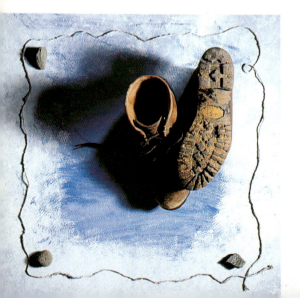

николаш Nora Scarlett
Represented By
Barbara Umlas
(212) 534-4008

252 WEST 30 ST
NEW YORK
NEW YORK 10001
212 947 9403

JAKE RAJS

Mark Thomas

MARK THOMAS

141 West 26th Street 4th floor New York, New York 10001 212-741-7252

Represented by BARBARA UMLAS 212-534-4008

JOHN BEA

N STUDIO
5 West 19th Street, New York, New York 10011 (212) 242-8106

JOSEPH MULLIGAN

239 CHESTNUT STREET
PHILADELPHIA, PA 19106
215 592-1359

REPRESENTED BY RALPH KERR

ELIZABETH

H E Y E R T

251 WEST 30 ST.
N.Y. N.Y. 10001
(212) 594-1008

The perfect combination of Vision, Quality and Execution has throughout history produced achievements that go beyond the ordinary.

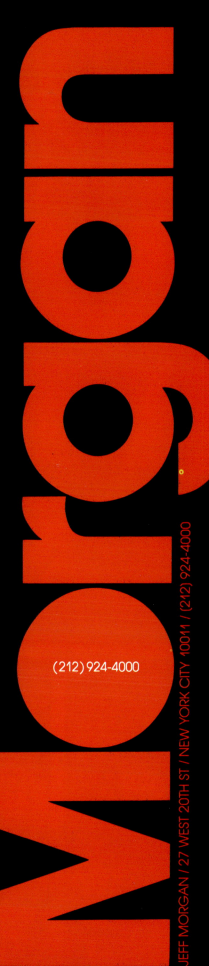

Morgan

(212) 924-4000

JEFF MORGAN / 27 WEST 20TH ST / NEW YORK CITY 10011 / (212) 924-4000

ALL PHOTOGRAPHS PRODUCED FOR SOVRAN FINANCIAL CORPORATION
BEATLEY & GRAVITT / ROBERT YOUNG

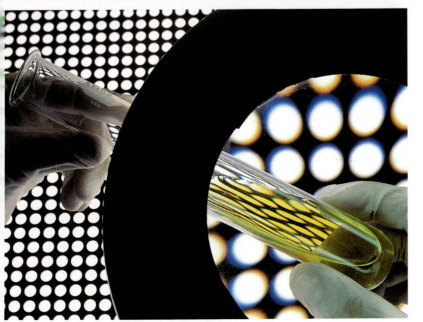

lou jones
22 randolph street
boston 02118 usa
617/426 6335
212/463 8971

clients:
bendix
ibm
pan am
kawasaki
lotus
polaroid
compaq
price waterhouse
reader's digest
esquire

RYSINSKI

109 W 27th Street, New York, NY 10001
(212) 807-7301

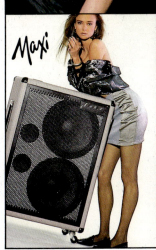

OSKAR MARTINEZ
303 Park Avenue South, Suite 408, New York, N.Y. 10010   212-529-7521

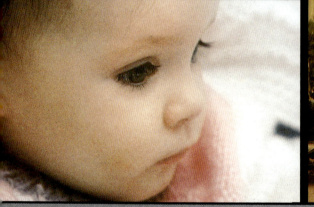

JEFF

CADGE

New York City
212•246•6155

LYNN GOLDSMITH • 241 W. 36TH ST. • NYC • 10018 • 212/736-4602 • TELEX: 971782

SUZANNE VEGA

TOM WOLFE

LYNN GOLDSMITH • 241 W. 36TH ST. • NYC • 10018 • 212/736-4602 • TELEX: 971782

SALLY, MY GODCHILD

EMO PHILIPS

ITZHAK PERLMAN

ERIC KAHAN 36 WEST 20 STREET N.Y.C. NY 10011 (212) 243-9727

TED MORRISON
PHOTOGRAPHY

To View a Portfolio Contact: Ralph/CoCo/Dennis/JoAnn (212) 239-1189
286 Fifth Avenue · New York, New York 10001

TED MORRISON
PHOTOGRAPHY

To View a Portfolio Contact: Ralph/CoCo/Dennis/JoAnn (212) 239-1189
286 Fifth Avenue · New York, New York 10001

CHRISTENSEN

Paul Christensen, 286 Fifth Avenue, New York, New York 10001
To view a portfolio contact: Ralph/CoCo/Dennis/JoAnn — 239-1189

Katrina
★★★

KATRINA DE LEON PHOTOGRAPHY
286 FIFTH AVENUE
NEW YORK, NY 10001

To View a Portfolio Contact: Ralph/CoCo/Dennis/JoAnn (212) 239-1189

KATRINA DE LEON PHOTOGRAPHY
286 FIFTH AVENUE
NEW YORK, NY 10001

To View a Portfolio Contact: Ralph/CoCo/Dennis/JoAnn (212) 239-1189

AUBRY

DANIEL AUBRY • PEOPLE ILLUSTRATION • WORLDWIDE STOCK AVAILABLE • (212) 598-4191

Michael Sahaida
Red Circle Studios
5 West 19th Street
New York, New York 10011
Represented by:
 Clinton Savage
 212-924-4545

© 1988 Michael Sahaida

Joe Standart
Red Circle Studios
5 West 19th Street
New York, New York 10011

In New York call:
    Clinton Savage   212-924-4545
In Chicago:
    Vince Kamin   312-787-8834

© 1988 Joe Standart

Robert A

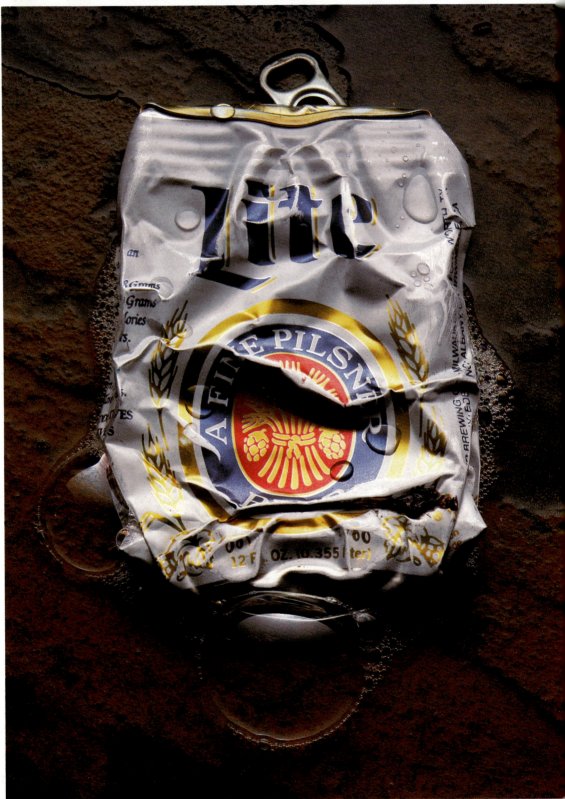

Robert Ammirati Studio, 568 Broadway N.Y., N.Y. 10012 (212) 925-58
Represented by Frank Meo (212) 353-0907

AMMIRATI

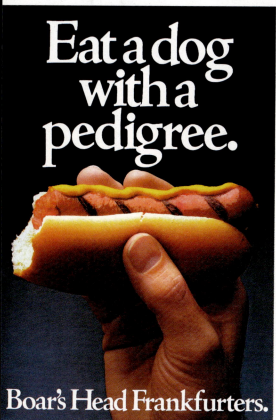

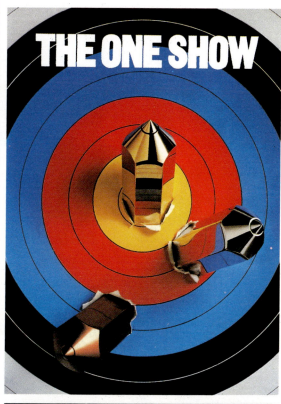

JOHN HUET

107 South Street, Boston, MA 02111 617-423-0908

327

REPRESENTATIVE
RICK WEISBROT
212-477-3333

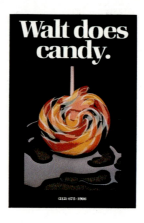
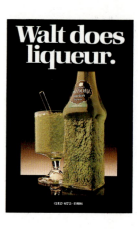
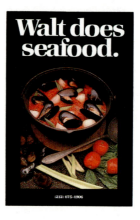

WALT CHRYNWSKI
154 WEST 18 ST NEW YORK, NY 10011 (212) 675-1906

331

Jeffrey E. Blackm

FOR ASSIGNMENTS AND
AN EXTENSIVE STOCK LIBRARY   718 769 0986

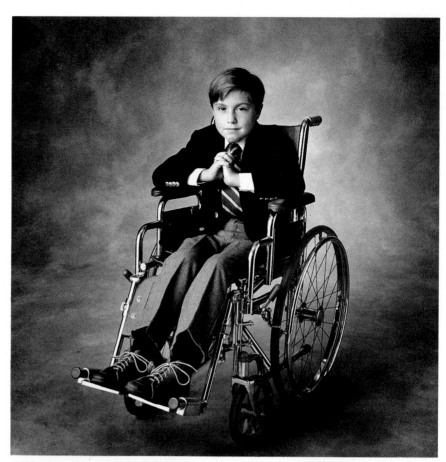

HUMANS BY UMANS

MARTY UMANS PHOTOGRAPHY
29 EAST 19 STREET NY NY 10003
212 · 995 · 0100
REPRESENTED BY DARIO SACRAMONE
212 · 929 · 0487

HUMANS BY UMANS

MARTY UMANS PHOTOGRAPHY
29 EAST 19 STREET NY NY 10003
212 · 995 · 0100
REPRESENTED BY DARIO SACRAMONE
212 · 929 · 0487

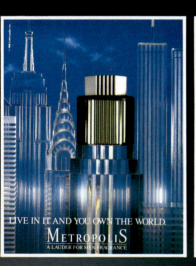
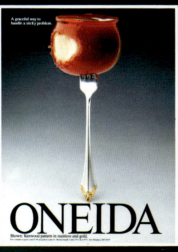
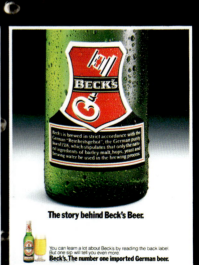

ROBBoston

Clients include:
Polaroid
Lotus
John Hancock
AT&T
American Tourister
Stratus Computer
Paper Mate
Data General

Steve Robb   535 Albany Street   Boston   MA   02118

To FAX: in US 1-800-544-0417, overseas 214-661-1096. Include our name and Bos-501.

617-542-6565

Excerpts from a summer diary...

I've been with Eric nearly everyday.

Sometimes we'll just ride for hours in his pickup.

Uncle Claude says that I'm a born farm girl.

I shall not easily forget my summer on this farm.

CONTRINO
PHOTOGRAPHY
212 · 947 · 4450

BRUNO PHOTOGRAPHY INCORPORATED

Roy Grace   Grace & Rothschild

Mike Travis   Bozell, Jacobs, K & E

Janet Sutherland   Kobs & Draft

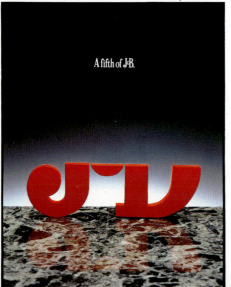

Roy Grace   Grace & Rothschild

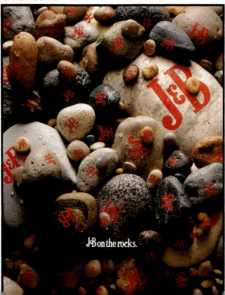

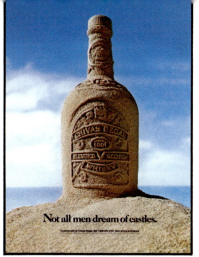
Lester Feldman DDB Needham

Harvey Baron Ally Gargano/MCA

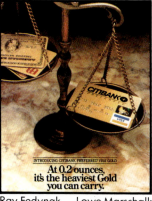
Ray Fedynak Lowe Marschalk

Susan Lipschutz Young & Rubicam

Raul Pina Della Femina, Travisano
& Partners

Keith Evans DDB Needham

Olga Arseniev TBWA

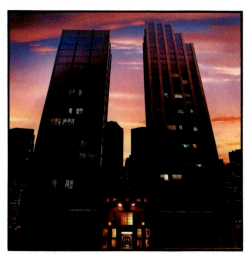
Guy Migliaccio, Donald Bow Young & Rubicam

Bruno Photography Incorporated

43 Crosby Street
NY, NY 10012

Represented by
Holly Kaplan

212-925-2929

343

Terry Niefield Studio
12 West 27th Street
New York 10001
(212) 686 8722

Represented by
Robert Feldman

N I E F

I E L D

MITCHELL FUNK
500 E 77ST. N.Y. N.Y. 10162 212-988-2886

Shel Secunda

112 Fourth Avenue, New York, New York 10003 (212) 477-0241

SUSUMU SATO

SUSUMU SATO PHOTOGRAPHY INC.
109 WEST 27TH STREET
NEW YORK, NEW YORK 10001
FAX: 212 633-9235

TEL: 212 741-0688

REPRESENTED BY:
REBECCA SEGERSTROM

TEL: 212 242-0181

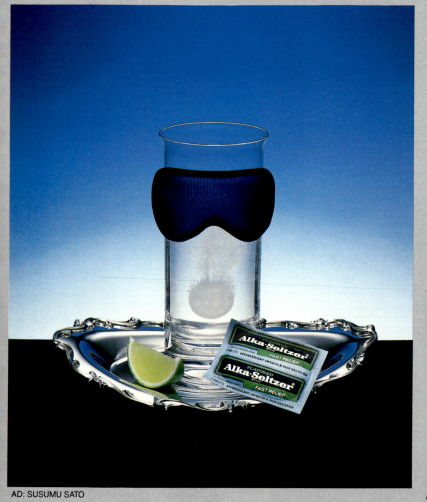

AD: SUSUMU SATO

AD: GRETTA GALLIVAN
COMMUNICATIONS DIVERSIFIED

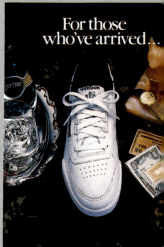

AD: BRUCE BURKE, EDWIN BIRD WILSON

AD: TOM BOTOKIN, NEW YORK TIMES

AD: JOY GREENE, YOUNG & RUBICAM/CYB

AD: JOY GREENE, YOUNG & RUBICAM/CYB

AD: GUS SAUTER, SAUTER&HIRSH

AD: SHIGEMITSU HAYASHI, MATRIX ADVERTISING

Douglas Foulke

DOUGLAS FOULKE PHOTOGRAPHY
140 WEST 22ND STREET NEW YORK CITY 10011 (212) 243-0822
REPRESENTED BY PAULA KRONGARD (212) 683-1020

ULF SKO
5 East 16th Street, New York

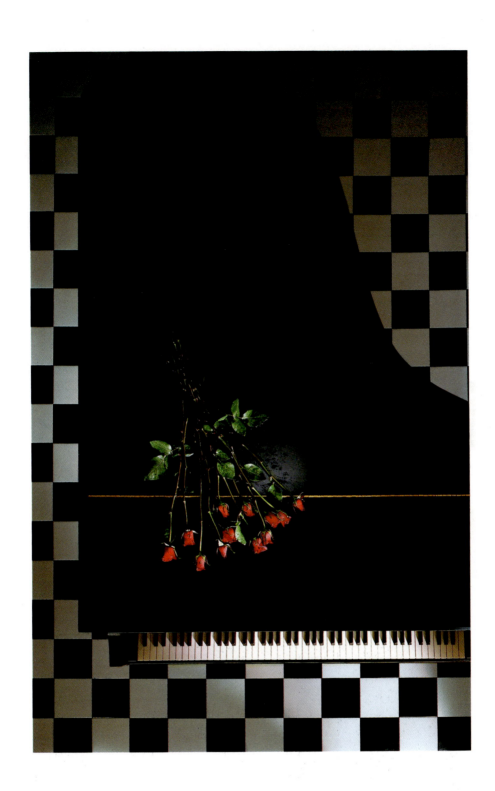

GSBERGH
NY 10003 • 212 255 7536

MICHAEL BELK

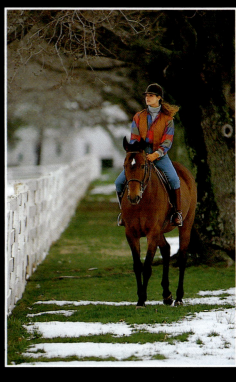

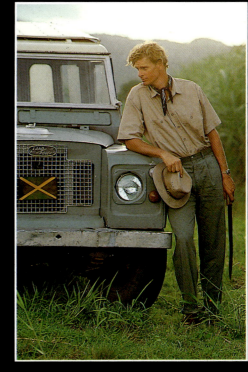

212-691-8255

THE BIG PICTURE

8 x 10 x EDAHL

ED EDAHL STUDIO   212 929-2002
236 WEST 27TH STREET NEW YORK, NEW YORK 10001

STEVEN EDSON

Microtrac Systems Inc.
ADS, Inc.
Weyerhaeuser Co.
CompuServe Data Technologies
Nestle Enterprises, Inc.
Allyn & Bacon
I Max Corporation

Fidelity Investments
Digital Equipment Corporation
Prime Computer, Inc.
Sheraton Hotels
Honeywell Bull
AT + T Bell Laboratories
New Balance

617 357-8032

107 South Street
Boston, Mass. 02111

Copyright 1989

Ron Brello Jr.

Photography, 400 Lafayette St. NYC 10003 (212) 982•0490
Represented by Mary Engel (212) 580•1051

RUM INVADES THE PROVINCE OF VODKA.

We took a chance. We challenged vodka on its "home ground": in orange juice and in ten leading vodka markets in the U.S.

Three rums of Puerto Rico were matched against the best-selling vodka in "blind" taste tests.

We crossed our fingers. Could an upstart like rum and orange juice stand a chance against a tradition like a screwdriver?

The outcome surprised even us. Of the hundreds of people tested, more preferred rum and orange juice, and the margin was substantial.

We think we know why. The rums of Puerto Rico, which are aged by law for one year, have a warmer, livelier character than vodka.

Their flavor is more naturally suited to orange juice. The result is the perfect marriage.

Isn't it amazing what can happen when people are guided by tastebuds instead of tradition?

RUMS OF PUERTO RICO

BRITISH AIRWAYS
The world's favourite airline

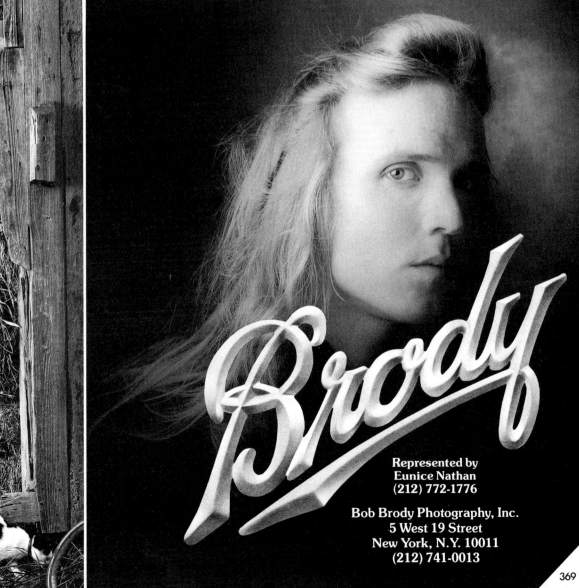

Brody

Represented by Eunice Nathan
(212) 772-1776

Bob Brody Photography, Inc.
5 West 19 Street
New York, N.Y. 10011
(212) 741-0013

E U R O P E E U R

KEVIN

OBLATTERWALLSTR. 44
(011 49) 821

VENICE

BRUSSELS

VENICE

E U R O P E E U R

GALVIN

8900 AUGSBURG, GERMANY,
156393

PARIS

BAVARIA

PARIS

MUNICH

**Represented by
Eunice Nathan
212-772-1776**

PAUL ARESU

PAUL ARESU

REPRESENTED BY TOM AFFATATO OR CALL BARRY GOLDRING AT **ARESU-GOLDRING STUDIO** 568 BROADWAY, NYC (212) 334-9494

365 FIRST AVENUE
NEW YORK, NY 10010
[212] 505-5688

REPRESENTED BY
EILEEN C TOGASHI
[212] 420-0206

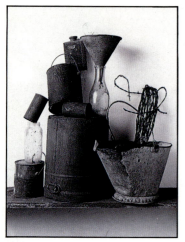

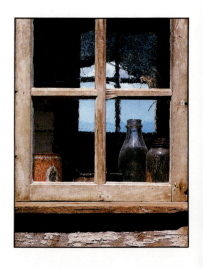

119 West 23rd Street New York, N.Y. 10011 (212) 206-0539

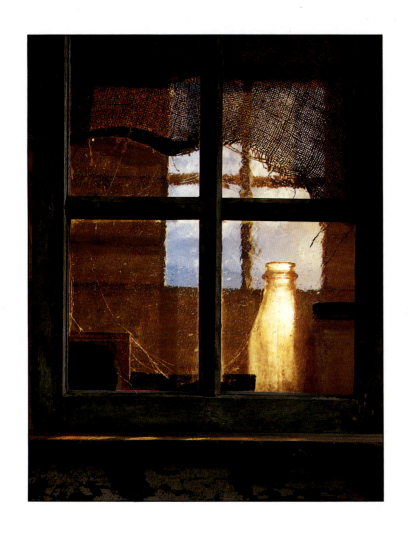

Kevin A. Logan

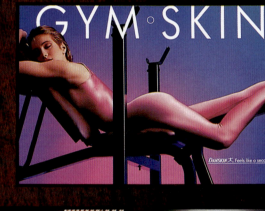

FORTUNATELY, HE FOUND A MORE ACCEPTABLE WAY TO DEAL WITH IT.

B A R D   M A R T I N

Stylist: Liz Deutsch

142 West 26 Street   New York NY 10001   **212.929.6712**

(212) 691-3364   126 WEST 22nd STREET   NEW YORK, NEW YORK 10011

KRAUS

PAUL BARTON PHOTOGRAPHY

111 West 19th St., NYC, NY 10011 (212) 691-1999. Studios in New York and Miami.

©PAUL BARTON 1989   A fine selection of stock photography available.

PAUL BARTON PHOTOGRAPHY

111 West 19th St., NYC, NY 10011 (212) 691-1999. Studios in New York and Miami.
©PAUL BARTON 1989   A fine selection of stock photography available.

JAMES
C O H E N
I N C O R P O R A T E D

36 EAST 20TH STREET NYC 10003
2 1 2 - 5 3 3 - 4 4 0 0

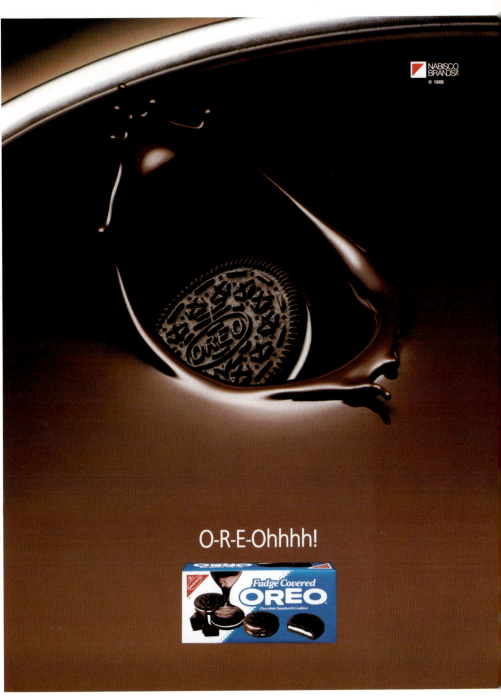

O-R-E-Ohhhh!

R E P R E S E N T E D   B Y
A R L E N E
R O S E N B E R G
2 1 2 - 6 7 5 - 7 9 8 3

MINH • 200 PARK AVE. SOUTH NEW YORK, NY 10003 (212) 477-0649
Represented by WENDY HANSEN (212) 684-7139

Golden Sin

(serves 4)

1 sheet frozen puff pastry, thawed
2 cups sugar
1 cup water
2 Golden Delicious apples
3 tbsps. butter
¼ cup brandy
candied lilacs or violets, silver and gold dragees

Preheat oven to 425 degrees. Cut 4 circles out of the puff pastry using a 4-inch tartlet pan. Place on a cookie sheet and cover with a sheet of parchment (or aluminum foil). Place another cookie sheet on top and weigh with something ovenproof. Bake for 20–25 minutes, until golden. Remove and let cool on wire rack.

Combine the sugar and water in a heavy saucepan. Dissolve the sugar over low heat. Increase heat to medium-high and let mixture boil until it turns pale gold color, about 20 minutes. Do not stir at any time. Transfer ½ cup of the caramelized sugar to a heat-proof measuring cup. Pour slowly over the back of a 3½-inch ladle (or other rounded, heat-proof form) criss-crossing back and forth to form a domed cage. Let cool completely and gently remove cage. Repeat with remaining sugar. Set aside until ready to use. Do not refrigerate.

Peel and core the apples. Cut ¼-inch slices. Melt butter in a large skillet. Add apples and saute until lightly browned on the edges, 5–7 minutes. Add the brandy and saute until almost evaporated.

To assemble, mound the apple slices on the pastry rounds, top with the cages and garnish with the crystallized lilacs.

Concept and Photograph by:
Dennis M. Gottlieb
137 West 25th Street
New York, NY 10001
(212) 620-7050
FAX (212) 242-6580

Concept, Food Styling and Recipe by:
Rick Ellis
(212) 228-3624

Prop Styling by:
Hannah Milman
(212) 475-4371

Painted Background by:
Chuck Hettinger

Design by:
Julio Vega
(718) 636-9042

One in a series of sixteen Gottlieb recipe cards ranging from startling appetizers to inspiring desserts.

To get your hands on the entire series, and feast your eyes on a portfolio that will make your mouth water, call **Judith Shepherd** at **(212) 242-6554**.

GLOBUS STUDIOS (212) 243-1008

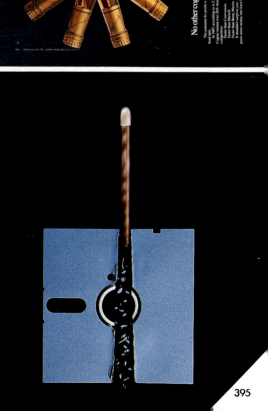

395

ZIMMERMAN

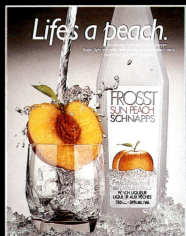

Represented by
Susan Miller
212.905.8400

David Zimmerman Studio
119 West 23rd Street
New York, NY 10011
Studio 212.243.2718

Washington D.C./Virginia/Baltimore:
Kiki Greka-Walter 703.569.0771

California:
Bruce Cohen 619.280.3513

Texas:
Nancy Stephens and Carol Considine
214.871.1316

London:
Suzana Podolska 011.441.624.4989

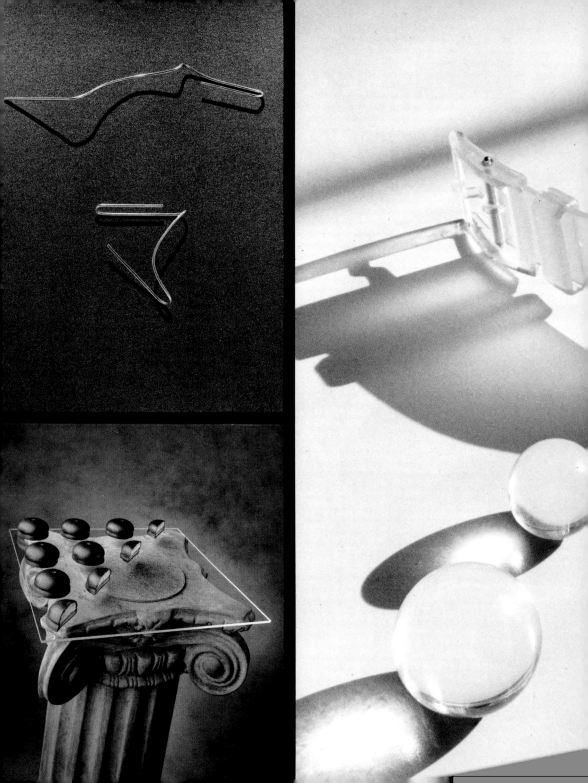

DOUGLAS WHYTE, 519 BROADWAY, NEW YORK, NY 10012 (212) 431-1667

Beth Galton Photography (212) 242-2266

Represented by Rosemary Samuels (212) 477-3567

FELLERMAN

STAN FELLERMAN 152 WEST 25TH STREET, NEW YORK, NY 10001 **(212)-243-0027**

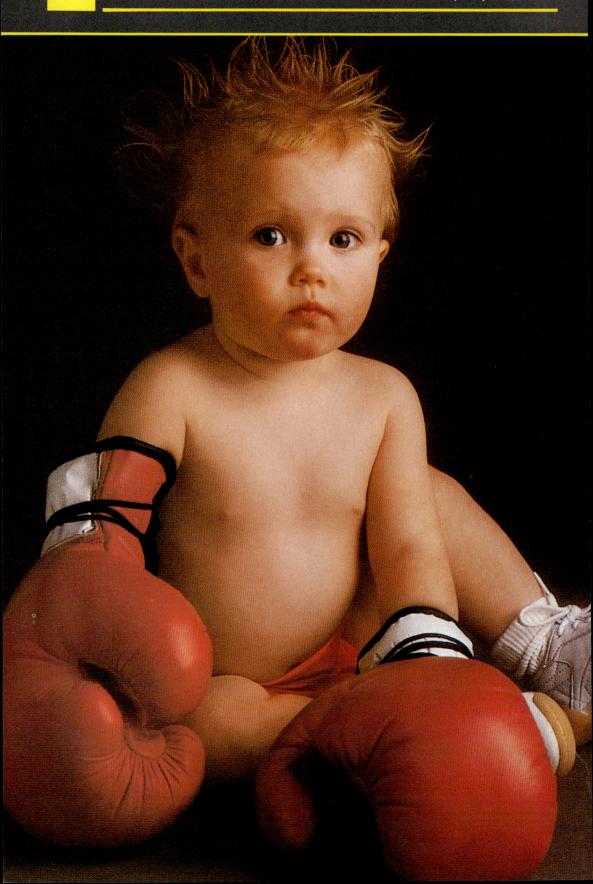

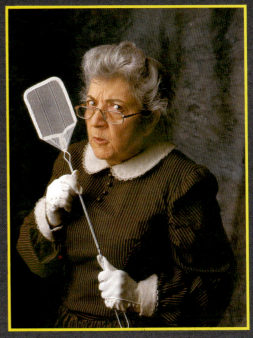

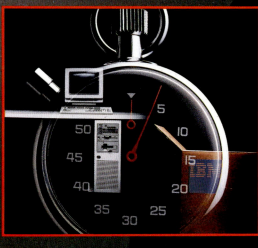

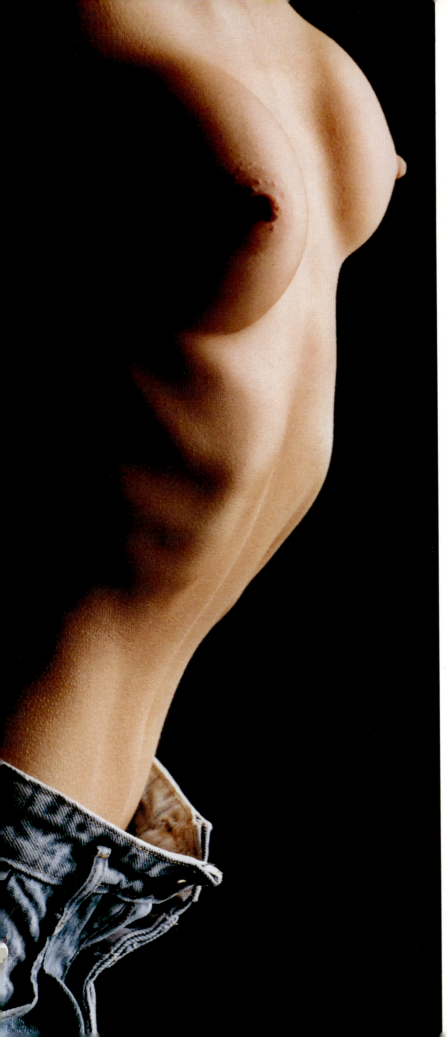

**George Kamper
Productions Limited**

15 W. 24th Street
New York, NY 10010
212-627-7171

Represented by
Ursula Kreis
212-562-8931

Additional work:
Showcase 11, p112–113

UHER

JOHN UHER
PHOTOGRAPHY

529 WEST 42nd STREET, NEW YORK, N.Y. 10036 • (212) 594-7377

IT'S COOL WHEN YOU'RE HOT.

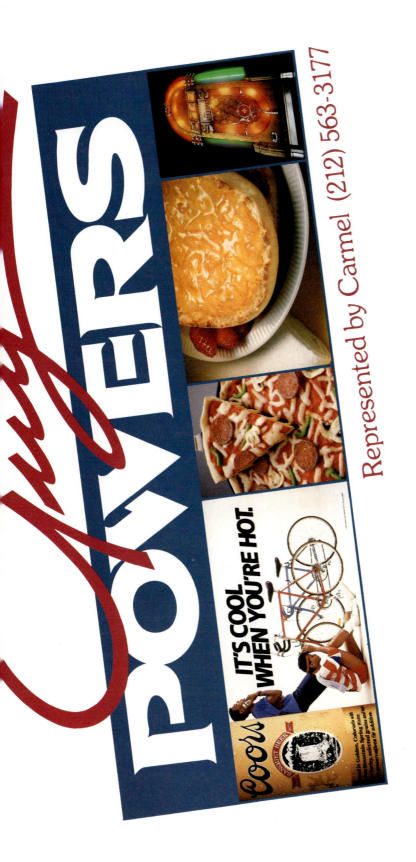

PLOTKIN'S
P E O P L E

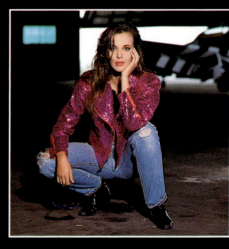

PLOTKIN'S
P E O P L E

REPRESENTED BY DOREEN GEBBIA 212·840·3686

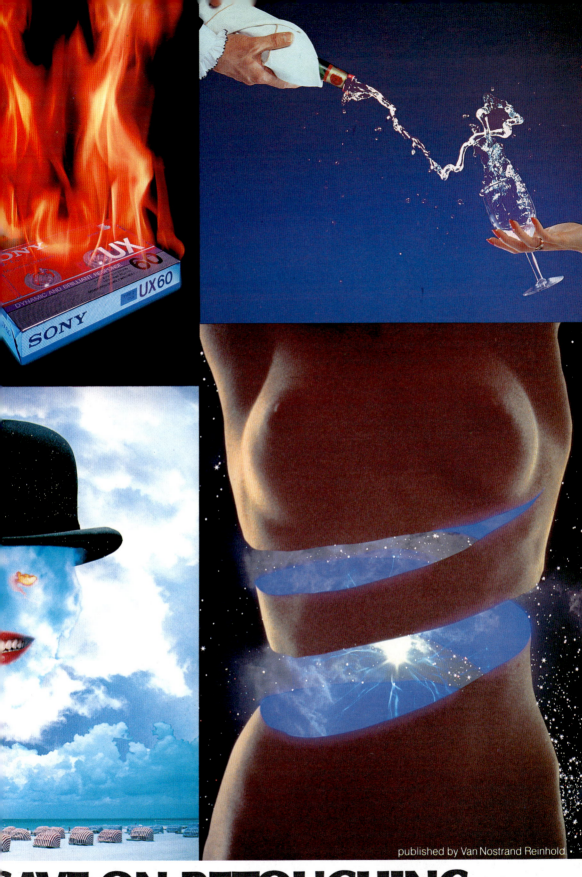

K A N

 KAN PHOTOGRAPHY INC.   122 WEST 26 STREET, N.Y.C.

Still photography that moves.

AGENT GEORGE WATSON 212-645-8616 STUDIO 212-989-1083

FAX
(212) 941-1558

MENDA INC.

GEORGE MENDA, INC./PHOTOGRAPHY/568 BROADWAY/NEW YORK, N.Y. 10012/(212) 431-7440

REPRESENTED BY SUSAN HAMILTON
(212) 431-7525

Carol Kaplan Studio
20 Beacon Street
Boston, MA 02108
617·720·4400
Represented by Robin Fernsell

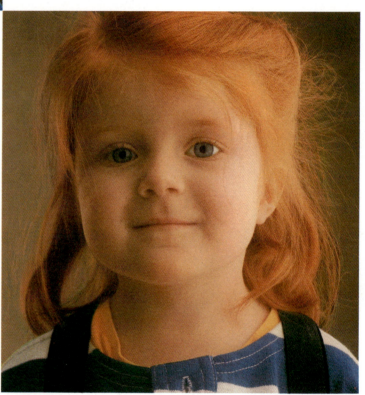

Kaplan

Carol Kaplan Studio
20 Beacon Street
Boston, MA 02108
617·720·4400
Represented by Robin Fernsell

Kaplan

RICK YOUNG

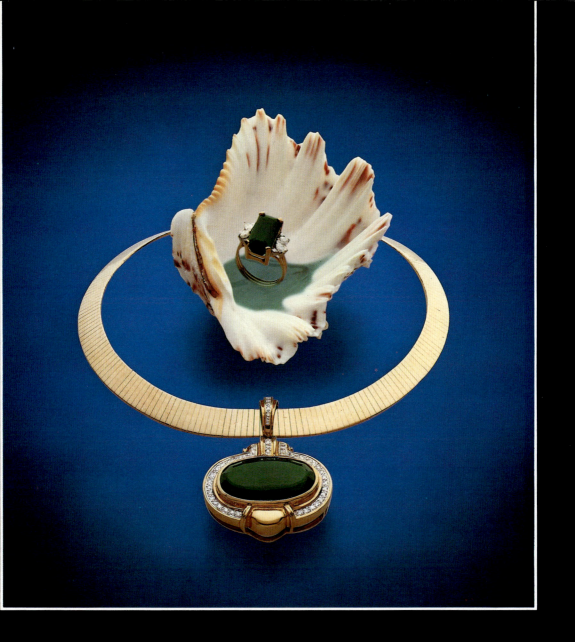

27 WEST 20TH ST. NY 10011
212-929-5701

REPRESENTED BY SONJA LASHUA

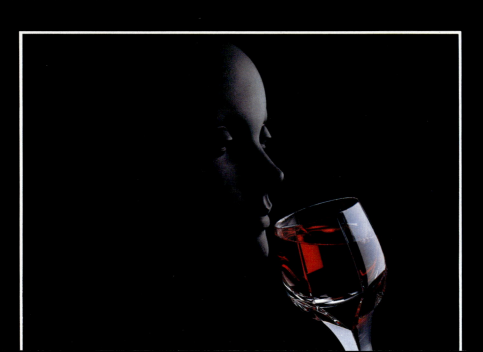

251 WEST 19TH STREET

NEW YORK CITY 10011

212/929/4355

DAVID BISHOP

REPRESENTED BY

ALISON KORMAN

KORMAN & COMPANY

212/633/8407

PALMA KOLANSKY

291 CHURCH STREET   NEW YORK CITY 10013   REPRESENTED BY CHUCK DORR   (212) 431-5858

Carl Fischer

Carl Fischer Photography, Inc.
121 East 83rd Street, New York, NY 10028-0803
(212) 794-0400 Fax (212) 794-0959

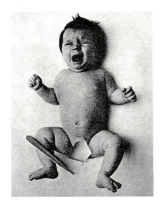

Copyright Carl Fischer 1989

STEVE KRONGARD
212-689-5634

212A EAST 26TH STREET · NEW YORK CITY · 10010

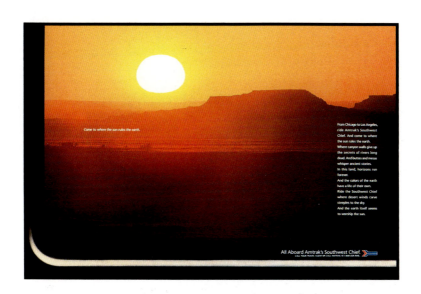

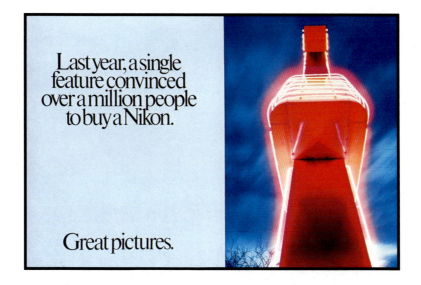

STEVE KRONGARD

212-689-5634

212A EAST 26TH STREET · NEW YORK CITY · 10010

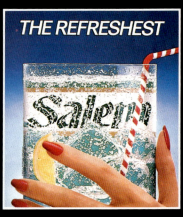

PERWEILER

New York 212 254 7247   Chicago 312 280 5134

Exit Productions Inc.   873 Broadway   New York, NY 10003

BRUCE LAURANCE

253 W. 28TH ST. NY, NY 10001 212-947-3451

JACKIE PAGE'S SHOOTERS

John Zimmerman
L.A.

Bill Summer
Dallas

Gert Wagner
Germany

Sam Haskins
London

212-772-0346

ALSO REPRESENTING: Smith Garner/Atlanta, Jim Raycroft/Boston, Lincoln Potter/Hong Kong, John Thornton/London, Honolulu Creative Group: Bob Abraham, David Cornwell, Michael Horikawa, Rick Peterson, Franco Salmoiraghi, Phil Uhl, William Waterfall, Steve Wilkings.

PAGE ASSOCIATES 219 E. 69 ST. N.Y., N.Y. 10021   STOCK AVAILABLE

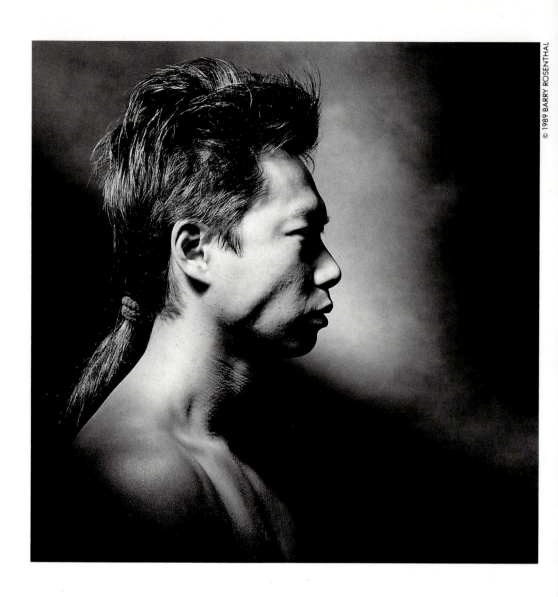

BARRY ROSENTHAL STUDIO REPRESENTED BY ELYN ZELMAN

205 WEST 19TH STREET   NEW YORK CITY   10011   212·645·0433

Richard Pierce

HARPER'S BAZAAR

ELLE

ELLE

WELLS, RICH, GREENE

241
West 36
Street
New York
NY 10018

© 1988 GEORGE HAUSMAN

Hausman
FOR VERY SPECIAL PEOPLE

GEORGE HAUSMAN PHOTOGRAPHY
1181 BROADWAY NEW YORK, N.Y. 10001
(212) 686-4810

REPRESENTATIVE ERIC FRIEDMAN
IN CHICAGO: RON AHLBERG (312) 329-1920

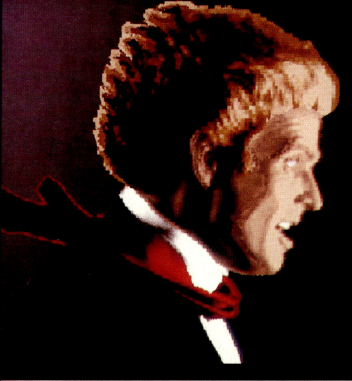
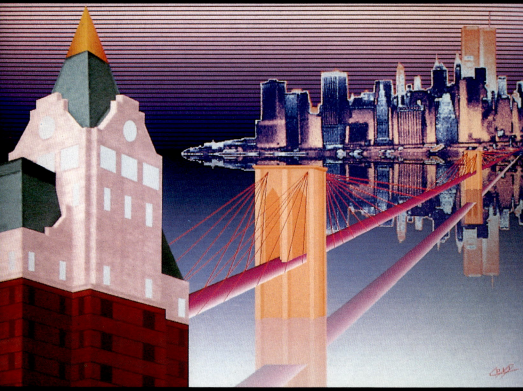

FRANCK LEVY
(212) 557-8256

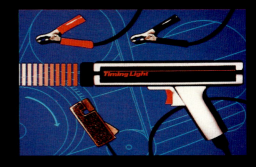

FRANCK LEVY
(212) 557-8256

CHUCK BAKER

Chuck Baker Inc.,
1630 York Avenue, New York City, 10021

"I LIKE NEW IDEAS.
AND HERE ARE SOME BEAUTIFUL ONES
FROM MAX FACTOR…"

OUTBACK · RED

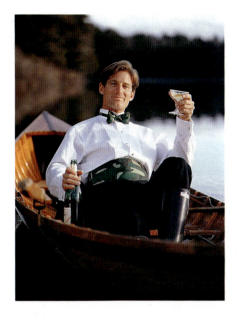

Clients include:
Horchow, De Beers Diamonds, Tiffany's, Self Magazine,
The New York Times, Glamour Magazine, Neiman Marcus, Macy's, Max Factor,
Outback Red, Conde Nast Traveler, Gold Council, Gerber.

LARRY LAWFER

107 SOUTH STREET

BOSTON, MA

02111

617-451-6093

FOOD
IN THE STUDIO

MICHAEL **SKOTT**
244 FIFTH AVENUE, N.Y., N.Y. 10001 (212) 686-4807

JIM RAYCROFT
PHOTOGRAPHY

BOSTON:
617-542-7229
FAX:
617-542-3936

NEW YORK CITY:
PAGE ASSOCIATES
212-772-0346

PHOTOGRAPHY WORLDWIDE

453

S K I P C

A P L A N

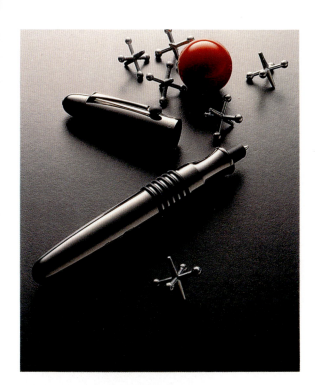

Skip Caplan
124 West 24 Street
New York, N.Y. 10011
212·463·0541

Cailor·Resnick Studio

237 WEST 54TH STREET, NEW YORK, NEW YORK 10019, (212) 977-4300

Photographers Jerry Cailor and Elliott Resnick. Studio representative Bob Altamore (212) 977-4300. FAX (212) 247-2815

MALYSZKO

Mike Malyszko

Represented by Judy Hughes

90 South Street

Boston, Massachusetts 02111

617 426 9111

CHARLES MASTERS

ST. JOHN ASSOCIATES
308 EAST 59TH ST. NYC 10022
TELEPHONE (212) 308-7744

REPRESENTED BY MARY LARKIN

LYNN ST. JOHN

ST. JOHN ASSOCIATES
308 EAST 59TH ST. NYC 10022
TELEPHONE (212) 308-7744

REPRESENTED BY MARY LARKIN

People on Location

Tom Kelly/Gail Mooney

212 360 2576
201 757 5924

WHEN YOUR IDEA IS BIG. REALLY BIG.
NOT PALTRY…

MICHAEL ENGLERT

REPRESENTED BY TIMOTHY ENGLERT
142 WEST 24TH STREET ◆ NEW YORK, N.Y. ◆ (212) 243-3446

MARK HAMILTON

119 WEST 23RD STREET, NEW YORK, NEW YORK 10011 • (212) 242-9814

KENNAHOUM 212·219·0592

Dial For Gold. Charl

Charles Gold, Inc.
56 West 22nd Street,
New York, N.Y. 10010.
212-242-2600.

Represented by
Karen Russo
212-749-6382

475

CLINT·CLEMENS

— CLIENT–LOTUS —

*Represented
by
Harvey Kahn*
212 • 752 • 8490
617 • 482 • 3838

CLIENT—NATIONAL CAR RENTAL

CLINT·CLEMENS

CLIENT — LEE JEANS

*Represented
by
Harvey Kahn*
212 • 752 • 8490
617 • 482 • 3838

CLIENT—HONDA

CLIENT—BARRY BRICKEN

CLIENT—TOYO LTD.

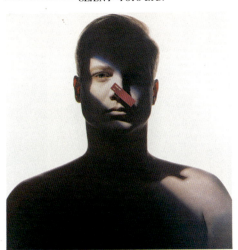

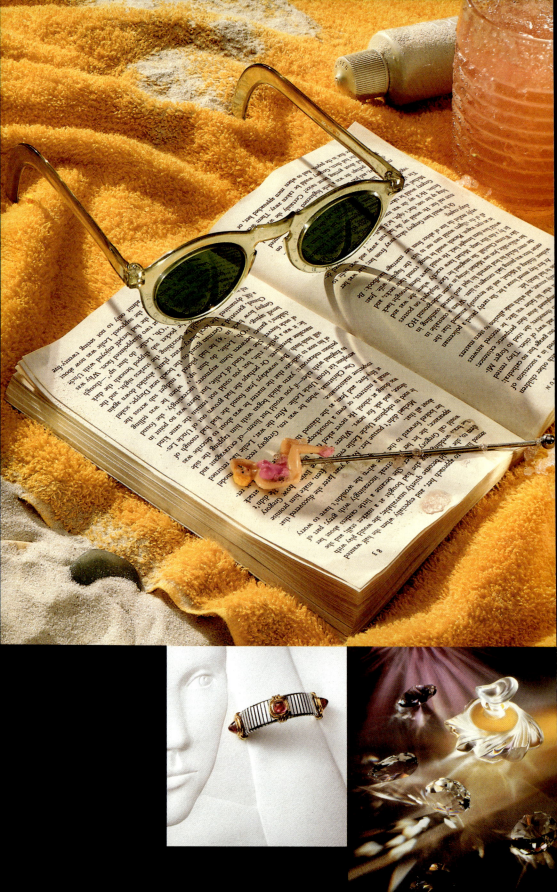

RIC COHN
137 WEST 25 STREET NEW YORK, N.Y. 10001 212/924-4450

Elizabeth Hathon Photography

Stock Available
All photographs © 1989 Elizabeth Hathon

8 Greene St   NY NY 10013   212 219 0685

Elizabeth Hathon Photography

All photographs © 1989 Elizabeth Hathon

8 Greene St NY NY 10013 212 219 0685

REPRESENTED BY MICHELLE DeMUTH   212 627 4797
443 WEST 18TH STREET, NEW YORK, NY 10011   212 242 7825

DUCOTÉ

212-989-3680

487

Last year we dropped, draped, balanced and rigged 47 ads for Tiffany. We also poured, spilled, smeared and smudged for Cover Girl, made Town & Country, Nina Ricci and Revlon ravishing, ice cream and Pam delectable, Hennessy tantalizing and DeBeers Diamonds dazzling. And that was on Tuesday. To see what we did the rest of the year, call Shelley Spierman.

Cy Gross

Photography
59 West 19th Street, New York, N.Y. 10011
212·243·2556

Represented by Shelley Spierman 212·749·8911

haiman

Todd Merritt Haiman, Inc.   Photography   212·391·0810

LINDA BOHM

7 Park Street
Montclair, NJ 07042
201 746•3434
212 349•5650
Fax 201•746•4905

YUTAKA KAWACHI   33 W. 17 ST., N.Y.C. NY 10011 (212) 929-4825

ALL PHOTOS © YUTAKA KANACHI

JAMIE HANKIN
PHOTOGRAPHY

PHILADELPHIA (215) 238-9076 NEW YORK CITY (212) 687-1120

Benefits For The Young And The Restless.

499

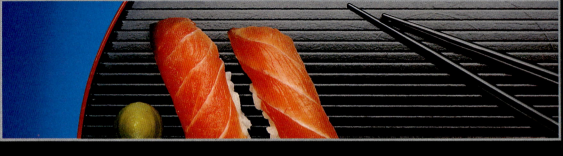
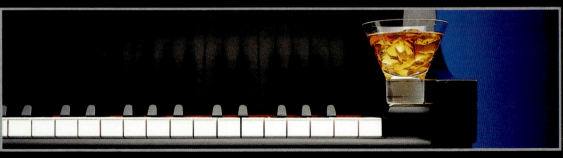
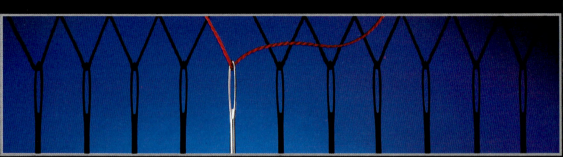

DCA ADVERTISING INC.
KEITH BENNETT, SENIOR ART DIRECTOR

McCAFFREY & McCALL, INC.
JAY COOPER, ART DIRECTOR

LISA CHARLES
STILL LIFE

119 WEST 23 NEW YORK 10011 (212) 807-8600

LISA CHARLES
STILL LIFE

119 WEST 23 NEW YORK 10011 (212) 807-8600

■ GEOFFREY CLIFFORD

REPRESENTED BY:

MARGE CASEY 212-486-9575 NEW YORK

STOCK/EDITORIAL WHEELER PICTURES 212-564-5430 NEW YORK

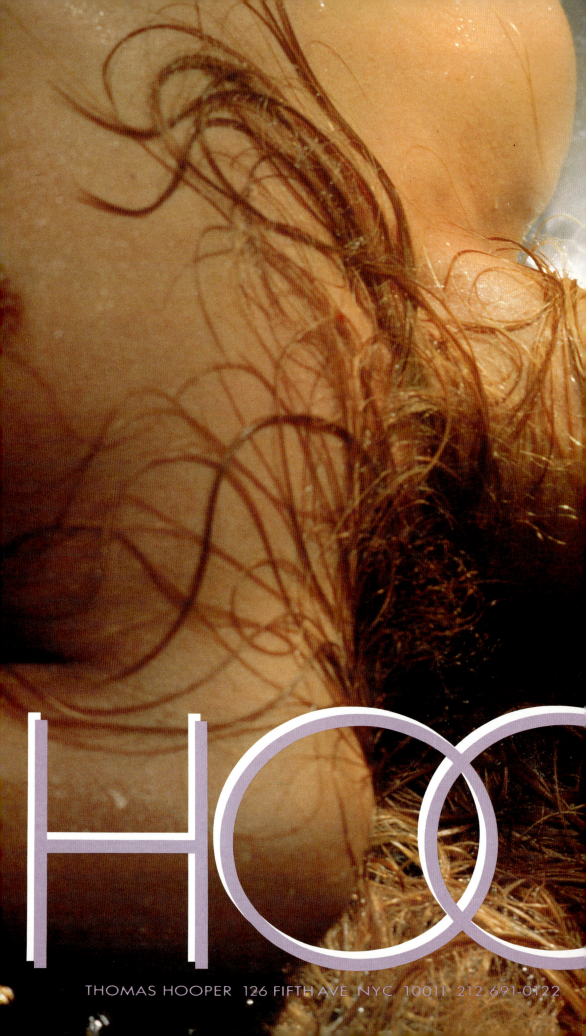

THOMAS HOOPER 126 FIFTH AVE NYC 10011 212 691-0122

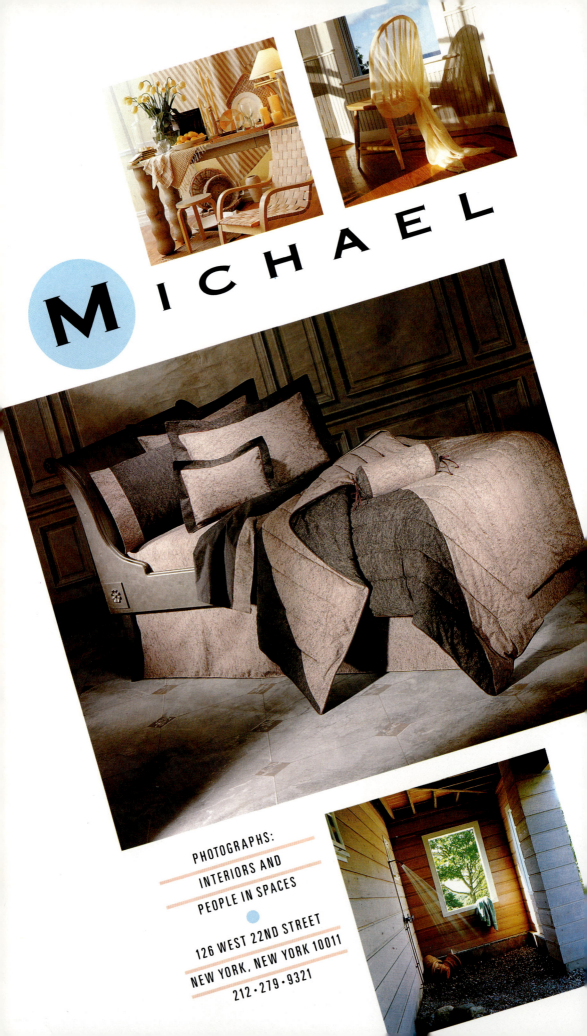

DAVID

118 West Twenty Seventh Street • New York City • 10001
212•924•1030

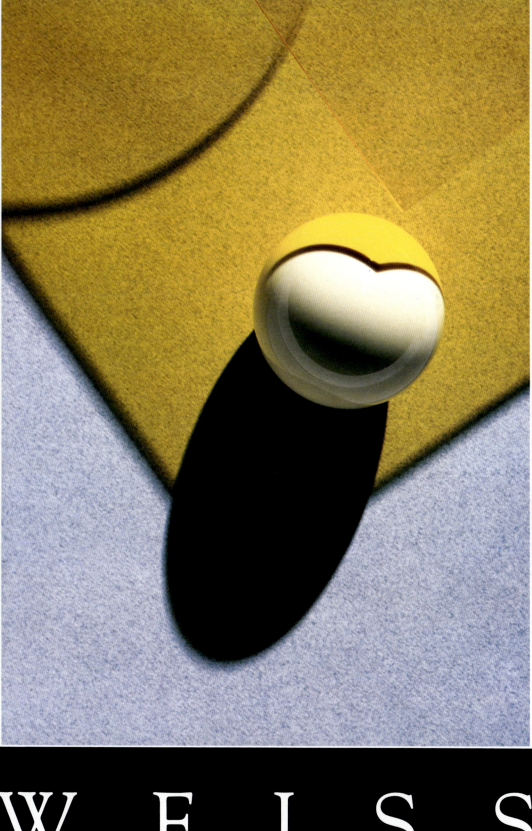

FRANK

5 EAST 16th STREET, NEW YORK CITY (212) 675-5960

REPRESENTED BY
MARGE CASEY AND ASSOCIATES

COWAN

SUN, COAL AND CATTLE. Powder River Basin has been called cattle country and coal country. And a lot of people call it home. People like Dwight Knott.

"I've got a special reason to love Wyoming. My family homesteaded this land. So when Sun Company came here to build the Cordero coal mine we wondered about the future of the land. And the cattle. But Sun also started a Land Reclamation and Research Center. Today our experiments are making sure the land and cattle are in better shape than ever.

"I run the place. So I'm part of Sun's future. And Wyoming's."

At Sun we think putting our energy back into the land is just as important as getting it out.

Dwight Knott, Sun Company manager of the Big Horn Ranch and Reclamation Research Center.

WHERE THERE'S SUN THERE'S ENERGY.

It must be Dole.

Represented by Marge Casey Associates (212) 486-9575
FAX 838-5751

Milan: Hillary Bradford, 54-69-141

Michael Geiger

H O W A R D

MENKEN STUDIOS
119 WEST 22 STREET
NYC 10011
(212) 924-4240

PHYLLIS GOODWIN
NEW YORK
(212) 570-6021

ELLA
BOSTON
(617) 266-3858

VICKI PETERSON
CHICAGO
(312) 467-0780

INGE METZGER
GERMANY
211/575053

MENKEN

C A R L

CARL ZAPP IN ASSOCIATION WITH **MENKEN STUDIOS**
119 WEST 22 STREET, NYC 10011 (212) 924-4240

PHYLLIS GOODWIN, NEW YORK (212) 570-6021
ELLA, BOSTON (617) 266-3858
VICKI PETERSON, CHICAGO (312) 467 0780
INGE METZGER, GERMANY 211/575053

Z A P P

M A R I L I

REPRESENTED BY
COLLEEN M^cKAY
(212) 598-0469
STUDIO: (212) 431-1840

FORASTIERI

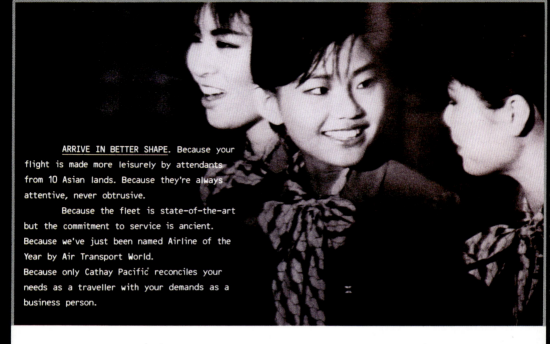

MALCOLM MARCUS: Leo Burnett Ltd.—Toronto

STEVE SCHOLEM:
Lord Geller Federico and Einstein, Inc.

SCOTT SOROKIN: Lowe Marschalk

VALERIE SILKA: Ogilvy and Mather

BOB DEGAETANO: Della Femina Travisano

DAVID L
S   T   U

The auto industry just ran into a major obstacle.

BOB BARRIE: Fallon McElligott

STEVE BASEMORE: Backer Spielvogel Bates

BARBARA DIBUE: Young and Rubicam

STEVE SCHOLEM:
Lord Geller Federico and Einstein, Inc.

TEL: 212 581 3933 • FAX: 212 265 8205

REPRESENTED BY JERRY ANTON 212·633·9880

REZNY

AARON REZNY, INC • 119 WEST 23RD ST • NY, NY 10011 • 212 691 1894

DANA DUKE • 212 260-3334

Acme Electric • AIG • Allendale Insurance • Allied Corp. • American Bakeries • American Brands • American Can Company • American Express Company • Avnet • Bank of Commerce • Bankers Trust • Becton Dickinson • Bear Stearns • Sanford Bernstein • Black & Decker • Bradford National • Calvillo, Shevack, Goldbert & Partners • The Carter Organization • Celanese • Charterhouse Group International • Chase Manhattan • Citicorp • Citytrust • Cole, Yeager & Wood • Collins & Aikman • Colt Industries • Comex • Computer Data Services • Comstock • Connecticut General • Crane • Creamer, Towbridge, Case & Basford • Data General • Dexter • Diagnon • Dillon Read • Discover Magazine • Engelhard • Federal Express • Fidelity Union • Fieldcrest • Financial World Magazine • First Boston • First Jersey National Bank • First Mississippi Corp. • Fortune Magazine • Fuji Bank • G.B. Fermentation • GTE • General Foods • General Reinsurance • HBO & Co. • H. J. Heinz • Frank B. Hall • Hart Schaffner & Marx • Hartford Insurance • Harvey Hubbell • Hi-Shear • Hill, Holiday, Connors & Cosmopulos • IBM • Ingersoll-Rand • International Paper • Irving Trust • Jerrico • Kekst & Company • Key Pharmaceuticals • Korn/Ferry International • Life Magazine •

DANA DUKE • 212 260-3334

Lowe's • Machine Technology • Managistics • Marine Midland • Merrill Lynch • Midlantic • Mohasco • Morgan Guaranty • Morgan Stanley • MONY • Nabisco Brands • National Patent • New England Life Insurance • New Jersey Bell • N.Y. Stock Exchange • Newmont Mining • S. E. Nichols • Nicor Inc. • Nordic American Bank • Northstar Reinsurance • Norton Simon • Ogden • Olin • Oxford Industries • Paine Webber • Papercraft • Phibro-Salomon • Playboy • Private Satellite Network • Reeves Communications • Rexham • Richardson-Vicks • Saatchi & Saatchi Compton • RP Scherer • J. Henry Schroder • Science Digest Magazine • Scott Paper • Scovill • Sea-Land • Seligman Securities • Shearson • Smith Barney • The Southern Company • Standard Oil of Ohio • Stanadyne • Sun Chemical • Sunrise Savings & Loan • Tambrands • Telerate • Telesis • Tyco • UMC Industries • Union Carbide • Uniroyal • United Energy Resources • United Industrial Corp. • U.S. Industries • U.S. Surgical • Verus International • Viacom • View Magazine • Vornado • Ward Howell • Warner-Lambert • Wertheim • Xerox Credit Corp. •

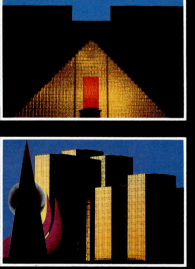
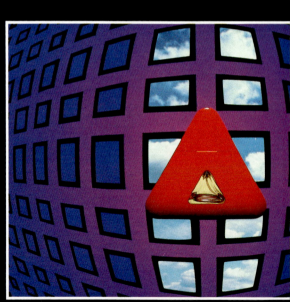

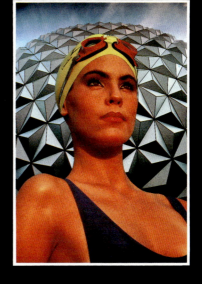

CREATES HIGH IMPACT GRAPHICS FOR COLORFUL CLIENTS.
XEROX • DU PONT • MITSUBISHI • CITIBANK • RCA • CHILTON
SMITHKLINE BECKMAN • ROHM & HAAS • TURNER CONSTRUCTION
ARM & HAMMER • SHARED MEDICAL SYSTEMS • FMC

STEVE UZZELL
1419 TRAP ROAD
VIENNA, VA 22180
703-759-5432

UZZELL

R O B E R T   F A R B E R

Landscapes / Still Life

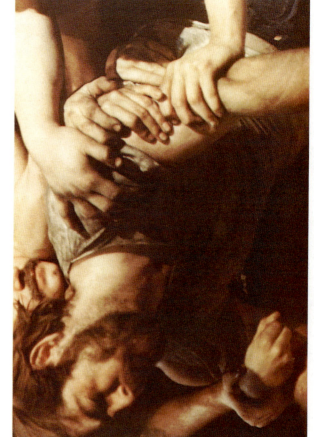

N.Y. 212/486 9090

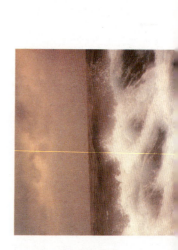

ROBERT FARBER

Fashion / Advertising

R O B E R T   F A R B E R

Beauty / Nudes

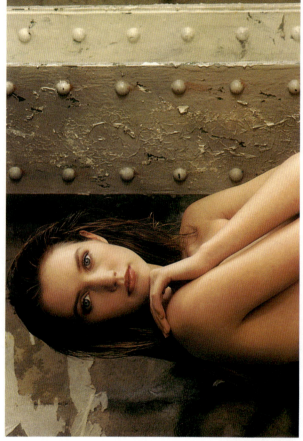

N.Y. 212/486 9090

ROBERT FARBER

Books / Posters

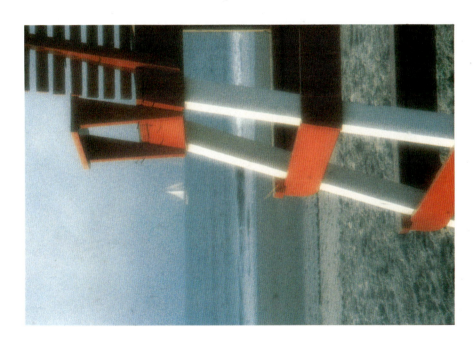

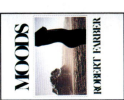

Donna Aristo
360 Manville Road
Pleasantville, NY 10570
Westchester 914-747-1422
NYC 212-643-9206

Jerry Errico
360 Manville Road
Pleasantville, NY 10570
Westchester 914-747-1422
NYC 212-643-9206

537

473 BROOME STREET, NEW YORK CITY 10013, 212 941-8582, STOCK AVAILABL

Chuck Fishman

Shig Ikeda

636 AVE. OF AMERICAS
NEW YORK N.Y. 10011
212-924-4744

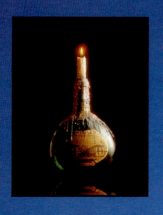

REPRESENTED BY:
JOE CAHILL, STEVE RYAN
212-751-0529

REEL AVAILABLE
ON REQUEST

Chip Forelli

Chip Forelli Studio
316 Fifth Avenue
New York, New York 10001
212.564.1835

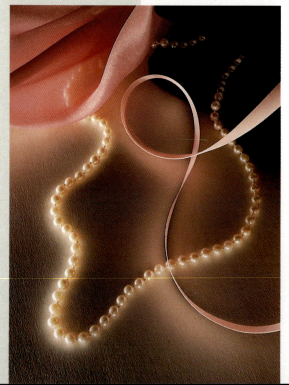

DRAKKAR NOIR

M A R E S C A
36 W. 26th STREET • NEW YORK, N.Y. 10001 • 212/620•0955
TO SEE ADDITIONAL IMAGES PLEASE REFER TO THE GOLD BOOK

Location: Jackson, Mississippi
See us also in Black Book 1984–1988 as well as GRAPHIS Magazine.
Please call for a copy of our mini-portfolio and in NYC call Michelle DeMuth for a look at our book.

RICHMOND

JACK RICHMOND STUDIO•12 FARNSWORTH STREET•BOSTON,MA 02210 • 617-482-5974

549

SKIP HINE
PHOTOGRAPHY
34 West 17th St., NY, NY 10011 212-691-5903

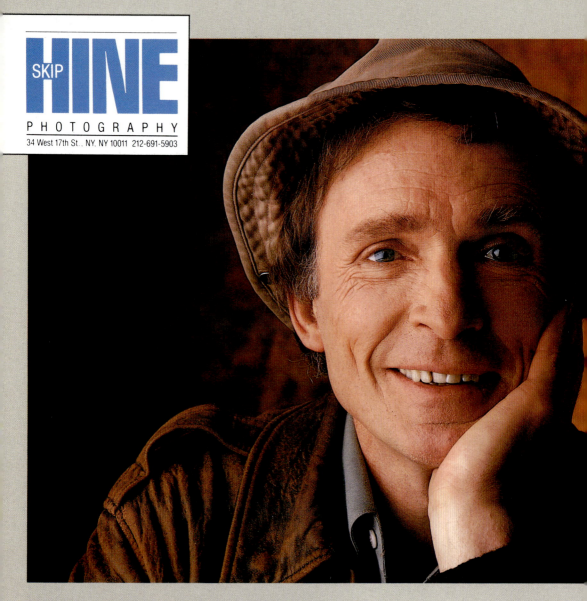

*SPECIAL THANKS TO LORETTA SAL

DENNIS GALANTE

STUDIO:
133 WEST 22ND ST.
NEW YORK, N.Y. 10011

212-463-0938

© 1989 DENNIS GALANTE

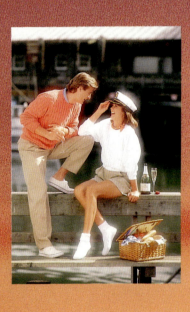

A former staff photographer for National Geographic now shooting for major agencies and corporations all over the world. Represented by Karen Russo (212) 749-6382. Represented in Chicago by Vincent Kamin (312) 787-8834. For stock call Woodfin Camp and Associates (212) 481-6900.

DICK DURRANCE II

TEL 212 683 4258
FAX 212 481 3812

Clients include:

	Chase Manhattan	Macy's
A.T.&T.		
	Estée Lauder	Loreal
Champion Spark Plugs		
	Brawny/James River	
Avon	Continental Airlines	I.B.M.

hing/norton

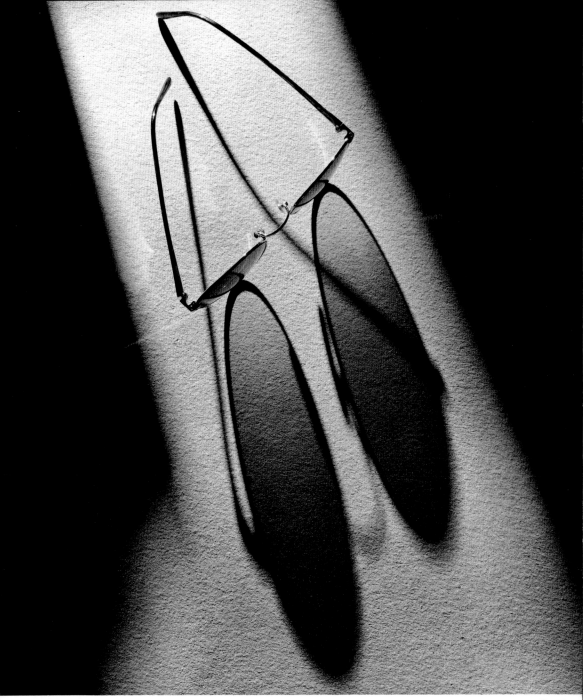

©1989

Perdue Samsung Electronics Stereo Review

Nikon Sharp Electronics

Singer U.S. Mint

N.W. Orient Parker Pens Volvo

ERIC MICHELSON

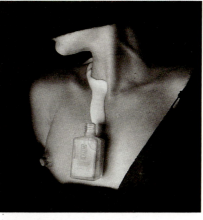
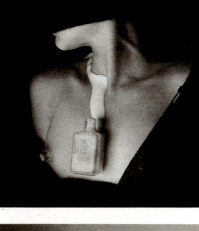
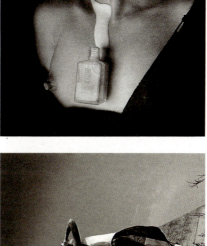

Row 1: Kent International/*Ogilvy & Mather* Editorial/*France* Editorial/*England* Lanvin/*Egypt*

Row 2: Evan-Picone Clarion/*Lintas S.S.C.B.* Evan-Picone Intergold/*Geers Gross*

Row 3: Editorial/*Italy* Evan-Picone Germaine Monteil/*Revlon* Editorial/*Africa* Editorial/*U.S.A.*

Row 4: Aziza/*Ogilvy & Mather* Editorial/*Africa* Charles of the Ritz Charles Jourdan/*Ted Bates*

212.223.0948

NORWEGIAN CRUISE LINE

JORDAN MARSH

CHARLES HEIDSIECK

ESTEE LAUDER

GRANT PETERSON

568 Broadway   New York, New York 10012   212. 219. 0004

A TWENTY-FOUR PAGE PICTURE BOOK

ELLIE BYRON-HALEY

AT&T

Agent: Kathy Bruml 212. 874-5659

R O B I

JAMES ROBINSON   (212) 580•1793   155 RIVERSIDE DRIVE, NEW YORK CITY 10029   • STOCK AVAILABLE •   CLIENTS: CONDÉ NAS

© JAMES ROBINSON 1989

N S O N

ER · U.S. ARMY · POLAROID · AT&T · CHRYSLER FIRST · AVON PRODUCTS · LANE FURNITURE · REPRESENTED BY STEPHEN MADRIS

FABIO

F A B I O

FABIO MUCCHI PHOTOGRAPHY

5 West 20th Street NY. NY. 10011 PH:212 620.0167-242.0942
FAX: 212 463.7825

RON WU

179 St. Paul St.

Rochester

New York 14604

716 454 5600

Clients include: Bausch & Lomb, Corning Glass Works, Champion Athletic Products, Champion International, Coleman, Curtice Burns Foods, Eastman Kodak Co., Foster Grant, Gannett Co., Remington, Shimano American Corp., Xerox.

Jerry Simpson
STUDIO

244 Mulberry Street New York City 10012 212.941.1255

Clients include:

American Express
Beatrice Foods
Benson & Hedges
Calvin Klein
Campbell's
Food & Wine
General Foods
Good Food
Good Housekeeping
Gorton's
House Beautiful
Nabisco Brands
New York Telephone
Red Book
Seagram
Stouffers
Weight Watchers

TV reel
available upon request.

James Porto

Photographe

212 966 4407

87 Franklin Street

New York, N.Y. 10013

Stock Photography Available

melillo

nicholas melillo
118 west 27th st. n.y., n.y. 10001
212 691 7612

Stephen Wilkes

TRAVEL & LEISURE / BIG SUR

MAGAZINE PUBLISHERS OF AMERICA / JOHN EMMERLING INC.

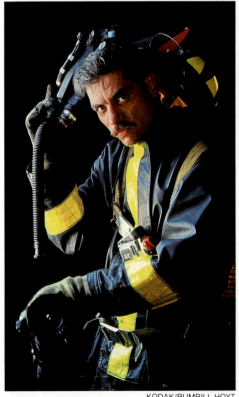

KODAK / RUMRILL HOYT

48 E.13th Street, NYC
(212) 475-4010

Assignments for both advertising
and corporate photography. Stock: (212) 475-4839

KODAK/J.W. THOMPSON

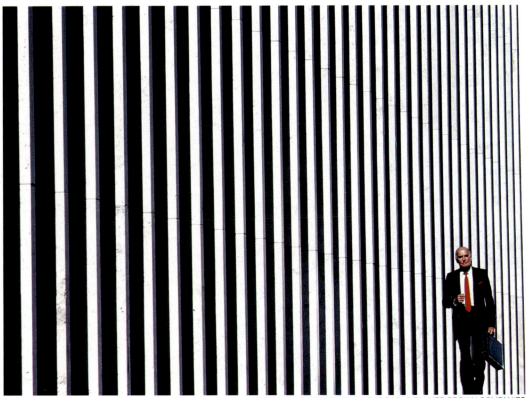

AMERICAN SECURITY BANK/THE EARLE PALMER BROWN COMPANIES

ALL PHOTOS © STEPHEN WILKES 1989

Stephen Wilkes

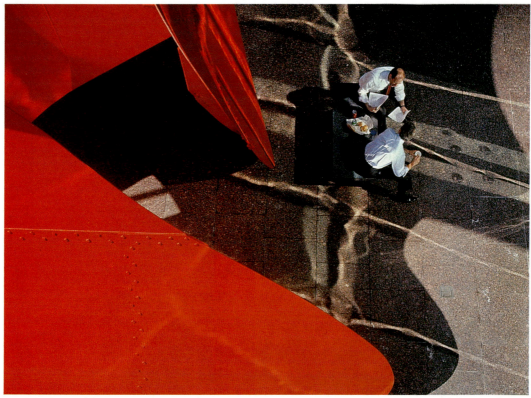

AT&T/YOUNG & RUBICAM

LORILLARD/SAATCHI & SAATCHI

48 E.13th Street, NYC
(212) 475-4010

Assignments for both advertising and corporate photography. Stock: (212) 475-4839

MAGAZINE PUBLISHERS OF AMERICA/JOHN EMMERLING INC

ALL PHOTOS © STEPHEN WILKES 1989

David Leach

ALLY & GARGANO/MCA ∺ AMERICAN EXPRESS ∺ BBD & O ∺ BOZE

GREY ⇒ HONDA ⇒ LEVINE HUNTLEY SCHMIDT & BEAVER ⇒ LORIMAR ⇒ McCANN ERICKSON ⇒ OGILVY & MATHER ⇒ J.WALTER THOMP

TRANSAMERICA ☰ YOUNG & RUBICAM/DENTSU

75 Spring Street, 9th Floor, New York, NY 10012
Telephone: (212) 288-1234

In New York, Arlene Johnson: (212) 966-8600
In The Midwest, Randi Fiat & Associates: (312) 784-2343
In Los Angeles: (213) 932-1234

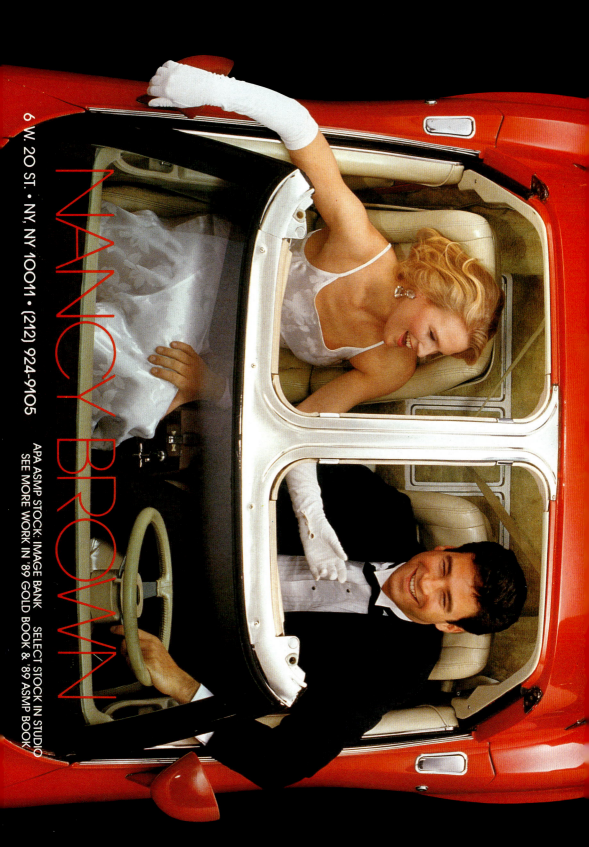

"I shot the moon."

...Mark Alexander

Mark Alexander Studio
412 Central Avenue, Cincinnati, Ohio 45202, 513-651-5020.

ARNDT

JIM ARNDT PHOTOGRAPHY

400 FIRST AVENUE NORTH #510, MINNEAPOLIS, MN 55401
(612) 332·5050

©1988 Jim Arndt

ARNDT

JIM ARNDT PHOTOGRAPHY
400 FIRST AVENUE NORTH #510, MINNEAPOLIS, MN 55401
(612) 332·5050

SHOTWELL

SHOTWELL

Charles Shotwell Photography   2111 North Clifton   Chicago, Illinois 60614   312 929-0168

HOLLIS OFFICER

PHOTOGRAPHY
816·474·5501

RADENCICH

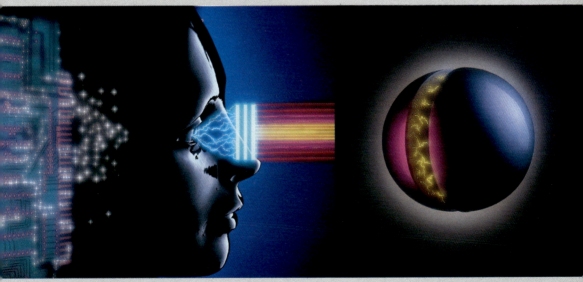

Represented
by
Linda
Pool
216 East
9th Street
Kansas City,
Missouri
64134

816-761-7314
or 816-756-1992   FAX 816-756-1186

NOZICKA

STEVE NOZICKA PHOTOGRAPHY LTD 314 W INSTITUTE PLACE CHICAGO, IL 60610 312 787 8925

REPRESENTED BY JOEL HARLIB AND ASSOCIATES, INC. 312 329 1370

LAURIE

LAURIE RUBIN REPRESENTED B

RUBIN

ANDI FIAT 312.784.2343

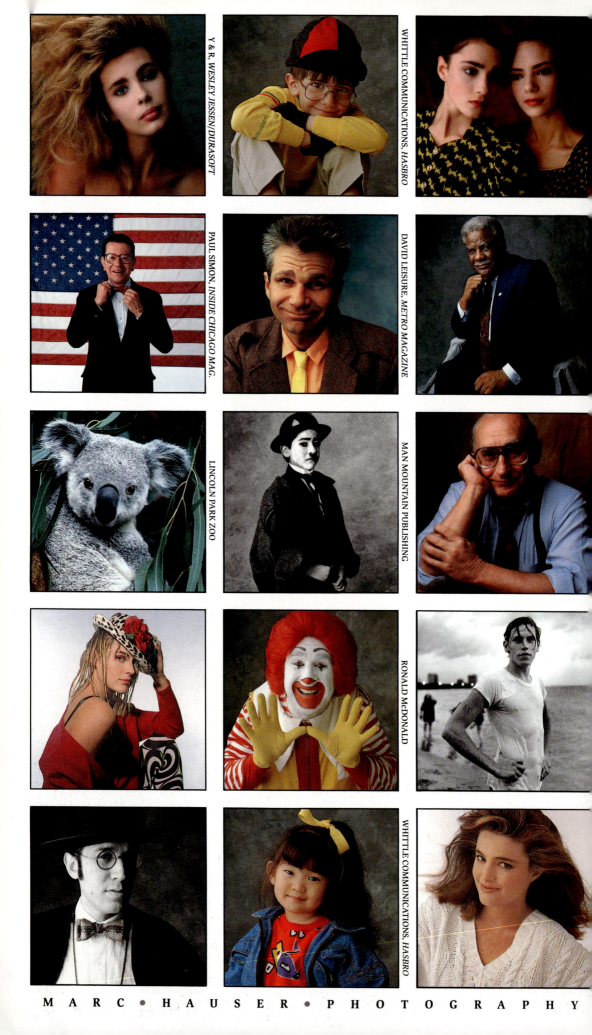

MARC • HAUSER • PHOTOGRAPHY

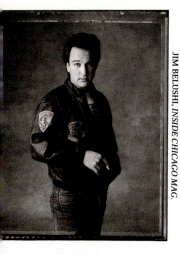
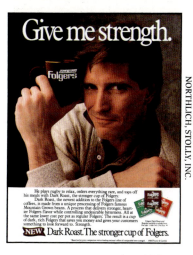
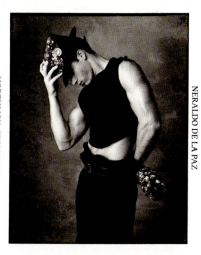

Marc Hauser Photography

MARC HAUSER PHOTOGRAPHY 312 486-4381 1810 WEST CORTLAND CHICAGO, IL 60622

REPRESENTED BY RANDI FIAT & ASSOCIATES CHICAGO 312 784-2343 CALL FOR THE REEL

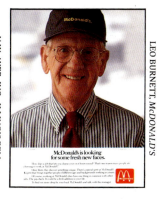

M A R C • H A U S E R • P H O T O G R A P H Y

CASALINI

☎ R A N D I F I A T 3 1 2 . 7 8 4 . 2 3 4 3

GIORGIO VENTOLA

230 WEST HURON CHICAGO 60610
PRINT & FILM 312-951-0880

FAX # 312 938-2072

D'ORIO

Tony D'Orio Photography Chicago 312 421-5532
Represented by Skillicorn Associates 312 856-1626

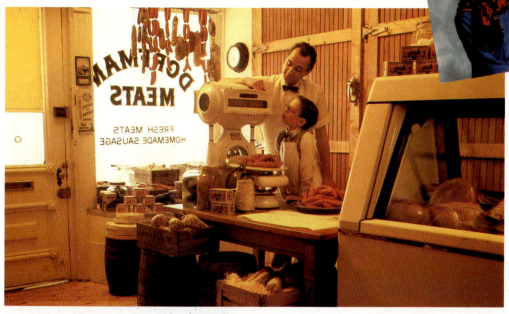

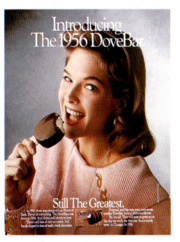

Call for the reel.

TONY D'ORIO PHOTOGRAPHY 312 421-5532 REPRESENTED BY SKILLICORN ASSOCIATES 312 856-1626

JANIS TRACY PHOTOGRAPHY 213 W. INSTITUTE PLACE, CHICAGO, IL 60610 312•787•7166

JANIS татарCY

JANIS TRACY REPRESENTED BY SKILLICORN ASSOCIATES 312•856•1626

WE SHOOT TRUCKS!

TOO!

Bieber

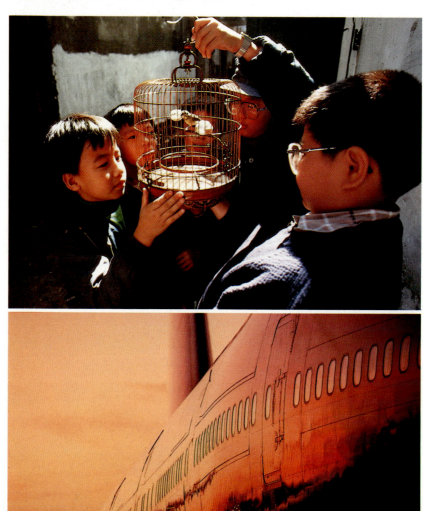

Tim Bieber Inc.
Chicago: Ann Snowberger 312-463-3590
New York: Michael Ash 212-807-6286
Minneapolis: Arlene Corcoran 612-823-4821

TERRY DAVID DREW
Photographer

FEDERATED DEPARTMENT STORES
WILSON SPORTING GOODS CO.
CARSON PIRIE SCOTT AND CO
KEROFF AND ROSENBERG
SEARS, ROEBUCK AND CO
BURRELL ADVERTISING
WATER TOWER PLACE
LEO BURNETT U.S.A.
COCA-COLA/SPRITE
PHILLIP MORRIS
WBBM-TV (CBS)
ILLINOIS BELL
WLS-TV (ABC)

452 NORTH MORGAN
SUITE 2E
CHICAGO, IL 60622
312 829-1630

REPRESENTED BY
C.W. GLENN & ASSOCIATES
312 787-4459

624

"When you visit my photo studio, watch your step."
—*Rick Dublin*

Dublin Photography • 414 Third Ave. N., Minneapolis, MN 55401 • phone (612) 332-8924

H A W K E R

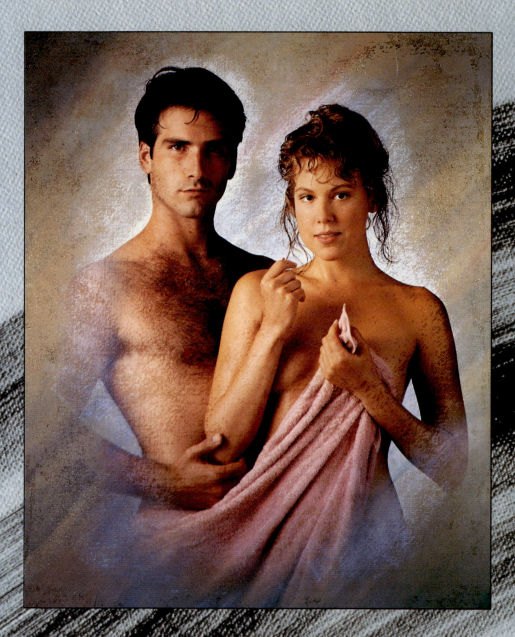

KAZU

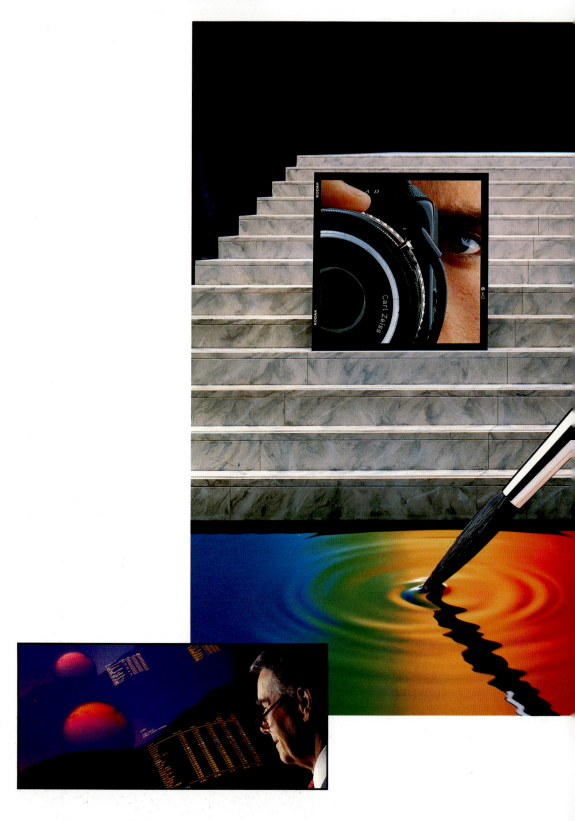

1211 West Webster, Chicago, IL 60614   312.348.5393

Representative: Janice Tepke   312.348.5393

PHOTOGRAPHY DEBOLD.

1801 North Halsted Street, Chicago, Illinois 60614 · Contact: Cindy Debold & Associates 312/337-1177

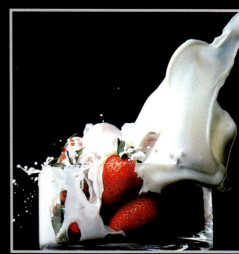

PHOTOGRAPHY
DEBOLD.

1801 North Halsted Street, Chicago, Illinois 60614 · Contact: Cindy Debold & Associates 312/337-1177

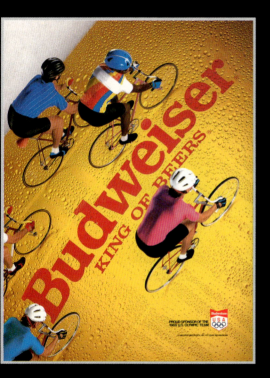

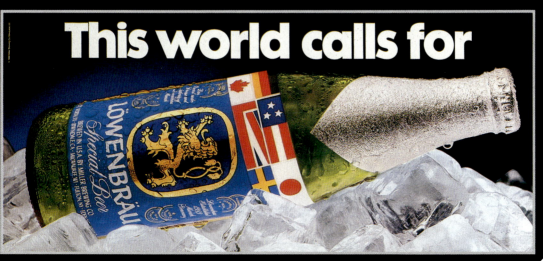

NORTHERN TELECOM/J. Siebert, A.D.

SHARPER CUSTOMER FOCUS

Nothing is more important to the success of any business—large or small—than one-to-one, responsive customer contact. And Northern Telecom offers a variety of networking products and services that keeps your customers' needs in sight.

Besides already popular features such as 800-number services, least cost routing and Meridian* Digital Centrex, your phone company now offers many advanced new services through Northern Telecom systems. Network-wide automatic call distribution instantly routes customer calls to where you can serve them immediately—anywhere on your network. Calling line identification even tells you who's calling before you pick up the phone. So you can offer immediate, customized assistance.

For networking that lets you create one-of-a-kind products and services for your customers, call 1-800-453-9806 in the U.S. or 1-800-387-1487 in Canada.

nt northern telecom

FLEXIBLE NETWORKING FROM NORTHERN TELECOM

WASHINGTON POST/J. Noone, A.D.

JAK MAKRAL

ACE HARDWARE/R. Kimmel, A.D.

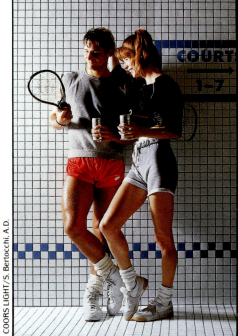

COORS LIGHT/S. Bertocchi, A.D.

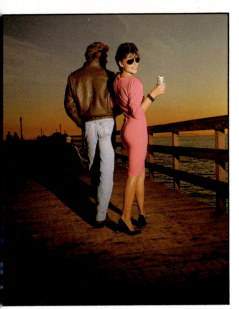

SUZANNE

JOANN CARNEY PHOTOGRAPHY 312 829-2332

JOANN CARNEY
photography

REPRESENTED BY BILL RABIN & ASSOCIATES 312 944-6655

CALL FOR OUR *CARNEY FILM* SAMPLE REEL

SPG

Abby Sadin

Abby

represented by:

Elizabeth Altman Associates

312 266 8661

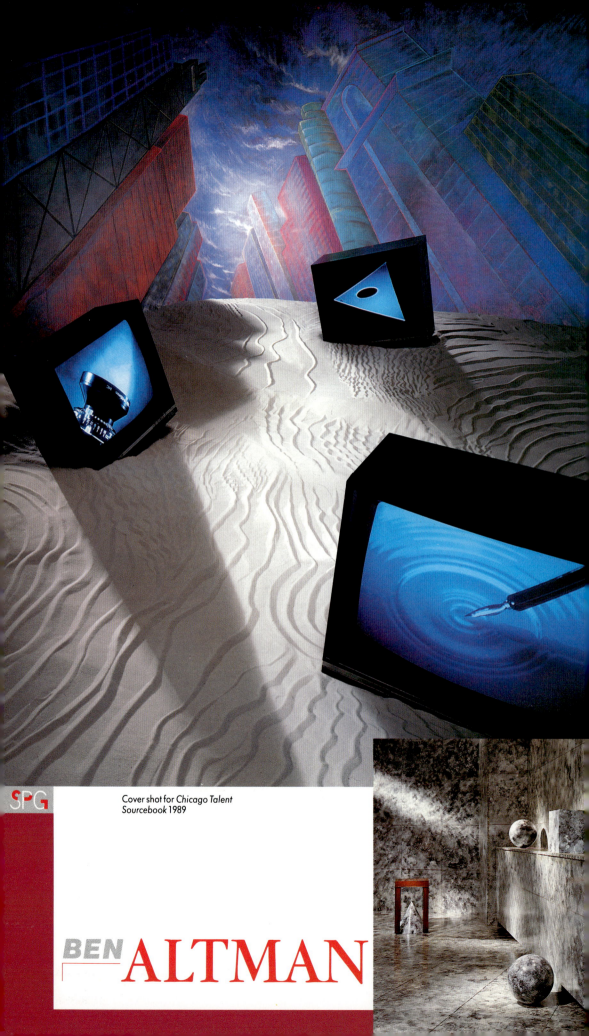

Cover shot for *Chicago Talent Sourcebook 1989*

BEN ALTMAN

Handcoloring: Russell Thurston

represented by:

Elizabeth Altman Associates
312 266 8661

H A R R I S O N

FOR MORE THAN A SLICE OF MY WO

J O N E S

CHICAGO   312 337 4997

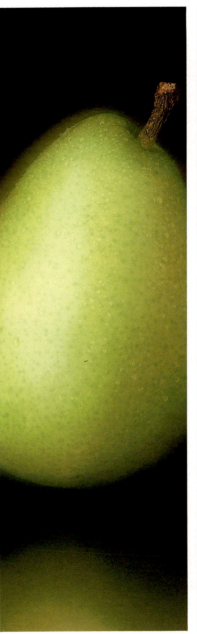

EASE CALL:

MARY ANN **BARASA & ASSOCIATES**   312 280 2289

Richard Hamilton Smith
612-645-9199

© 1989 RICHARD HAMILTON SMITH

FOR STOCK CALL:
Jan Bliss
612-645-5070
St. Paul, Minnesota

CHICAGO AGENTS:
Mary Atols, John Hoffman
312-281-7124

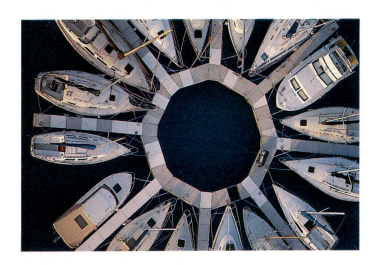

RICHARD HAMILTON SMITH
612-645-9199

FOR STOCK CALL:
Jan Bliss
612-645-5070
St. Paul, Minnesota

CHICAGO AGENTS:
Mary Atols, John Hoffman
312-281-7124

647

216 West Ohio Street
Chicago, IL 60610 USA
312.467.5663

Print and Film Agent
Jim Hill
312.866.6440
TV Reel Available

SUSAN

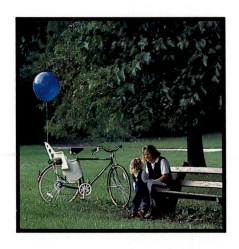

DavidWagenaar
CHICAGO

DAVID WAGENAAR PHOTOGRAPHY ▲ CHICAGO ▲ 312-942-0943

653

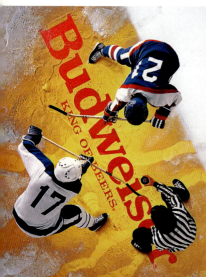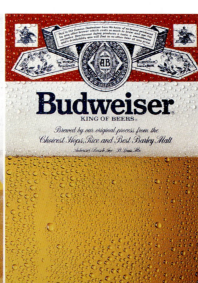

SCHEWE

Jeff Schewe Photography

624 West Willow

Chicago,

Illinois

60614

Phone:

312-951-6334

Fax:

312-787-6814

655

©1988. Courtesy of PLAYBOY Magazine.

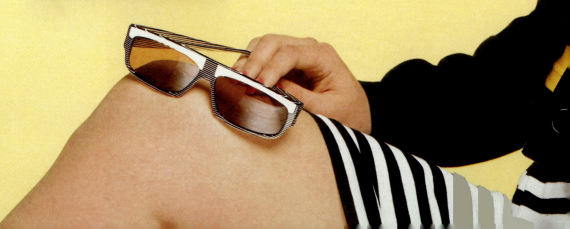

Variety flavors

all that we see,

think and feel.

People to sea.

Places to sew.

Things to eat.

Walter Gray Photography, Inc.
1035 West Lake. Chicago, Illinois 60607. 312.733.3800
Represented by: Doug Stieber & Company. 312.222.9595

JAMES HAEFNER

PHOTOGRAPHY

313-583-4747

1407 ALLEN
TROY, MICHIGAN 48083

NICK VEDROS 1988

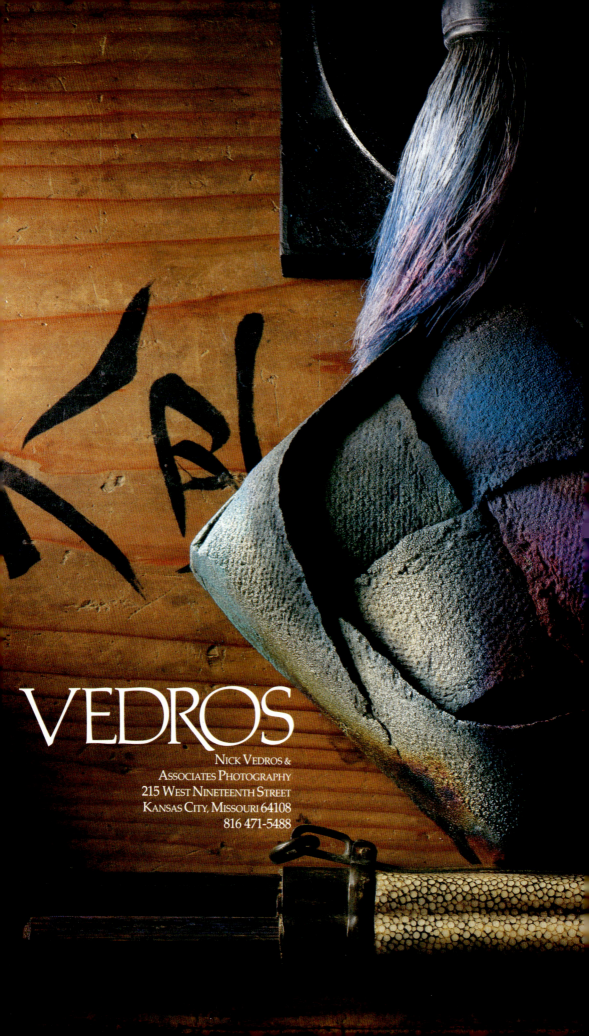

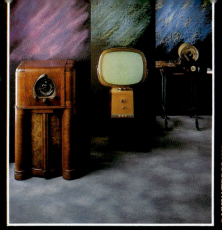

© NICK VEDROS 1988

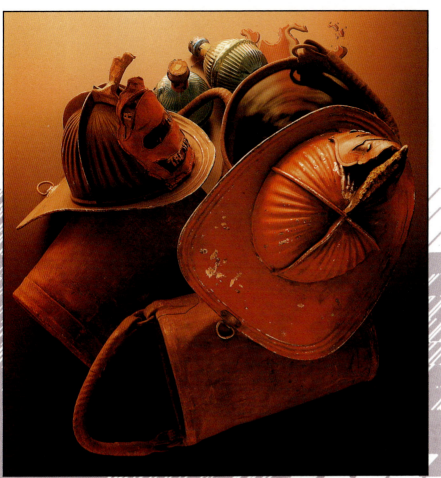

JIM KRANTZ STUDIOS, INC.
5017 S 24 STREET
OMAHA, NE 68107
402 734-4848

Design Photography

1324 HAMILTON AVENUE • CLEVELAND, OHIO 44114 • (216) 687-0099
521 SIXTH STREET • SAN FRANCISCO, CA 94103 • (415) 543-1504

Photographers: Carl Fowler, Jim Lawson • Representative: Kathryn Anderson

SEE OUR AD IN THE WEST: NEW
SAN FRANCISCO STUDIO OPEN.

312.256.7862

BILL CROFTON

CHICAGO

© Bill Crofton 1988

326R Linden Avenue Wilmette, Illinois 60091

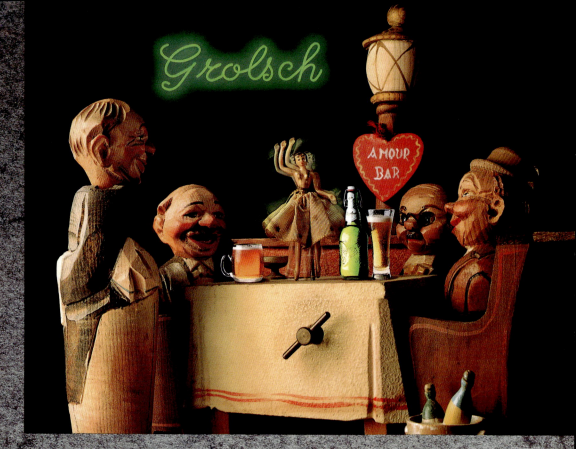

9 WEST HUBBARD, CHICAGO 60610 312/836-0411

REPRESENTED BY

SANDRA NICOLINI 312/346-1648

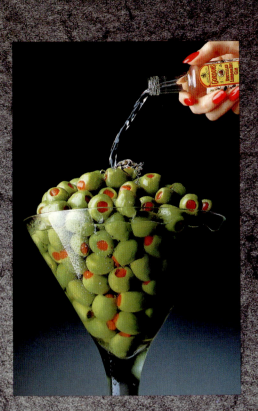

PETROFF

Dave Jordano Photography, 1335 North Wells, Chicago Illinois 60610
Represented by Vincent J. Kamin & Associates, 312.787.8834

Jordano

ARCHITECTURAL DIGEST©

TONY SOLURI

HADDON ADVERTISING

TOWN & COUNTRY MAGAZINE

ARCHITECTURAL DIGEST©

LORD, GELLER, FEDERICO, EINSTEIN, INC.

SCHNADIG

OGILVY MATHER

1147 W. Ohio, Chicago 60622 △ (312) 243-6580
Represented by: Judy McGrath △ (312) 944-5116

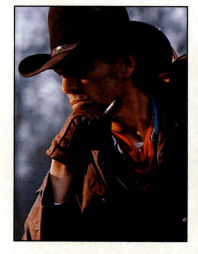

PERNO

1956 WEST GRAND AVENUE
CHICAGO, IL 60622
312 666-4345

PERNO

REPRESENTED BY
JUDY McGRATH
312 944-5116

FAX # 312 421-7036

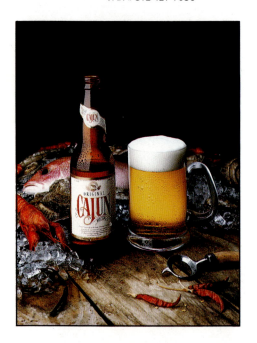

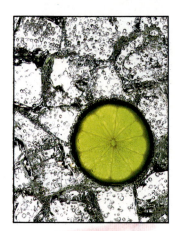

REPRESENTED BY

JUDY McGRATH

312 944-5116

RAY PERKINS

PHOTOGRAPHY

222 S. MORGAN

CHICAGO 60607

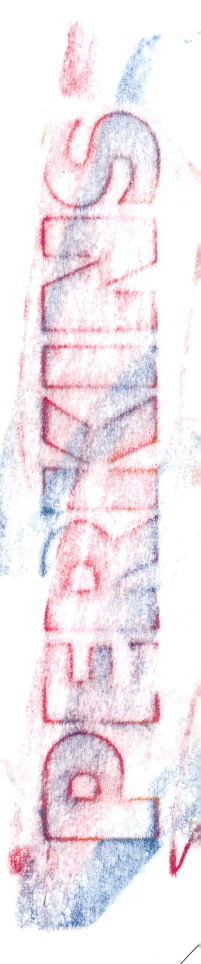

COREY
P H O T O G R A P H Y
F I L M

CARL COREY PHOTOGRAPHY, INC.
222 SOUTH MORGAN STREET CHICAGO, ILLINOIS 60607
REPRESENTED BY WENDY HANSON
312/421-3232

COREY
PHOTOGRAPHY
FILM

CARL COREY PHOTOGRAPHY, INC.
222 SOUTH MORGAN STREET CHICAGO, ILLINOIS 60607
REPRESENTED BY WENDY HANSON
312/421-3232

COREY
F I L M
P H O T O G R A P H Y

CARL COREY FILM, INC.
222 SOUTH MORGAN STREET   CHICAGO, ILLINOIS 60607
WENDY HANSON
EXECUTIVE PRODUCER
312/421-3232

COREY

FILM
PHOTOGRAPHY

CARL COREY FILM, INC.
222 SOUTH MORGAN STREET CHICAGO, ILLINOIS 60607
WENDY HANSON
EXECUTIVE PRODUCER
312/421-3232

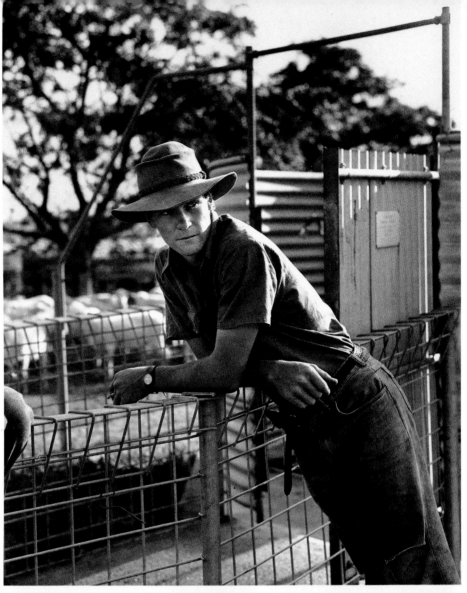

DON GETSUG STUDIOS • 1255 S. MICHIGAN AVE. • CHICAGO 60605
312 939 1477 ■ AGENT: TOM MALONEY & ASSOCS. • 312 321 1900

Eileen Glenn

EILEEN GLENN PHOTOGRAPHIC ILLUSTRATION

PURINA 100 CAT FOOD
CENTRA ADVERTISING

JORDAN, TAMARAZ,
CARUSO ADVERTISING

PORTRAIT

PURINA PUPPY CHOW
CENTRA ADVERTISING

PURINA PUPPY CHOW
CENTRA ADVERTISING

MUTUAL OF OMAHA
BJK&E

RALSTON PURINA, ST. LOUIS

312-944-1756

300 WEST SUPERIOR, SUITE 203, CHICAGO, IL 60610

TUAL OF OMAHA
&E

PORTRAIT

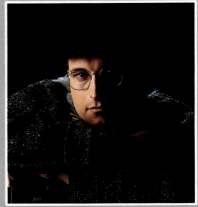
PORTRAIT

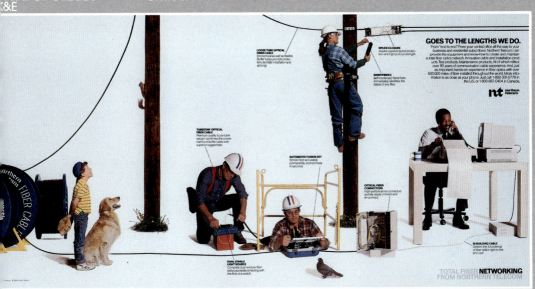
RTHERN TELECOM
/ALTER THOMPSON/CHICAGO

ID
NDERSON ADVERTISING

OSCAR MAYER
J. WALTER THOMPSON/CHICAGO

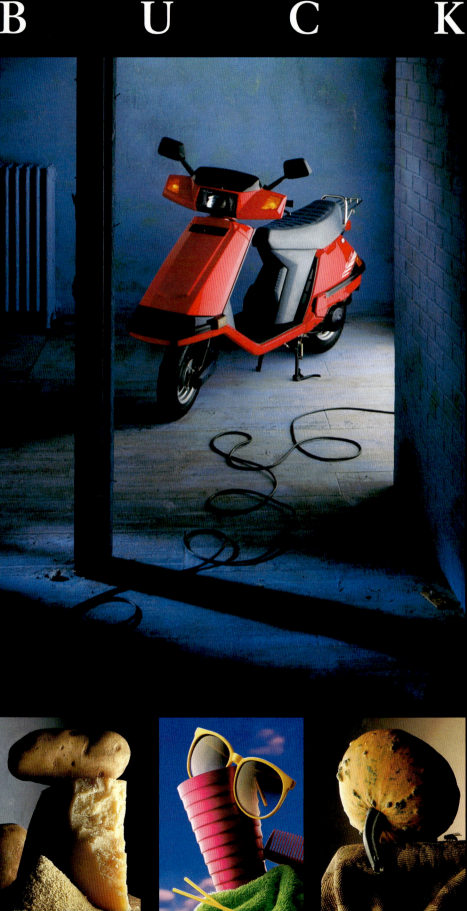

KLOCWORKS
PHOTOGRAPHY

Howard Kloc
Photographer
Anna Biernat
Representative

520 W. 11 Mile Road
Royal Oak, Michigan
48067
313-541-1704

HAND COLORING: CHERYL WINSOR

1808 WEST GRAND AVENUE
CHICAGO, IL 60622
312 733-8021

Paul Elledge

REPRESENTED BY
ANN SNOWBERGER
312 463-3590

HAND COLORING: CHERYL WINSOR

LIFT YOUR CONFIDENCE WHEREVER YOU GO.

Proven Dandruff Care and Great Looking Hair.

1808 WEST GRAND AVENUE
CHICAGO, IL 60622
312 733-8021

Paul Elledge

REPRESENTED BY
ANN SNOWBERGER
312 463-3590

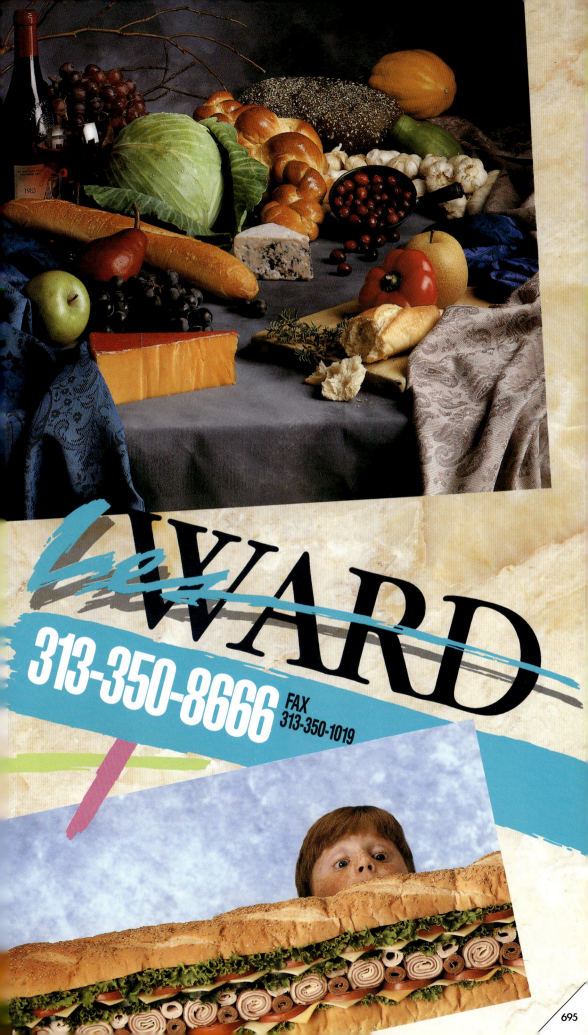

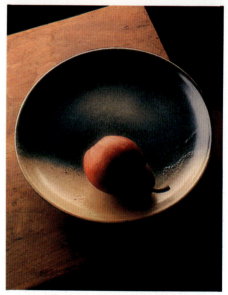

WANS STUDIO, INC.

325 West 40th Street
Kansas City, Missouri 64111
(816) 931-8905
FAX: (816) 931-6899

REID

312.235.4343

1651 W. NORTH AVENUE 60622

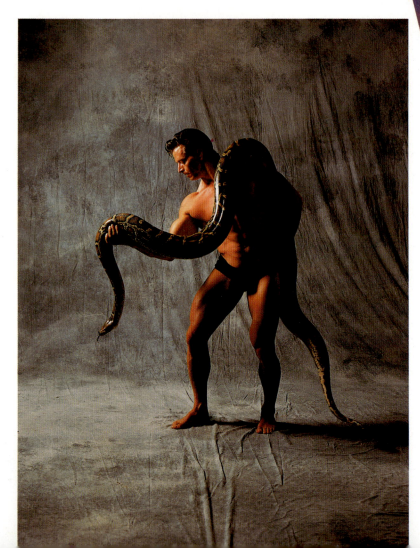

F15E : 8 x 10 Kodak Ektachrome

represented by **ken FELDMAN** 312 337.0447

699

Bruce André

PHOTOGRAPHY · 432 NORTH CLARK STREET
CHICAGO, ILLINOIS 60610 · PHONE (312) 661-1060
REPRESENTED BY: RICK SOLDAT

PAUL Poplis
PHOTOGRAPHY

Paul Poplis Photography   **(614) 231-2942, FAX (614) 231-1698**
3599 Refugee Road, Columbus, Ohio 43232

When you need to set a mood, capture a moment or tell a story; it's a Rush job

©Rush, 1988

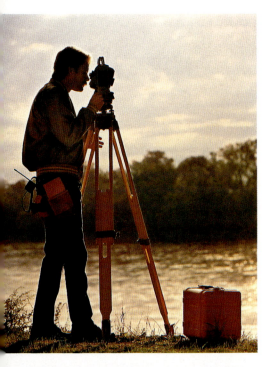
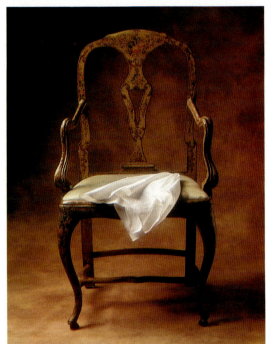

Michael Rush Photography
415 Delaware St.
Kansas City, MO 64105
816•471•1200
ASMP

EWERT

Steve Ewert Photo/Photomatics/Film
17 North Elizabeth, Chicago, Illinois 60607, (312) 733-5762
Represented by: Sally Murphy & Assoc., (312) 346-0720

McCALLUM

REPRESENTED BY
CAROLYN POTTS
& ASSOCIATES
312 935-1707

Bill Tucker Studio, Inc.

# Bill Tucker Studio, Inc.

114 West Illinois 312-321-1570
Chicago, Illinois 60610 Fax: 312-321-9549

WESTERMAN

CHARLIE WESTERMAN · CHICAGO (312) 248-5709 · NEW YORK (212) 353-1235

JENNIFER KING
9709 East Jewell Avenue #106　　Denver, Colorado 80231　　303-337-3137

RICHARD NOBLE

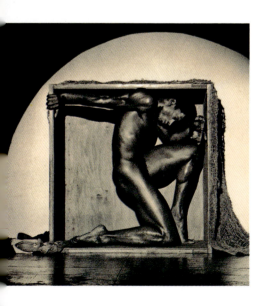

518 MELROSE AVENUE LOS ANGELES CA 90046 213•655•4711

REPRESENTED IN NEW YORK BY MICHAEL ASH 212•807•6286

FILM

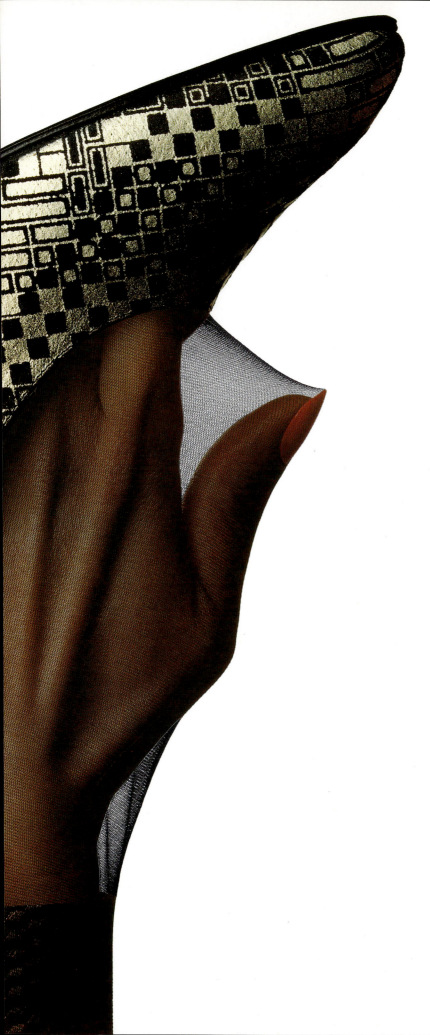

HEFFERNAN
415.626.1999

PRINT

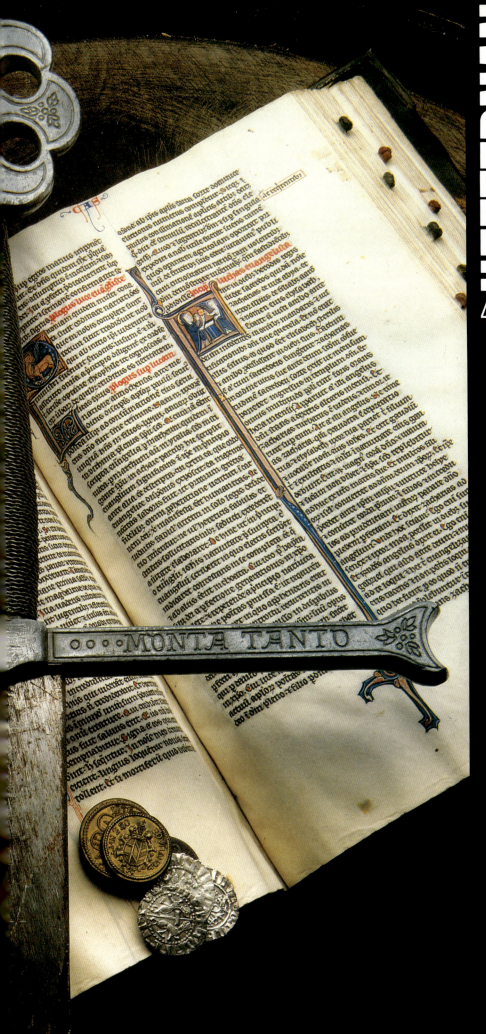

HEFFERNAN
415.626.1999

125 King Street
San Francisco
California 94107
415 541 9050

Representation
By Freda Scott
Please Call
415 621 2992

VICTOR BUDNIK

125 King Street
San Francisco
California 94107
415 541 9050

Representation
By Freda Scott
Please Call
415 621 2992

VICTOR BUDNIK

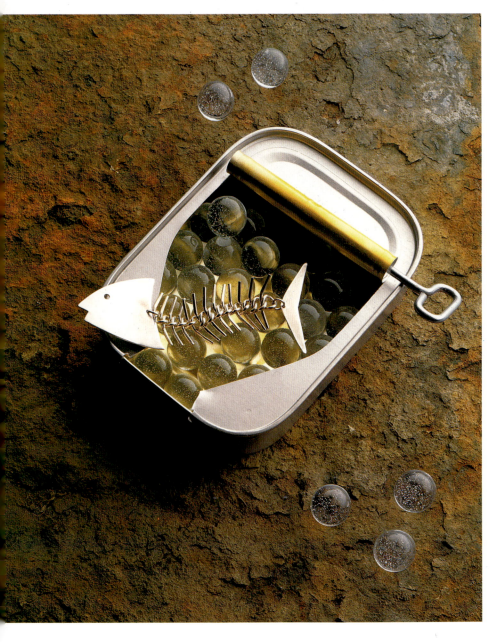

RJ·Muna

415·328·1131

Photo Illustration

Represented by
Freda Scott
415·621·2992

RJ ⁊ Muna

415 ⁊ 328 ⁊ 1131

Black & White

Represented by
Freda Scott
415 · 621 · 2992

SCHELLING

SAN FRANCISCO 415 • 441 • 3662

FRED A SCOTT

Artists Representative
244 Ninth Street
San Francisco,
California 94103-9879

415 621 2992

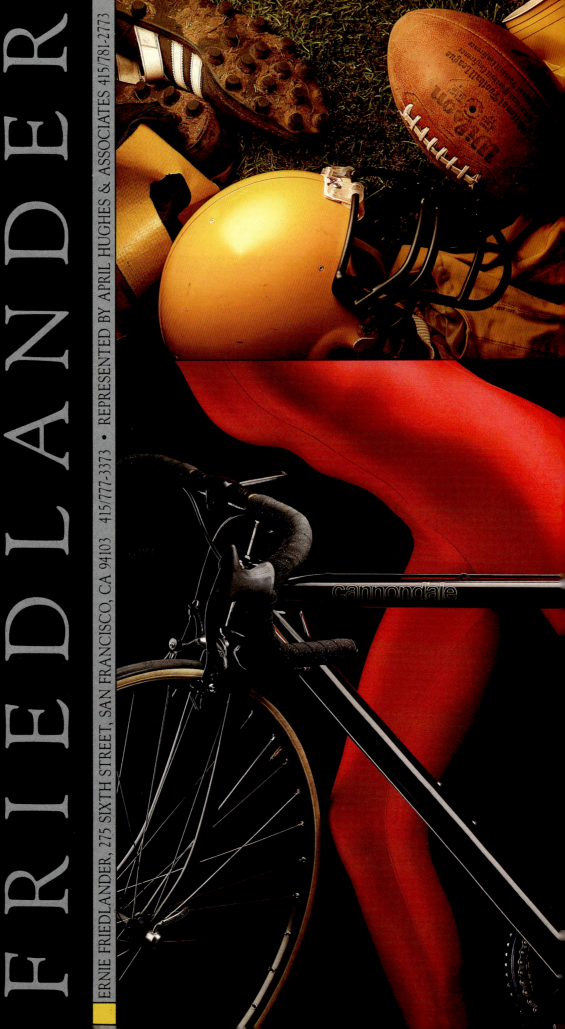

BILL RO

Bill Robbins Photography
7016 Santa Monica Blvd., Los Angeles, CA 90038   Fax: 213-465-8394

OBBINS

We've got personality

For additional work see 1979-88 Black Books
Stock & Photomatic reel available

Studio: 213-466-0377

739

© APPLE/MACINTOSH

© KING WORLD

© ARCO

DOMINIC Marsden

213 · 464 2492
Jean Gardner
REPRESENTS

FAX (818) 508 · 0036

RODNEY RASCONA

4232 SOUTH 36TH PLACE — SUITE 4232 — PHOENIX, ARIZONA 85040 — 602·437·0866

743

PAUL HOFFMAN

4500 19th Street, San Francisco, California 94114

415-863-3575

Represented by Mary Busacca

415-381-9047

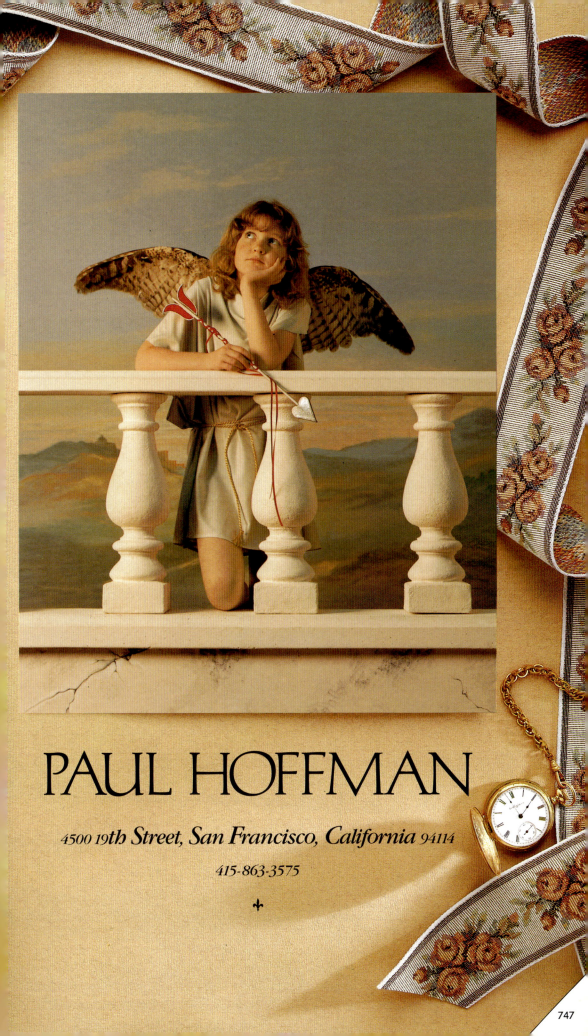

G R i G

NISSAN • THE DESIGNORY • TIM MERAZ

MERCEDES • McCAFFREY AND McCALL, INC. • STEVE HORMAN

RCEDES • McCAFFREY AND McCALL, INC. • STEVE HORMAN

F PROMOTION

OP • VICKERS & BENSON/FKQ • KEN ANDREWLAVAGE

bert L. Grigg
otography Inc.
50 N. Wilcox Avenue
llywood, CA 90038
3-469 6316

New York
Representative
Michael Ash
212·807 6286

Los Angeles
Representative
Tricia Burlingham
213·271 3982

Detroit
Representative
Mike Morawski
313·543 9440

Chicago
Representative
Joel Harlib
312·329 1370

CARIN KRASNER

PHOTOGRAPHY • 3239 HELMS AVENUE • LOS ANGELES CA 90034 • 213/280-0082
REPRESENTED BY TRICIA BURLINGHAM • 213/271-3982

CARIN KRASNER

PHOTOGRAPHY • 3239 HELMS AVENUE • LOS ANGELES CA 90034 • 213/280-0082

© JOHN LAWLOR 1989

JOHN LAWLOR ON LOCATION

Office (213) 468-9050 FAX (213) 468-1003
Representatives:
New York: BERT YELLEN (212) 838-3170
West Coast: TRICIA BURLINGHAM (213) 271-3982
Chicago: SKILLICORN ASSOC. (312) 856-1626
Television: BASSINSON PRODUCTIONS (213) 466-2171
Assistants phone for appointment (213) 465-6815

LOCATION ASSIGNMENTS FOR
ADVERTISING AND
CORPORATE PHOTOGRAPHY

CALL FOR
OUR MONOCHROME AND
COLOR PORTFOLIO

LONNIE DUKA PHOTOGRAPHY
919 ORIOLE DRIVE
LAGUNA BEACH, CA 92651
714-494-7057

ALLAN

ALLAN LAIDMAN · PHOTOGRAPHY

110 Free Silver Court, A102 Aspen, Colorado 81611 303-925-4791

Represented by

East & Central: David Munk 303-925-1945

West: McBAIN SHARPE 213-392-9341, 474-9820

Animals. Domestic, wild, exotic and dangerous. With people or product.

KIMBALL

Ron Kimball Photography · 2582 Sun-Mor Avenue, Mountain View, California 94040 · 415/969-0682

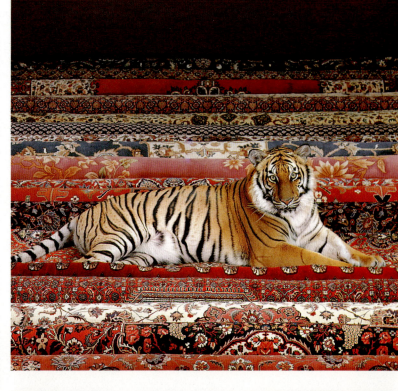

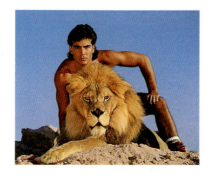

KIMBALL

Ron Kimball Photography • 2582 Sun-Mor Avenue, Mountain View, California 94040 • 415/969-0682

Over 200,000 stock shots available of the highest quality.

1.

2.

3.

1. MAGAZINE
ART DIRECTOR
Doug Patterson
COPYWRITER
Martin MacDonald
AGENCY
Hal Riney & Partners
San Francisco
CLIENT
Sterling

2. MAGAZINE
ART DIRECTOR
Dennis Lim
COPYWRITER
Bob Ancona
Brent Bouchez
AGENCY
Ketchum Advertising
Los Angeles
CLIENT
Acura

3. BROCHURE
ART DIRECTOR
Colleen Leonhard
COPYWRITER
Fred Stafford
AGENCY
Young & Rubicam
Detroit
CLIENT
Lincoln-Mercury

4. BROCHURE
ART DIRECTOR
David Stokes
COPYWRITER
Craig Caldwell
AGENCY
Ketchum Advertising
Los Angeles
CLIENT
Acura

5. MAGAZINE
ART DIRECTOR
Mas Yamashita
COPYWRITER
Dave Butler
AGENCY
Chiat/Day
Los Angeles
CLIENT
Yamaha

If this picture has already convinced you to buy a new Yamaha Virago, don't bother turning the page.

PHOTOGRAPHY
Bo Hylén
STUDIO
1640 S. La Cienega Blvd.
Los Angeles, Ca. 90035

For portfolio and reel call

(213) 271-6543
TELEFAX
(213) 271-6470

Jay Silverman Production

Silver

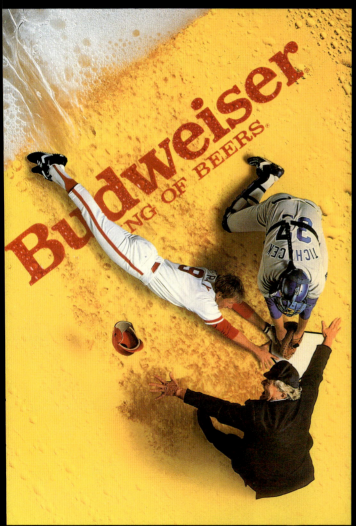

Represented and Produced by Tony Rotundo (213) 466-6030   FAX 466-7139   CALL FOR OUR REEL

man

Jay Silverman Studios
920 North Citrus Ave.
Hollywood, CA 90038-2402

Last Year, Fred Flew Over 100,000 Miles To 17 Foreign Countries. Just To Buy You The Perfect Gift.

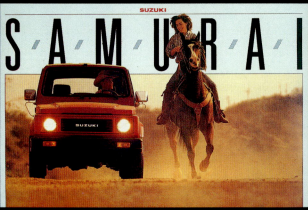

TASTE THE HIGH LIFE

Jay Silverman Production

Silver

Represented and Produced by Tony Rotundo (213) 466-6030   FAX 466-7139   CALL FOR OUR REEL

man

Jay Silverman Studios
920 North Citrus Ave.
Hollywood, CA 90038-2402

Milroy/McAleer

NEWPORT BEACH CA
714·722·6402

Milroy/McAleer

LAWDER

Food Stylist: Elvie Wilkenson

JOHN LAWDER PHOTOGRAPHY

2672 South Grand
Santa Ana, CA 92705
714-557-3657

Represented by
Laurie Hampton
FAX 714-557-2143

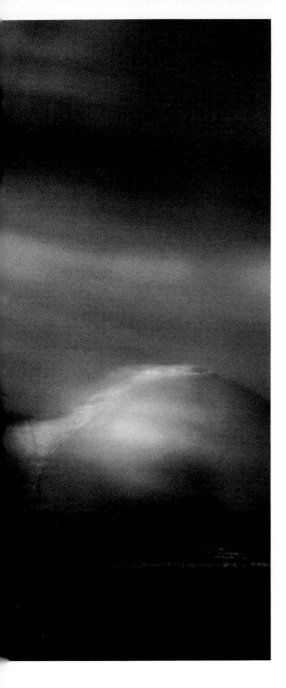

Mizono

Robert Mizono

650 Alabama

San Francisco 94110

415 648 3993

Mizono

Robert Mizono

650 Alabama

San Francisco 94110

415 648 3993

PERSONAL WORK

BUDWEISER/DMB&B-ST. LOUIS/
NORM SIMON-AD

MOUNTAIN DEW/BBDO-NY/RON PALUMBO-A

KUHN

New York:
Madeleine Robinson 212-243-3138
Chicago:
Ken Feldman 312-337-0447
Dallas:
Melissa Hopson 214-747-3122
Los Angeles:
Ann Koeffler 213-850-8222
San Francisco:
Corey Graham 415-956-4750
West Coast:
Carol Sund 206-624-4706
The Image Bank 212-529-6700

Shooting for major agencies and corporations all over the world

MJB/HAL RINEY & ASSOC.-SF

PENTAX CORP./THE BLOOM AGENCY/
DEBORAH HOVHANNESIAN-AD

EGGHEAD SOFTWARE/THE RICHARDS COMPANY/PETER RICHARDS-AD

U.S. ARMY

WEST

For existing work see Black Book '88, '87, '86, '85, '84, '83, '82.

Chuck Kuhn
Photography, Inc.

Represented by Warren Cook
(714) 770-4619

P.O. Box 2159
Laguna Hills, California 92654

For additional examples, see
Showcase 4 thru 12 and Black Book '88
© 1988 Kathleen Norris Cook

Assignment and Stock / Landscapes / Aerials / Panoramics

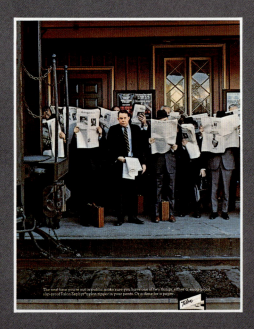

PETRUCELLI ASSOCIATES INC.

TONY PETRUCELLI   714-458-6914

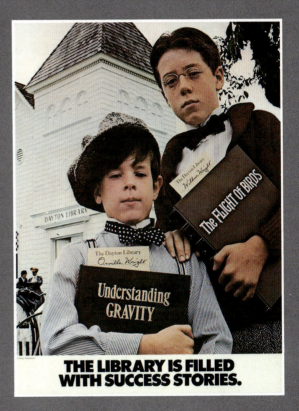

TO SEE MORE OF THE PORTFOLIO SEE CALIFORNIA WORKBOOK AND BLACK BOOK PAGES 132-133 NORTHEAST SECTION.

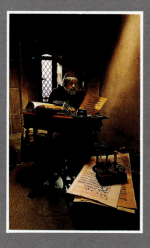

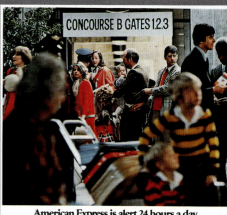

PETRUCELLI ASSOCIATES INC.

TONY PETRUCELLI 714-458-6914

TO SEE MORE OF THE PORTFOLIO SEE CALIFORNIA WORKBOOK AND BLACK BOOK PAGES 132-133 NORTHEAST SECTION.

Tom Landecker Photography
282 Seventh Street
San Francisco, Ca. 94103
(415) 864 8888

LANDECKER

© LANDECKER 1989

© LANDECKER 1989

KEVIN SANCHEZ STUDIOS   SAN FRANCISCO   415.285.1770

DIRK DOUGLASS
PHOTOGRAPHY

2755 SOUTH 300 WEST SUITE D
SALT LAKE CITY, UTAH 84115
(801) 485-5691

STOCK AVAILABLE AT SHARP SHOOTERS 800-666-1266

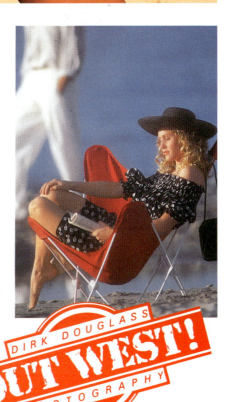

DIRK DOUGLASS OUT WEST! PHOTOGRAPHY

AIR LA

VANTAGE

MERCEDES BENZ

CHAMPION

PORSCHE

VANTAGE

MILLER

ZWART
REPRESENTED BY CELIA S. SNYDER

JEFFREY R. ZWART
ZWART STUDIOS INC.
1900-E EAST WARNER
SANTA ANA, CA 92705
TEL (714) 261-5844
FAX (714) 261-5973

PONTIAC/DMB&B

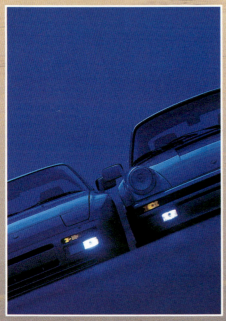
AUTOMOBILE

MOTOR TREND

AUTOM

MAZDA/FCB

HUBER

REPRESENTED BY CELIA S. SNYDER

VIC HUBER
ZWART STUDIOS INC.
1900-E EAST WARNER
SANTA ANA, CA 92705
TEL (714) 261-5844
FAX (714) 261-5973

OBILES

793

For Years, People Have Been Telling Me To Get Out Of Town.

Honeywell, American Airlines, Sheraton, Polaroid Corp, Gates-Learjet, General Motors, just to name a few. I feel at home on the road. Shooting locations. Some with people. Some without. Whether it's here in Arizona, or wherever. I'm ready. Let's talk, and I'll be out of town by sundown.

Gerczynski Photographs

2211 N. 7th Avenue, Phoenix, AZ 85007 (602) 252-9229
Stock photography available

Design Photography

1324 HAMILTON AVENUE • CLEVELAND, OHIO 44114 • (216) 687-0099
521 SIXTH STREET • SAN FRANCISCO, CA 94103 • (415) 543-1504

Photographers: Carl Fowler, Jim Lawson • Representative: Kathryn Anderson

TO SEE ADDITIONAL IMAGES SEE OUR AD IN THE MIDWEST

KNUDSON

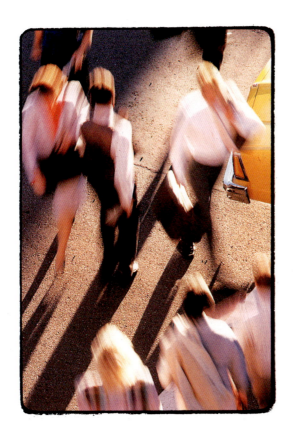

CLIENTS INCLUDE:

AMERICAN EXPRESS

AUDI OF AMERICA

CLUB MED

DOW CHEMICAL

NORFOLK SOUTHERN

PRINCESS CRUISES

SHERATON RESORTS

SPERRY FLIGHT SYSTEMS

TABASCO

US WEST

ASSIGNMENT & STOCK

PO BOX 10397

PHOENIX, ARIZONA 85064

602·277·7701

JOHN McDERMOTT

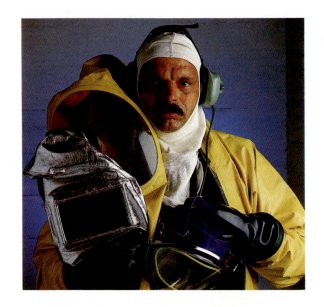

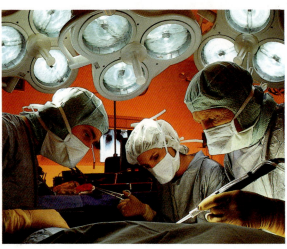

415.982.2010

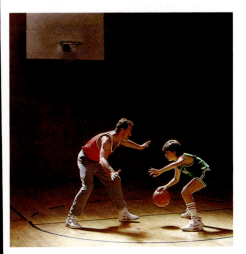

Pacific Northwest

Sun Valley Company

Saturdays

John Terence Turner

All photos © John Terence Turner 1988

(206) 325-9073
173 37th Ave. E.
Seattle, WA 98112
FAX (206) 322-1356

Represented by Yoko Tao
Tokyo (03) 550-8788

Marni Hall & Associates
Los Angeles (213) 934-9420

New York Portfolio Depot
(212) 989-8588

Clients include:
AT&T, Canon Cameras, NIKE,
Seagram's and Southern Bell.

Shots set up to look as if they weren't.

See other work in Black Book
'83, '84, '85, '86, '87, '88.

Richard Wahlstrom Photography, 650 Alabama Street, San Francisco, CA 94110, 415/550-1400, FAX 415/282-9133

WAHLSTROM

Richard Wahlstrom Photography, 650 Alabama Street, San Francisco, CA 94110, 415/550-1400, FAX 415/282-9133
Reps: San Francisco 415/441-3769, Chicago 312/337-7770, Dallas 214/428-8781

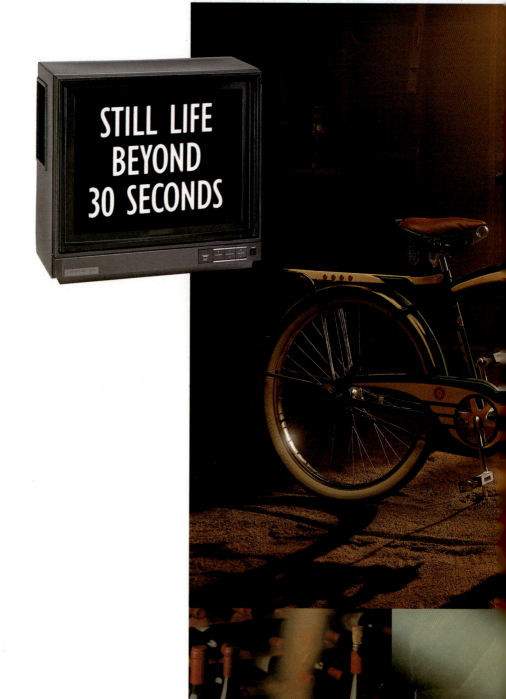

LEE
PEARSON PHOTOGRAPHY

1746 N. IVAR AVE. L.A. CA 90028

(213) 461-3861

James B. WOOD

(213) 461-3861   1746 N. IVAR AVE. L.A. CA 90028

LOS ANGELES: STACY WEISS (213)939-9797

SAN FRANCISCO: RON SWEET (415)433-1222

MIDWEST: TONI MC NAUGHTON (312)938-2148

MICHAEL HORIKAWA
shoots the best of Hawaii.

Luxury resorts, travel, fashion, product.
Location, studio and aerial.
See also: Showcase 1986–88

Thanks to AT&T, AMFAC, Aston Hotels, Catalina, Dole International, Eastern Airlines, Fuji Film, General Foods, Hawaiian Airlines, Hilton Hotels, Hyatt Hotels, Lever Brothers, Mauna Lani Resort, Mercedes-Benz (Europe), Nissan (Japan), Pan Am, Panasonic, Playboy, Sheraton Hotels, Shiseido, Toshiba, United Airlines, and many others.

Studio: 508 Kamakee Street, Honolulu, Hawaii 96814
808 / 538-7378, 226-3256

Represented by:
Gene O'Rourke
Honolulu Creative Group
808 / 924-2513

New York:
O'Rourke Page Associates
212 / 772-0346

Chicago:
Jim Hanson
312 / 527-1114

ZAJACK STUDIOS, INC.

SPECIALIZING IN

AUTOMOTIVE

PHOTOGRAPHY

ZAJ

1517 W. ALTON AVE.

SANTA ANA, CA 92704

714·432·8400

FAX 714·432·1809

Jim Blakeley Photographer, Inc.
Telephone 415 558 9300

1061 Folsom Street
San Francisco, CA 94103

Represented by Ivy Glick
Telephone 415 543 6056

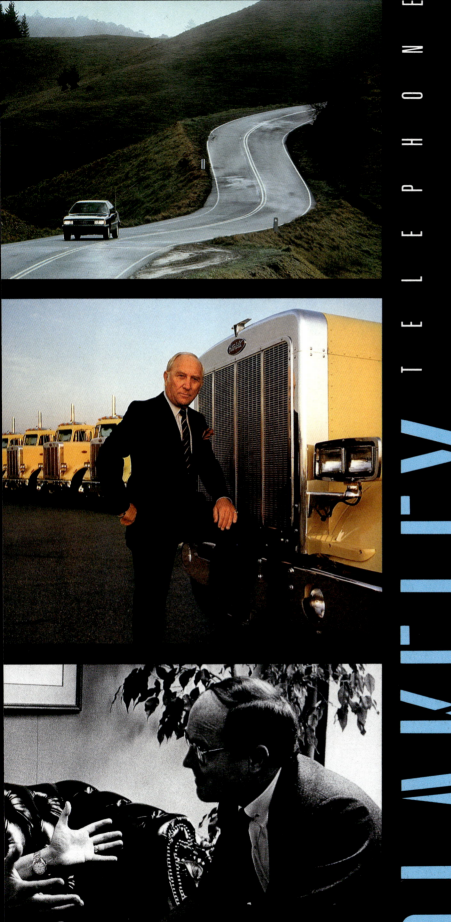

MICHAEL LAMOTTE
STUDIOS, INC.
828 MISSION STREET
SAN FRANCISCO
CALIFORNIA 94103
415.777.1443

REPRESENTED BY
MILLICENT
CHASE-LALANNE
415.986.6121

AGFA
AIM
AIR FRANCE
ALBERTO-
CULVER
ALL STATE
AMOCO
ARCO
ARMOUR-
ALL
AT&T
AUSTRIAN-
LOTTO
AVIANCA
BACTINE
BANK OF -
AMERICA
BETTY-
CROCKER
BILLY / KID
BLUE CROSS
BORDENS
BUDWEISER
BUSCH
CABALLERO
CADBURY
CAMEL
CAMERON-
OIL TOOLS
CANADA DRY
CATALINA
CENTURY 21
CHUNG KING
CHANTELLE
CHEVY
CLOROX
COKE
COLDWELL-
BANKER
CNT FRANCE
CORONA
CONTINENTAL
CREDIT-
AGRICOLE
CROWN-
ZELLERBACH
DANIEL-
HECHTER
DATSON
DELCO
DEL MAR-
BLINDS
DEL MONTE
DISNEY
DOLE
DITTO
DRAKKER
DR. PEPPER
DUNLOPILLO
DUPONT-
WATCHES
EASTER-
SEALS
FANTA
EUROCARD
ESQUIRE
FIAT
FRITO LAY
GATORADE
GAVISCON

INTERNAT'L-
HARVESTER
JEEP
KAWASAKI
KELLOGGS
KNOOR
KRAFT
KRONEN-
BORG
LEVI'S
L.A. TIMES
LITTER-
GREEN
MAXWELL-
HOUSE
MANWICH
MAZDA
MARTELL
MATTEL
MASTER-
CARD
MCDONALDS
MERCEDES-
BENZ
MOTEL 6
MICHELOB
MICRORIM
MUSTANG
NATIONAL-
CAR RENTAL
NBC
OBERNAI
OLSMOBILE
OSCAR-
MEYER
PAC BELL
PHILLIPS-
ELECTRON.
PHILLIPS 66
PEPSI
PILLSBURY
PIONEER
PLAYERS
PUCH-
MOPEDS
PUREX
PURINA
PROTO-
TOOLS
RAISON-
BOARD
RALEIGH
RAYBAN
REDKIN
ROYAL-
VIKING
RENAULT
REDSON
RC COLA
SAFECO
SEARS
SEVEN UP
SHELL OIL
SIMCA
SHERWIN-
WILLIAMS
SITMAR
CRUISES
STOUFFER
SLICE

TWENTY YEARS ON LOCATION...FROM GRIFFITH PARK TO KATHMANDU

MARTY EVANS

6850 Vineland Ave. Suite K; N. Hollywood, Ca 91605   (818) 762-5400 Telex 6831319
Reps: **New York:** Joan Jedell (212) 861-7861   **Chicago:** Joel Harlib (312) 329-1370
San Francisco: Nadine Hyatt (415) 456-7711   **Paris:** Star Studios 47570932
W. Germany: Ute Rockenfeller 211-689009   T.V. Reel Available

GOODYEAR
GENERAL-
MILLS
GENIE
GEORGIA-
PACIFIC
GINGESS
GREYHOUND
GRUNDIG
HAGGAR
HAMILTON-
BEACH
HEINEKIN
HERTZ
HONDA
HORLICKS
HOME -
SAVINGS
HUNT-
WESSON
IBM
ILLINOIS-
LOTTERY
INTERFLORA
INTERPACE
INTERNAT'L-

SUNBEAM
SUNKIST
SUZUKI
TRANS-
AMERICA
TWICE-
AS FRESH
TWA
UNION OIL
UNITED-
ARTISTS
VISA
VISICORP
VOLKSWAGON
V-8
VON'S
VAGABOND
WARNER
WATERPIC
WELLS-
FARGO
WESTERN-
AIRLINES
WINSTON
WRIGLEY
XEROX

817

CHARLES WILLIAM BUSH

940 NORTH HIGHLAND, LOS ANGELES, CALIFORNIA 90038. 213.466.6630. FAX 213.466.0144. SAN FRANCISCO, NADINE HYATT 415.456.7711. LOS ANGELES, RHONI EPSTEIN 213.663.2388. CHICAGO, BILL RABIN & ASSOC. 312.944.6655. DALLAS, LARRY & ANDREA LYNCH 214.521.6169. NEW YORK, JOAN JEDELL 212.861.7861.

PERSONALITIES

HARRY ANDERSON
RICHARD DEAN ANDERSON
MEREDITH BAXTER-BIRNEY
SHARI BELAFONTE-HARPER
CORBIN BERNSEN
JACQUELINE BISSET
ELAINE BOOSLER
BARRY BOSTWICK
BEAU BRIDGES
JAMES BROLIN
JAMES CAAN
JOHNNY CARSON
RICHARD CHAMBERLAIN
RAY CHARLES
JANE CURTAIN
TED DANSON
BETTE DAVIS
TONY DENNISON
BRUCE DERN
LAURA DERN
PHIL DONAHUE
JILL EIKENBERRY
FARRAH FAWCETT
SALLY FIELD
JANE FONDA
CATHY GISEWHITE
SHARON GLESS
ELLIOT GOULD
DAVID HALLIDAY
LINDA HAMILTON
DARRYL HANNAH
MARK HARMON
KATHRYN HARROLD
CHARLESTON HESTON
KATHERINE HICKS
QUINCY JONES
SALLY KELLERMAN
CHERYL LADD
MICHAEL LANDON
ANGELA LANSBURY
JOHN LARROQUETTE
JUDITH LIGHT
HEATHER LOCKLEAR
SHELLY LONG
SOPHIA LOREN
LORETTA LYNN
SHIRLEY MacLAINE
HOWIE MANDELL
ANN-MARGRET
ALI McGRAW
JONI MITCHELL
DUDLEY MOORE
ESAI MORALES
JUICE NEWTON
DOLLY PARTON
GREGORY PECK
CHYNNA PHILLIPS
VINCENT PRICE
DEBORAH RAFFIN
JAMES READ
JOHN RITTER
KENNY ROGERS
DIANA ROSS
SUSAN SARANDAN
JACK SCALIA
TRACY SCOGGINS
CONNIE SELLECCA
TOM SELLECK
JANE SEYMOUR
WILLIAM SHATNER
MARTIN SHEEN
CYBIL SHEPHERD
JACLYN SMITH
SISSY SPACEK
SUSAN ST. JAMES
JIMMY STEWART
DONALD SUTHERLAND
DONNA SUMMER
PATRICK SWAYZE
ALLEN THICKE
JOHN TRAVOLTA
MICHAEL TUCKER
CHRISTY TURLINGTON
CICELY TYSON
BEN VEREEN
ROBERT WAGNER
RACHEL WARD
LESLIE ANN WARREN
RAQUEL WELCH
BILLY DEE WILLIAMS
ROBIN WILLIAMS
SHEREE WILSON

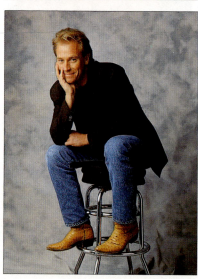

CHARLES WILLIAM BUSH

940 NORTH HIGHLAND, LOS ANGELES, CALIFORNIA 90038. 213.466.6630. FAX 213.466.0144. SAN FRANCISCO, NADINE HYATT 415.456.7711. LOS ANGELES, RHONI EPSTEIN 213.663.2388. CHICAGO, BILL RABIN & ASSOC. 312.944.6655. DALLAS, LARRY & ANDREA LYNCH 214.521.6169. NEW YORK, JOAN JEDELL 212.861.7861.

CLIENTS

ABC ENTERTAINMENT CENTER
ANHEUSER-BUSCH INC.
BAKER WINOKUR RYDER
BBDO
J. BERNSTEIN INC.
THE BLOOM AGENCY
BOZELL & JACOBS/
KENYON & ECKHARDT
BRIGHT AND ASSOCIATES
BULLOCKS WILSHIRE
LEO BURNETT U.S.A.
BUTLER KOSH BROOKS
CBS ENTERTAINMENT
CAPITOL RECORDS
CAESARS PALACE
CELANESE
CHATELAINE MAGAZINE
CHIAT/DAY
CLARION COSMETICS
COLUMBIA PICTURES
COMMERCIAL GRAPHICS
COTY
D'ARCY MASIUS BENTON & BOWLES
DAILEY & ASSOCIATES
EMI AMERICA RECORDS
EISAMAN, JOHNS & LAWS
EVE CIGARETTES
FAMILY CIRCLE
FOOTE, CONE & BELDING
FOX BROADCASTING
GIORGIO PARFUM
GLAMOUR MAGAZINE
GOOD HOUSEKEEPING
GUMPERTZ/BENTLEY/FRIED
HOECHST FIBERS INDUSTRIES
INTERNATIONAL PLAYTEX INC.
ITALIAN TAXI MAGAZINE
KODAK
LEVI STRAUSS
L'OFFICIEL
LORIMAR
LOS ANGELES MAGAZINE
MCA RECORDS
McCALL'S MAGAZINE
MGM/UNITED ARTISTS
MTM
MAX FACTOR & CO.
MAY COMPANY
MAYBELLINE
McCANN-ERICKSON INC.
MERLE NORMAN COSMETICS
MODE O'DAY FASHIONS
MOTOWN RECORDS
NBC
NEEDHAM HARPER
WORLDWIDE INC.
NEUTROGENA CORP.
NOXEMA
OGILVY & MATHER
PARAMOUNT PICTURES
PARIS MATCH
PERT SHAMPOO
PICKWICK, MASLANSKY,
KOENIGSBURG
PURINA
RCA COMPUTERS
RCA RECORDS
REDKEN
RICHARD GRANT & ASSOC.
ROC COSMETICS
ROGERS & COWAN
7UP
SIMON & SCHUSTER
SPIEGEL
SSC&B/NY
TARLOW ADVERTISING
TELEDYNE
TIME-LIFE BOOKS
TROPICAL
TV GUIDE
ULTRA MAGAZINE
UNIWORLD
VIDAL SASSOON INC.
VISA INC.
WALT DISNEY STUDIOS
WARNER BOOKS INC.
WARNER BROTHERS
WELLS RICH GREENE INC.
WHITTLE COMMUNICATIONS
WOMANS DAY MAGAZINE
WRANGLERS INC.
YOUNG & RUBICAM

819

Elyse Lewin

820 N. FAIRFAX LOS ANGELES, CALIFORNIA 90046 (213) 655-4214

REPRESENTED BY
LOS ANGELES MARNI HALL (213) 934-9420 **CHICAGO** VICKI PETERSON (312) 467-0780
NEW YORK JOAN JEDELL (212) 861-7861

SEND FOR OUR FILM REEL

Twelve years of award

JEFF NADLER STUDIO, INC.
520 N. WESTERN AVE.
LOS ANGELES, CALIFORNIA 90004
213-467-2135

winning photography.

WEST COAST REPRESENTATIVE: ELLEN KNABLE & ASSOCIATES 213-855-8855
EAST COAST REPRESENTATIVE: JOAN JEDELL 212-861-7861

Vince Streano

COMMERCIAL AND ADVERTISING LOCATION ASSIGNMENTS. Services available include location scouting, talent searching and full production. Recent clients include: Sony Corporation, Arco Marine, Raymond Corporation, Smithsonian Magazine, Impell Corporation, Great Western Bank, Thortek, International Transportation Services, Airco.

Call Michelle at STREANO/HAVENS for access to our extensive stock photo file.

714/497-1908
P.O. Box 662, Laguna Beach, CA 92652

© V. STREANO 1988

Jay P. Morgan
PHOTOGRAPHY

213-224-8288

Jay P. Morgan Photography
618 D Moulton Ave., Los Angeles, CA 90031
Represented in Los Angeles by
Kelly Keith (213) 224-8288
FAX #(213) 224-8386

Let our monthly calendar
promotion invade your office.
Call or write to add your
name to our mailing list.

For additional work see '89 California Workbook
and '88 American Showcase.

Call for our film reel.

CUMMINS

1527 13th Avenue, Seattle, WA 98122, 206-322-4944

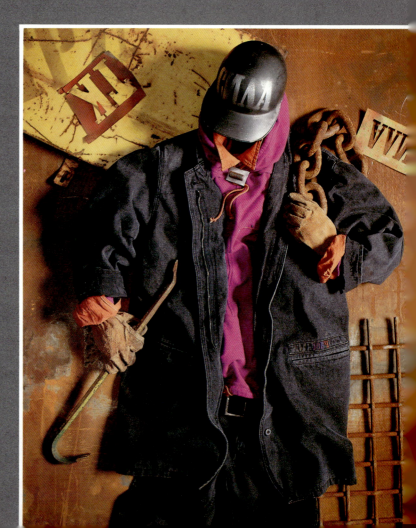

CUMMINS

Represented in the Midwest by: Skillicorn Associates, 312-856-1626.

M A R T I N
P H O T O G

8615 Commerce Avenue
San Diego, California 92121

© 1988 Martin Trailer

TRAILER
G R A P H I C S

Phone 619 **549 8881**
FAX 619 **549 0758**

© 1988 Martin Trailer

Siegel

Siegel Photographic, a full scale Photographic Design Studio, People! Product! Locations! Our studio has 8,000 sq. ft. of shooting space, B/W lab, conference rooms and a complete kitchen. The Southwest provides year round location photography with beautiful mountain and desert vistas. (Portfolio upon request.)

Siegel Photographic, Inc.
David M. Siegel
224 North 5th Avenue
Phoenix, Arizona 85003
Tel: 602-257-9509

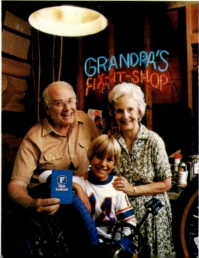

GENERAL ACCOUNTS

Arizona Bank	Discount Tire	Intel	SRP	Wells Rich & Greene
Arizona Tourism	First Interstate	Mattel Toys	Vincents Restaurant	Chiat-Day
Arvin	Garrett Air	McLain Airlines	Westcourt Hotels	J. Walter Thomson
Blue Cross	Goldwaters	Motorola	Western Savings	Ray Vote Graphics U.S.A.
Boy Scouts of America	Greyhound	Nationwide Liquor		Thomas-Tvert, Inc.
Circle K	Hilton Hotels	Oaxaca	Cramer/Krasselt	
Coventry Homes	Honeywell	Red Cross	Ogilvy & Mather	
	Humana	Scuba Pro	Phillips-Ramsey	

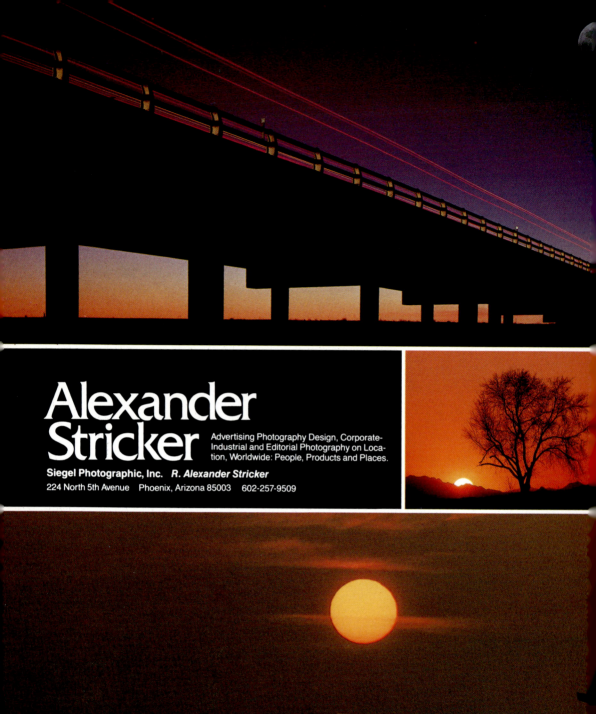

Alexander Stricker

Advertising Photography Design, Corporate-Industrial and Editorial Photography on Location, Worldwide: People, Products and Places.

Siegel Photographic, Inc. *R. Alexander Stricker*
224 North 5th Avenue   Phoenix, Arizona 85003   602-257-9509

Yong Mo, Peoples Republic of China

Cusco, Peru

Grand Canyon, Arizona

PAUL LOVEN

Paul Loven Photography, Inc.
(602) 253-0335 / Phoenix, Arizona

Represented by Mary Holland
(602) 275-3563

RON DERHACOPIAN
FOOD & PRODUCT PHOTOGRAPHY (213) 388-6724

MARKOWS

SOUTHWEST

Paul Markow shoots for print, photomatics and stock on location. Anywhere. Represented in Phoenix by Marjorie Rosenman at 602/273-7985.

RON COPPOCK

Bozell Jacobs

KMGH-TV

Broyles Allebaugh Davis

Indiana Bankcorp

Colorado Tourism

Lee Reedy Design

PHOTOGRAPHY

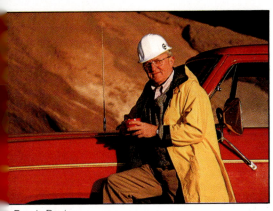
Reedy Design

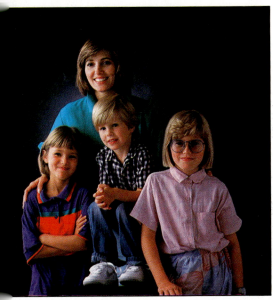
Cable Television

PHC, Pasadena

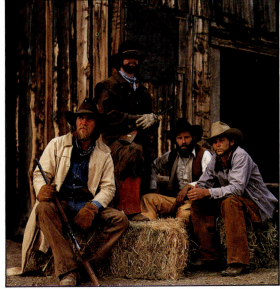
Wyoming Tourism

Multi Media, Plus System

Denver and the West / 303·477·3343
Midwest: Casalini and Coppock / 317·873·4858

841

Olympic Diver

Aerobic Rings/Fitness Dimensions

Charlie Joiner/General Instruments

Americas Cup/San Diego Yacht Club

*For more winning shots
contact Lois Harrington
2775 Kurtz St., Studio 2
San Diego, CA 92110
Telephone 619/291-2775*

Marshall Harrington　　Studio

Jumping & Sitting Dogs/Great American First Savings Bank

*For more winning shots
contact Lois Harrington
2775 Kurtz St., Studio 2
San Diego, CA 92110
Telephone 619/291-2775*

S A M E

Peter Samerjan, Inc./743 N. Fairfax Avenue Los Angele

RJAN

A 90046/USA/213-653-2940 Fax: 213-653-2905

David LeBon Photography
(213) 375-4877

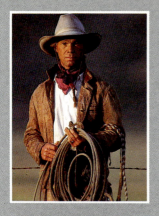

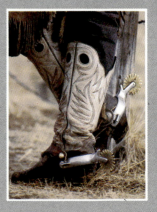

IN THE WEST, FOR ASSIGNMENTS CALL:
DAVID R. STOECKLEIN PHOTOGRAPHY
208-726-5191

IN THE EAST, FOR ASSIGNMENTS CALL:
DON STOGO/STOGO ASSOCIATES
212-490-1034

David R. Stoecklein

DAVID R. STOECKLEIN PHOTOGRAPHY
P.O. BOX 856
KETCHUM, ID 83340

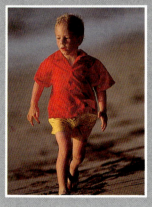

IN THE WEST, FOR ASSIGNMENTS CALL:
DAVID R. STOECKLEIN PHOTOGRAPHY
208-726-5191

IN THE EAST, FOR ASSIGNMENTS CALL:
DON STOGO/STOGO ASSOCIATES
212-490-1034

DAVID R. STOECKLEIN PHOTOGRAPHY
P.O. BOX 856
KETCHUM, ID 83340

849

HAWAII

Turner & deVries

From resorts to sports, we make the good life look great!

A partial list of our clients includes; America-Hawaii Cruises, Continental Airlines, Hilton Hotels, Simpson Paper Company, State of Hawaii, Toshiba, Toyota and United Airlines.

Cindy Turner and Hugo deVries
1200 College Walk, Suite 212, Honolulu, Hawaii 96817
Telephone: (808) 537-3115

K. D. Lange

Roy Orbison

Quincy Jones

Peter Darley Miller Photography

Telephone
213
460 4876

Represented by

Visages

Telephone
213
650-8880

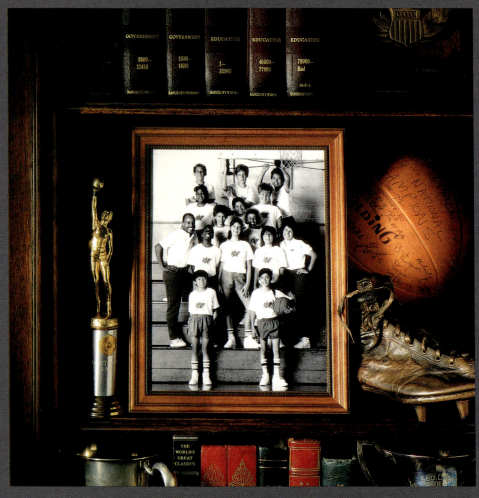

McGuire

GARY McGUIRE 1248 S. FAIRFAX LOS ANGELES CA 213-938-2481

ANDRE

HOLDEN (714) 553-9455

17911 SKY PARK CIRCLE, SUITE M, IRVINE, CA 92714

C H U N G

KEN LEI

Prints & Film

© 1988 KEN CHUNG
For more work
please refer to 88,87,86
Black Book, Work Book

Represented by

CHRISTINE

tel 213 938-9117
fax 213 938-4306

5200 Venice Blvd
Los Angeles
CA 90019

857

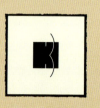

Hank Benson

653 Bryant

San Francisco

California

94107

415.543.8153

Fax 415.543.8244

Elma Garcia
AMERICAN CLASSICS

IF YOU DON'T SURF, DON'T START.

IF YOU DON'T SURF, DON'T START.

The Shalek Agency

LA Style Magazine

Elma Garcia
2565 Third Street
#308
San Francisco
California 94107
Tel: (415) 641-9992
Fax: (415) 641-0260

Elma Garcia
AMERICAN CLASSICS

CBS

MOJO/MDA

McCann Erickson

Elma Garcia
2565 Third Street
#308
San Francisco
California 94107
Tel: (415) 641-9992
Fax: (415) 641-0260

RUSING

→2   →2A

FOR THE REST OF THE STORY, GET THE REST OF THE BOOK. CALL FOR RICK'S PORTFOLIO.
REPRESENTED IN SAN FRANCISCO BY KURT GRUBAUGH. 415.381.3038
REPRESENTED IN CHICAGO BY VINCE KAMIN. 312.787.8834
PHOENIX STUDIO. 602.967.1864.

GRAY IN

IN ITS MOST POTENT FORM,
THE CAR HAILED AS "THE BEST HANDLING PRODUCTION SPORTS CAR IN AMERICA"
IS EQUIPPED WITH TIRES OF EQUAL CALIBRE.

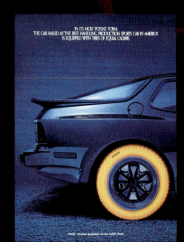

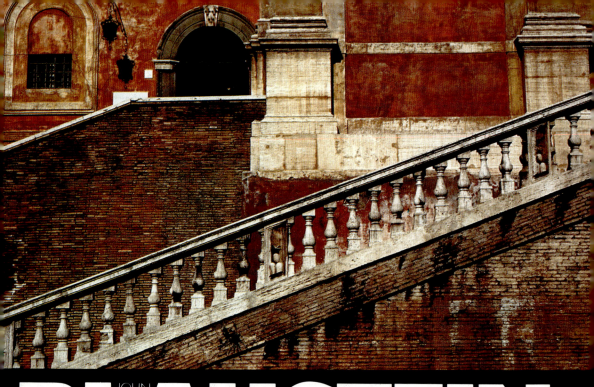

JOHN BLAUSTEIN

(415) 525-8133

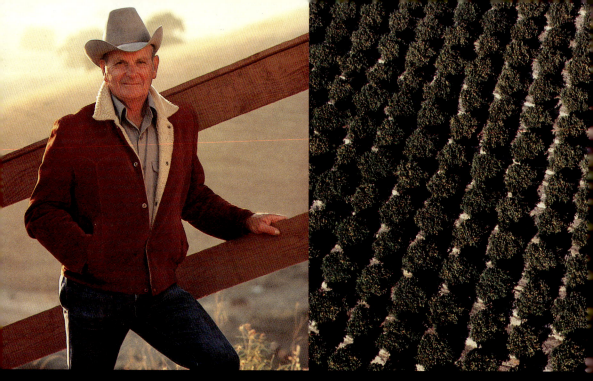

JOHN
BLAUSTEIN

(415) 525-8133

Photo by Ed Zak and Becker Bishop. Art direction and copy by Steve Diamant in exchange for a 1950's baseball jacket and a ride in the Speedster when it finally gets fixed. Typography by MasterType, S.F., Mechanical by Denis Ko S.F., out of the goodness of their hearts. Editorial assistance and moral support by Jerry Andelin, Rich Silverstein, Tom Whitworth and Cynthia Franco. Last-minute Reconstructive Type Surgery by Doctor Betsy Zimmerman. Special thanks to Red's Java. © 1988 Ed Zak Photo Inc. 80 Tehama St., S.F. Ca.

FIND OUT WHY YOU S
FRANCISCO TO SHOOT
WHO WILL MAKE YOU I
AND DRIVE YOU AF

A photo shoot with Ed Zak is a photo shoot like no other. But fear not, because you'll be travelling along a path well worn by San Francisco's finest Art Directors.

You can bounce along in dilapidated splendor in the very same seat occupied by Hal Riney's partner Jerry Andelin during countless shoots for Henry Weinhard's Beer, Yamaha, Olympia and MJB.

You can singe your lips on the same distinctive blend Red serve Rich Silverstein during his shoots for the Oakland Athletics, Cornnut and *The San Francisco Examiner*

OULD FLY OUT TO SAN
ITH A PHOTOGRAPHER
T AT RED'S JAVA HOUSE
UND IN THIS CAR.

And, when the day is done, ou can belly up to the bar in Ed's aloon, pop open a nice warm 3ud and contemplate tomorrow. It's actually a modern studio isguised as a saloon.)

At some point in the course of his singular experience, you might find yourself wondering exactly why you abandoned the comforts of home to do this crazy thing.

Then Ed will show you the shots, and you'll know.

To see Ed Zak's portfolio, call Ed at 415-781-1611.

ZAK IN THE WEST

YARBROUGH

Carl Yarbrough
stock & portfolio available
811 Mapleton Avenue
Boulder, Colorado 80302
303-444-1500

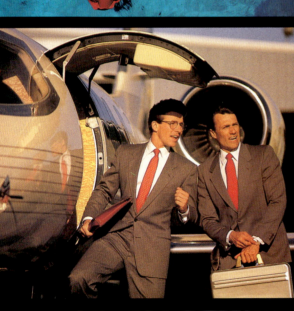

CONSTANTINOS
PHOTOGRAPHY

3232 S.W. 2nd Avenue • Bay 106 • Miami / Fort Lauderdale, Florida • 33315 • 305/467-3478

877

A.M.

COCA COLA/TOKYO

CABALLERO SKATEBOARDS/SAN DIEGO

NFL/NEW YORK

DISCOVERY MAGAZINE/SAN ANTONIO

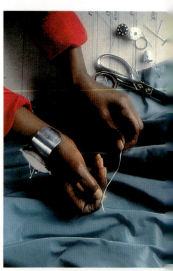

STEVEN'S INTERIORS/HOUSTON

For assignments and stock call
Arthur Meyerson Photography, Inc.

You have to get up pretty early in the morning to take better pictures than Arthur Meyerson.

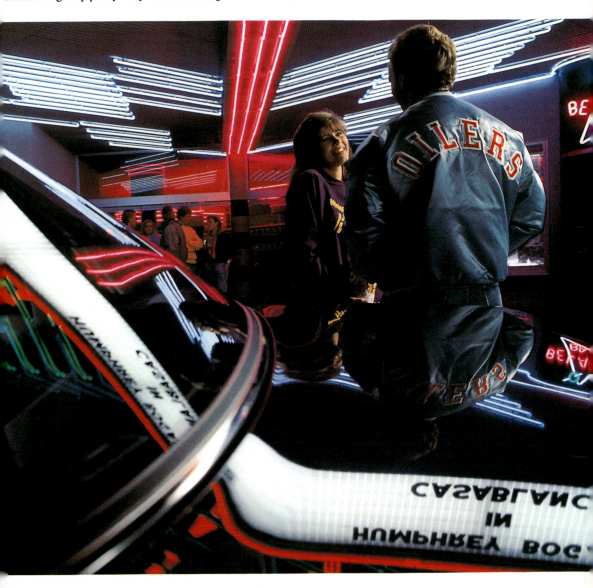

NFL/HOUSTON

PACIFIC CRUISES/SEOUL

15 Bellaire Blvd. Houston, Texas 77025
one: (713) 660-0405 Fax: (713) 660-9561

All photos ©1988 Arthur Meyerson

SCHIA

GEORGE SCHIAVONE
7340 S.W. 48 STREET
UNIT 102
MIAMI, FLORIDA 33155
305-662-6057

© George Schiavone 1988

BEEB(
BROTHERS ■ P

The brother who likes to go to out-of-the-way places capturing sensitive painterly images.

Additional work in The Creative Black Book 1985/1986/1987/1988

Specializing in Location Assignments

DWER
HOTOGRAPHY

IENTS: Remington
JCPenney
Nissan
Uniroyal
Young & Rubicam
General Electric
Frito-Lay
Johnson & Johnson
American Airlines

General Motors
Shell Oil
Dr Pepper
Pepisco
Alcoa Aluminum
Texas Instruments
Bell Helicopter
and others.

214/358-1219
Call for our portfolio.

9995 Monroe
Suite 209
Dallas, Texas 75220

BEEBO
BROTHERS P

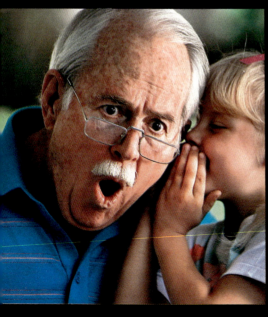

The brother who animates caricatures in a

Additional work in The Creative Black Book

Specializing In Location

FLIP CHALFANT

Represented by

Will Sumpter

404/874-2014

1728 N. Rock Springs Rd.

Atlanta, Ga. 30324

Studio 404/881-8510

All photos © 1989 Flip Chalfant

FRANK WHITE
2702 Sackett Street/Houston, Texas 77098/713-524-9250

Representative Client List:
Compaq Computer Corporation
Conoco, Inc.
Criterion Funds, Inc.
CRS Sirrine
Gulf Oil Company
Houston Ballet
Igloo Corporation
Laventhol & Horwath
Mitsubishi International Corporation
NASA
Shell Oil Company
Texas Instruments
Texas Opera Theatre

JOE WILLIS Photography

Miami & Ft. Lauderdale (305) 485-7185

M & M PRODUCTIONS

Stock at SharpShooters (800) 666-1266

Melissa Mimms

Miami & Ft. Lauderdale (305) 735-3739
M & M PRODUCTIONS

2700 ALBANY SUITE 303 HOUSTON, TX 77006
(713) 528-4334 IN NEW YORK (212) 319-3318

ROBB K

Location photography for

NDRICK

REPRESENTED BY RANDI FIAT & ASSOCIATES
IN CHICAGO (312) 881-7772

and advertising assignments

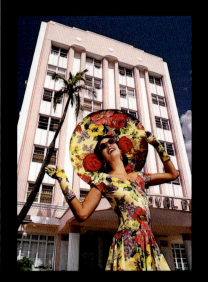

8533 N.W. 66th STREET
MIAMI, FLORIDA 33166
305 • **594 7516**

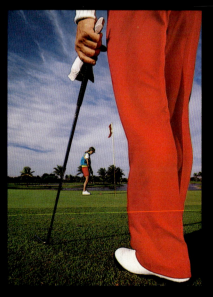

FERNANDO DIEZ
PHOTOGRAPHY

TOM JIMISON

NEW ORLEANS
5929 Annunciation, New Orleans, LA 70115, (504) 522-7955, 891-6760

Dakota is

OXMOX Design

Alice Springs

20 minutes into the future

Barcelona

Represented by Irene Dakota (305) 674-9975

Represented in Chicago by Vincent Kamin & Associates (312) 787-8834

in Miami

So are all these locations. *Call us and we'll take you anywhere in the world. Anytime of the year.*

Normandy

The Outback

Malibu

Michael Dakota
Miami, Florida (305) 325-8727

PELOSI

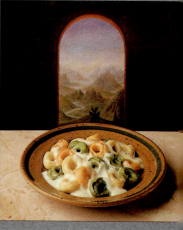

Steve Pelosi & Don Chambers.
684 Greenwood Ave. NE, Atlanta, Georgia 30306. Telephone: 404-872-8117. Fax: 404-872-2992

Clients include: American Express, Coca-Cola, Delta International, Arby's, Southern Bell, Dunlop, Kimberly Clark, Stouffer Marriott Hotels, Hardee's, Harland, Cellular One, Georgia-Pacific, Ryder Trucks, Masland Carpets, Cooper Tools.

Black and white portfolio available.

CHAMBERS

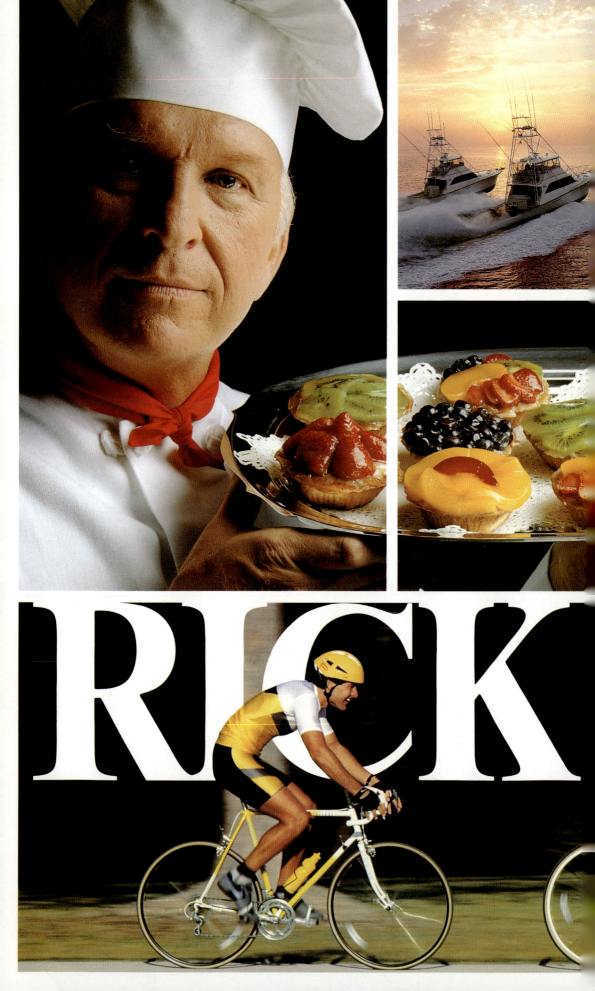
RICK

DIAZ *miami*

Rick Diaz Photography Inc.
7395 S.W. 42nd St.
Miami, Florida 33155
Phone 305 264 9761
Fax 305 264 9578

Stock through
SharpShooters
Miami, Florida
305 666 1266

913

ALL THE ADVANTAG
THE BIG CITY WITH

S OF SHOOTING IN
UT THE NEGATIVES.

Jimmy Williams

3801 Beryl Road · Raleigh, North Carolina 27607 · (919) 832-5971

Robin Hood

Independent Life

Northwest Airlines

Cracker Barrell

(615) 794-2041

Robin Hood

Independent Life

American Cyanamid

Jack Daniels

(615) 794-2041

8960 Southwest 114 Street
Miami, Florida 33176

305-233-1703
all areas except New York

Represented by:
Joan Jedell Assoc.
212-861-7861
New York area

Tom

Clients:
IBM, Nikon, Kodak, Coca-Cola, 7-Up, Hilton, Holiday Inns, Hertz, British Airways, Delta Airlines, Eastern Airlines, Bahamas, Mexico, Bacardi, Johnny Walker, Seagrams, Sears, Burger King, Lums, Lipton, Sanka, Pillsbury, DuPont, Hallmark, Salem, Time/Life, Royal Caribbean Cruise Line, Norwegian Caribbean Cruise Line, Sun Cruise Lines

Stock available

McCarthy

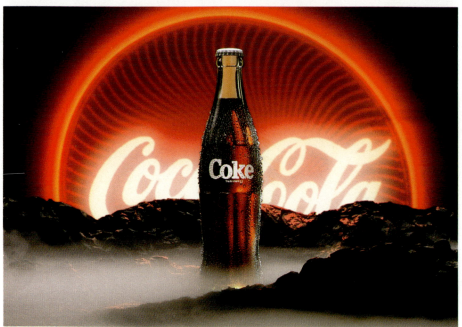

MARTY CLARK
1105 Peachtree St., Atlanta, Ga. 30309
Represented by Chris Kohler: 404 876-1223
Studio: 404 873-4618 FAX: 404 876-1224

TOM RICKLES

MIAMI BEACH

305-866-5762

DUPES: COLOR LAB MIAMI

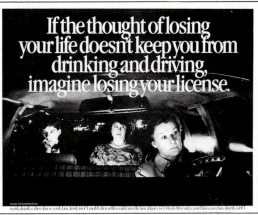

Martin Agency; Writer: Luke Sullivan; AD: Diane Tench

Ford & Westbrook; Writer: Bill Westbrook; AD: Kenny Sink

McKinney & Silver; Writer: Charlie Ashby; AD: Larry Bennett

Ford & Westbrook; Writer: Kerry Feuerman; AD: Kenny Sink

ERICKSON

117 South West Street
Raleigh, North Carolina 27603
Phone (919) 833-9955

923

George Schultz/Esquire

Dennis Quaid/LIFE

Willem Dafoe/Esquire

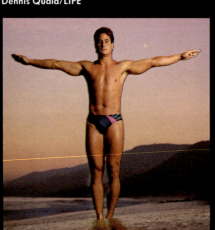
Greg Louganis/LA. Times Magazine

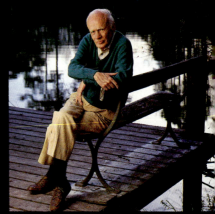
Walker Percy/N.Y. Times Magazine

LEE CRUM
1536 Terpsichore St. • New Orleans, LA 70130 • 504-529-2156

Robin Williams/Esquire

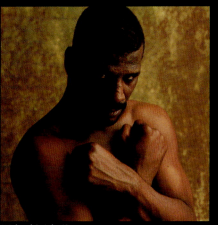
Michael Spinks/Sport

Carl Lewis/Runners World

Neville Brothers/Comet Rice

Dennis McGhee/Rolling Stone

LEE CRUM
1536 Terpsichore St. New Orleans, LA 70130 504-529-2156

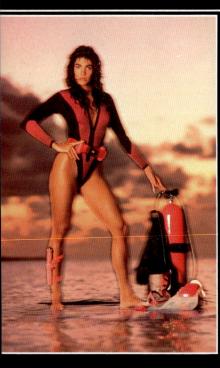

Miami
George Contoräkes
(305) 661-0731
Fax (305) 662-5752

New York
Rep. Doug Brown
(212) 953-0088

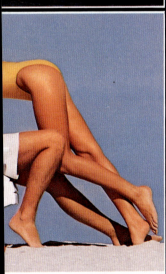

Now a faster way to a healthy-looking tan.

This summer, get a head start on a beautiful, healthy-looking tan. With new Sea & Ski® Natural

DUPLICATE TRANSPARENCIES BY COLORLAB • MIAMI

CONTORÄKES

BARABAN

Joe Baraban
2426 Bartlett #2
Houston, Texas 77098
713-526-0317

Represented By:
Bill Rabin in Chicago
312-944-6655

John Kenney & Associates
in New York
212-279-1515

Extensive Stock Available

© All photos 1988

Bob Gelberg

7035-E Southwest 47 Street
Miami, Florida 33155
305/665-3200 Fax 305/665-1638

DENNIS 101 HOWELL STREET DALLA

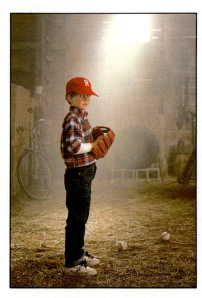

PARTIAL CLIENT LIST: SOUTHWEST AIRLINES, AMERICAN AIRLINES, CIGNA, XEROX, JACU

TEXAS 75207 • 214 651 7516 **MURPHY**

..., POULAN, WEEDEATER, NCAA, HAGGAR, GTE, DALLAS CONVENTION & VISITORS BUREAU

ERIC

ERIC HENDERSON PRODUCTIONS, 1200 FOSTER STREET, N.W. • ATLANTA, GEORGIA 30318 • 404/352-3615

HOMELINES CRUISES

HOMELINES CRUISES

WEST POINT PEPPERELL

MASLAND CARPETS

RYDER SYSTEM, INC.

THE RITZ-CARLTON HOTEL CO.

BLEYLE OF AMERICA

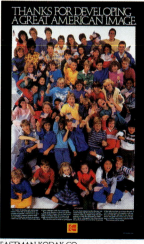
EASTMAN KODAK CO.

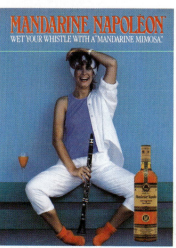
MANDARINE NAPOLEON LIQUEUR

CLIENTS INCLUDE: IBM, THE COCA-COLA COMPANY, PIPER AIRCRAFT CORP, PORSCHE OF AMERICA CORP, REEBOK VIACOM INTERNATIONAL, WEYERHAEUSER, HOLIDAY INNS INC., DAYS INN OF AMERICA, ATHLETE'S FOOT

wohrman

SCOTT WOHRMAN/P.O. BOX 9728/CORAL SPRINGS, FL 33075/(305)752-6297
SOUTH FLORIDA AND THE BAHAMAS

M ITCHELL K EARNEY

Studio
301 East 7th Street
Charlotte, NC 28202
704 377-7662

LANPHER

Lanpher Productions

Keith Lanpher

865 Monticello Avenue

Norfolk, Virginia 23510

804•627•3051

HOLLAND

ROBERT HOLLAND
P.O. BOX 162099
MIAMI • FLORIDA • 33116
305 • 255 • 6758

© Robert Holland 1989

80% OF JOE GEMIGNANI'S CLIENTS HAVE BEEN WITH HIM FOR OVER FIVE YEARS.

GET 50% OFF YOUR NEXT ASSIGNMENT AND FIND OUT WHY.

Out-of-town shooting can be filled with unknowns. Choosing a photographer shouldn't be one of them. Joe Gemignani delivers results. With creativity. Dedication. And technical excellence.

Joe's clients stay with him. Because he knows how to make them feel at home. 15 years. New York and Miami. Meeting deadlines. Producing knock-out visuals. Going the extra mile, Florida-style.

He can do it for you. Let Joe prove it and save you 50% off your first shoot. Call 305-685-7636 collect. Get acquainted, get a quote. Come and get South Florida with your eyes wide open.

Riunite
Florida
Piper Aircraft
Texaco
Rolls Royce
Gould Electronics
Harris Corp.
Ft. Lauderdale News
Uniroyal Tires

JOE GEMIGNANI
13833 N.W. 19 Ave.
Miami, FL 33054
305-685-7636

Stock Available • Sharp Shooters (800) 666-1266

PHOTO
RUTHE

Michael W. Rutherford

RAPHY
RFORD

therford Studios • 623 6th Avenue South • Nashville, TN 37203
presented by Ed Neaves • (615) 242-5953

N

Nick
Norwood

2500
Abaco Avenue

Miami
Florida, 33133

(305) 858-1510

STEWART
CHARLES
COHEN

**The Difference
Between Taking Pictures
And Making Pictures.**

2401 South Ervay, Suite 206 Dallas, Texas 75215
214-421-2186

ients include: Coca-Cola American Airlines American Express Braniff Airlines Exxon Fina Southwestern Bell Firestone Kodak Hilton Hotels Four Seasons Hotels Merrill Lynch Miller Brewing Co. Westin Hotels

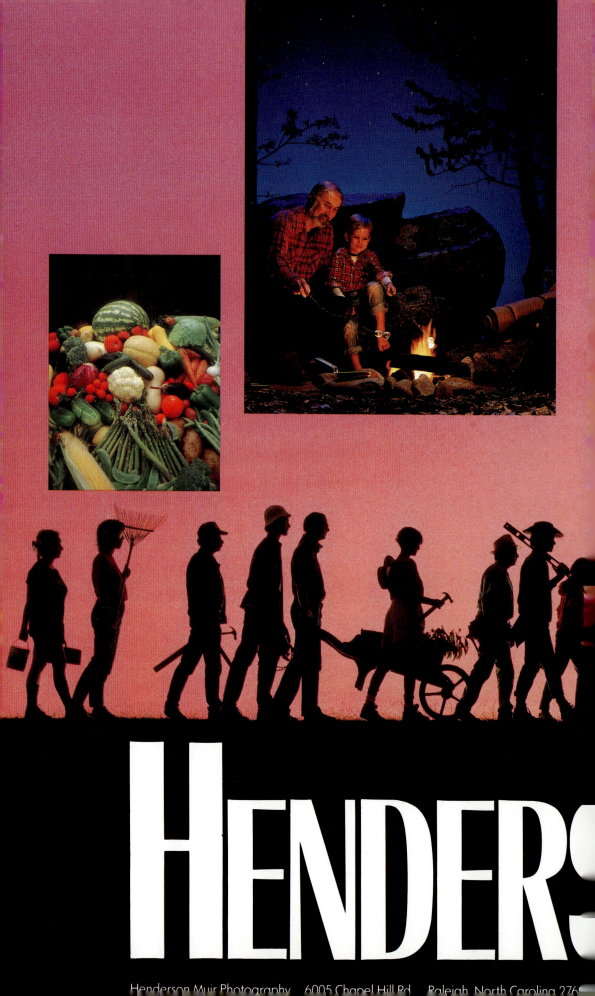

JEFF TURNAU

(305) 666-5454

STOCK/SHARPSHOOTERS (800) 688-1286

TURNAU/GOMEZ STUDIO, 4950 S.W. 72

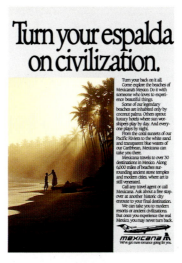

DUPES AND PROCESSING BY COLOR LAB MIAMI

VENUE, SUITE 114, MIAMI, FLORIDA 33155

951

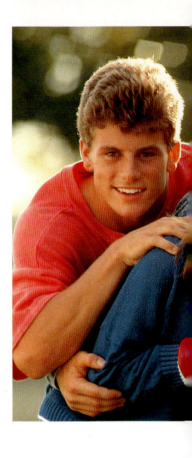

RICK GOMEZ

(305) 666-5454

STOCK/SHARPSHOOTERS (800) 666-1266

TURNAU/GOMEZ STUDIO, 4950 S.W. 72N

DUPES AND PROCESSING BY COLOR LAB MIAMI

AVENUE, SUITE 114, MIAMI, FLORIDA 33155

ROBERT LATORRE PRODUCTIONS

LATORRE

2336 FARRINGTON

DALLAS, TEXAS

75207

(214) 630-8977

REPRESENTED BY

JUDY WHALEN

(214) 828-1226

FAX NUMBER

(214) 638-3319

ASK TO SEE OUR TV REEL

CODY

MIAMI

©1988 Dennie Cody, Photographer • 5880 SW 53 Terrace, Miami, FL 33155
(305) 666-0247
Chromes by Color Lab Miami

HALLSTEIN
REPRESENTED BY YESAWICH AND WELSH

Orlando, Florida
407-422-9633
Specializing in
Location photography.

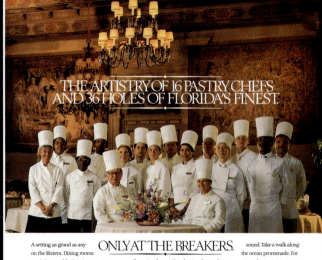

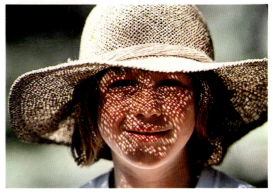
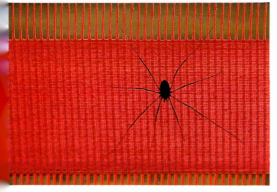

Jay Maisel sells
expensive stock pictures,
Call (212) 431-5157
and ask for Emily or Dan.

JAY MAISEL
190 The Bowery, NYC 10012

ALL PHOTOGRAPHS © 1988 JAY MAISEL

Sports Chrome Inc.
Stock Library and Assignment Center
In Sports Photography— we're in a league by ourselves!

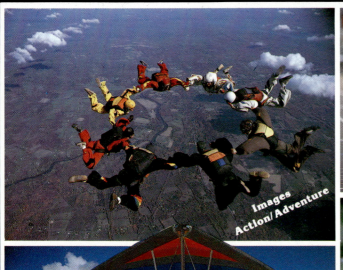

Images Action/Adventure

Images Professional

Images Leisure, Health Fitness

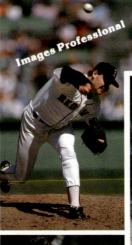

CONTACT: **JOYCE MEAD**
TONY AGUANNO
10 BRINKERHOFF AVENUE
PALISADES PARK, NJ 07650
(201) 568-1412

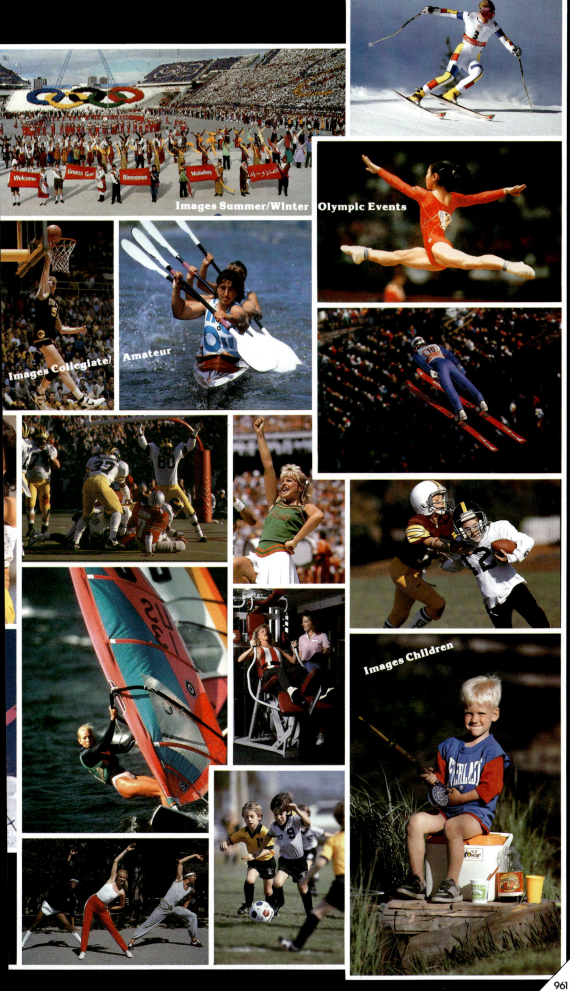

PHOTO RESEA

From left to right: Charlotte Raymond (Inset: Bill Longcore); Tom McHugh; Vandystadt (Courtesy: WGBH); John Veltri (Courtesy: Elkman Advert.); CDC/Bjornberg; Tom McHugh (Courtesy: Young & Rubicam and the U.S. Postal Office).

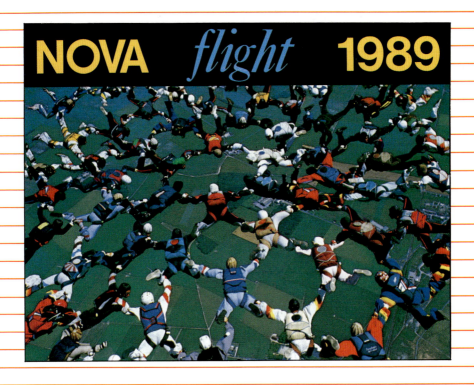
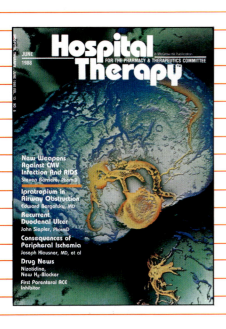

CHERS

60 East 56th Street
New York, NY 10022
212.758.3420
FAX: 212.355.0731

1 800 833.9033

"**THEY SENT JUST WHAT I ASKED FOR.**"
Mike McCabe/Assoc. Creative Director/Bader Rutter & Assoc./BROOKFIELD, WI

"**SUPER SHOTS AND A PLEASURE TO WORK WITH.**"
Ron Ballin/Art Director/Laurence Charles Free & Lawson, NYC

FOREST JOHNSON

"**OUTSTANDING COMPREHENSIVE SERVICE.**"
Paul Bleakney/Art Director/Sharp Hartwig/SEATTLE

"**UNBELIEVABLE CATALOG.**"
Francesca Lum/Art Director/Tromson Monroe Advertising/NYC

TOM CASALINI

Premium Stock Shots

DEAN LOUMAKIS   GEORGE CONTORAKES

4950 S.W. 72nd Avenue, Suite 114, Miami, Florida 33155

Tel: 305-666-1266, Toll Free: 1-800-666-1266, Call For Fax Number

RANDY MILLER

Catalog Available

Dupes and Processing by ColorLab, Miami.

JEFF TURNAU

JIM ULLRICH

JIM CASALINI

GARY KUFNER

RICK GOMEZ

MARC VAUGHN

PAUL MINSART

© Sharp Shooters 1989

967

ALL OF THESE FACES...
PLACES...SUBJECTS...

ABRASIONS
ABSTRACTS
ACCIDENTS
ACUPUNCTURE
ADDICTION
AERIALS
AEROBIC EXERCISE
AERONAUTICS
AFGHANISTAN
AGRICULTURE
AIRPLANES
AIRPORTS
ALABAMA
ALASKA
ALCOHOLISM
ALGERIA
ALLERGIES
AMBULANCES
AMERICANA
AMNIOCENTESIS
AMUSEMENT PARKS
ANATOMY
ANDORRA
ANESTHESIOLOGY
ANGIOGRAMS
ANIMALS
ANTIGUA
ANTIQUING
ARGENTINA
ARCHITECTURE
ARIZONA
ARKANSAS
ART
ARTERIOGRAMS
ARTHRITIS
ARTHROSCOPY
ARTIFICIAL JOINTS
ASCENSION
ASSEMBLY LINES
AUDITORY EVOKED
  POTENTIAL
AUSTRALIA
AUSTRIA
AUTOMOBILES
AUTO RACING
AZORES
BACKPACKING
BACTERIAL CULTURES
BAHA
BAHAMAS
BALI
BALLOON
  CATHETERIZATION
BALLOONING
BALLOONS
BANKING
BARBADOS
BARS
BASEBALL
BASKETBALL
BEACHES
BEAKERS
BEAM IMAGING
BELGIUM
BEQUIA
BERMUDA
BIKE RIDING
BIOFEEDBACK
BIOMECHANICS
BIRDS
BIRTH DEFECTS
BLOOD DONOR
BLOOD TEST/CELLS
BLOOD TRANSFUSION
BOATING
BOLIVIA
BONAIRE
BONE REPLACEMENT
BORA BORA
BOTTLES
BOXING
BRAILLE
BRAIN SURGERY
BRAIN TUMORS
BRAZIL

BREAST EXAMS
BREAST FEEDING
BREAST REPLACEMENT
BRIDGES
BROKEN BONES
BUILDINGS
BULGARIA
BULLFIGHTS
BURMA
BURN CENTERS
BUTTERFLIES
BUSINESS
CABLE CARS
CALIFORNIA
CAMELS
CAMEROON
CAMPFIRES
CAMPING
CANADA
CANARY ISLANDS
CANCER
CANCER TREATMENT
CANOEING
CANYONS
CAPILLARIES
CAPRI
CARGO SHIPPING
CARAVANS
CARNIVALS
CASINOS
CASTLES
CATALINA
CATARACT OPERATIONS
CAT SCANS
CATTLE
CAVERNS
CAVES
CELEBES
CELL DIVISION
CEMETERIES
CERAMICS
CHECK UPS
CHEMOTHERAPY
CHILDBIRTH
CHILDREN
CHINA
CHRISTMAS
CHROMOSOMES
CHURCHES
CIRCUS
CIRRHOSIS
CLOUDS
COLLAGEN TREATMENT
COLLEGES
COLORADO
COLOMBIA
COMMUNICATIONS
COMPUTERS
COMPUTERS IN
  MEDICINE
CONFERENCE ROOMS
CONNECTICUT
CONSTRUCTION
CONTACT LENS
CONTAINER SHIPPING
CONTRACEPTION
CORFU
CORNEAL TRANSPLANTS
CORSICA
COSTA RICA
COUPLES
COVERED BRIDGES
COWBOYS
CPR
CRAFTS
CRETE
CREWING
CROPS
CROP DUSTING
CROSS COUNTRY SKI
CROWDS
CRUISE SHIPS
CRYOSURGERY
CURACAO
CUBA

CYPRUS
CZECHOSLOVAKIA
DAHOMEY
DAIRY FARMING
DAMS
DANCING
DENMARK
DENTISTRY
DESERTS
DIAGNOSTIC IMAGING
DIALYSIS
DIETITIANS
DINING
DISCOTHEQUES
DISTRICT OF COLUMBIA
DOMINICA
DOMINICAN REPUBLIC
DSA
DISABLED
DISEASES
DOCTORS
DONORS
DNA
DREAM LABS
DRUG REHABILITATION
DRUGS
DSR
EASTER
EAST GERMANY
ECLIPSE
ECOLOGY
ECUADOR
EDUCATION
EEGS
E.E.N.T.
EGYPT
EKGS
ELBA
ELECTIONS
ELEUTHERA
EL SALVADOR
EMBRYOS
EMERGENCY ROOMS
EMOTIONAL DISORDERS
EMPHYSEMA
ENDOSCOPY
ENGLAND
ENTERTAINMENT
ETHIOPIA
EXECUTIVES
EXERCISE
EYE SURGERY
EYE TESTS
FACIAL EXPRESSIONS
FACTORIES
FAIRS
FALL
FAMILIES
FARMS
FENCES
FETAL DEVELOPMENT
FETAL MONITORING
FIJI
FINANCIAL
FINLAND
FIREMEN
FIREPLACES
FIRETRUCKS
FIREWORKS
FIRST AID
FISH
FISHING
FISH BOATS
FJORDS
FLAGS
FLAMENCO DANCING
FLOODS
FLORIDA
FLOWERS
FOOD
FOOTBALL
FOREIGN MEDICINE
FORESTS
FORMOSA
FOX HUNTING

FRANCE
FREEPORT
FROST
FRUIT
FUNDUSCOPY
GALAPAGOS ISLANDS
GAMBLING
GAMES
GAMMA SCANS
GANGRENE
GARDENING
GENETICS
GEOLOGY
GEORGIA
GERIATRIC MEDICINE
GERMANY
GHANA
GIBRALTAR
GLACIERS
GOLF
GRAND CAYMAN
GREECE
GREEK ISLES
GRENADA
GRENADINES
GROUP THERAPY
GUADELOUPE
GUAM
GUATEMALA
GYMNASTICS
GYNECOLOGY
HAIR TRANSPLANTS
HAITI
HANDICAPPED
HANGLIDING
HARBORS
HAWAII
HAYRIDE
HEALTH FOOD
HEALTH INSURANCE
HEART DISEASE
HEART SURGERY
HEART TRANSPLANTS
HERPES
HIGHWAYS
HIKING
HILTON HEAD
HOCKEY
HOLLAND
HOME NURSING
HONDURAS
HONG KONG
HORSEBACK RIDING
HORSE JUMPING
HORSE RACING
HOSPICES
HOSPITALS
HOTELS
HOUSEBOATS
HOUSING
HUMAN INTEREST
HUNGARY
HUNTING
HYGIENE
HYPERTHERMIA
HYPNOSIS
HYSTERECTOMIES
IBIZA
ICE
ICEBERGS
ICE BOATING
ICELAND
IDAHO
ILLINOIS
INDIA
INDIANA
INDIANS
INDONESIA
INJURIES
INTENSIVE CARE UNITS
IN VITRO FERTILIZATION
IOWA
IRAN
IRAQ
IRELAND

ISLANDS
ISLES DES SAINTES
ISLE OF MAN
ISRAEL
ISTANBUL
ITALY
IV
IVORY COAST
IWO JIMA
JAI ALAI
JAKARTA
JAMAICA
JAPAN
JAVA
JOGGING
JORDAN
KANSAS
KAYAKING
KENTUCKY
KENYA
KITE FLYING
KOREA
LABORATORIES
LABORATORY RESEARCH
LACROSSE
LAKES
LANDSCAPES
LA PALMA
LASER SURGERY
LAWN BOWLING
LEAVES
LEBANON
LEEWARD ISLANDS
LIBRARY
LEUKEMIA
LICHTENSTEIN
LIGHTHOUSES
LIGHTNING
LINEAR ACCELERATION
LIVESTOCK
LOUISIANA
LUNG CANCER
LUXEMBOURG
MACAO
MACHINERY
MADEIRA
MAILBOXES
MAINE
MAIN STREET, U.S.A.
MAJORCA
MALAYSIA
MALDIVES
MALTA
MAMMOGRAPHY
MANSIONS
MANUFACTURING
MARKETS
MARRIAGE COUNSEL
MARTIAL ARTS
MARTINIQUE
MARYLAND
MASSACHUSETTS
MASSAGE
MAURITIUS
MEDICAL
MEDICAL EQUIPMENT
MEN
MENTAL HEALTH
MEXICO
MICHIGAN
MICRONESIA
MICROPHOTOGRAPH
MILITARY
MINING
MINNESOTA
MISSISSIPPI
MISSOURI
MONACO
MONTANA
MOONS
MOOREA
MOROCCO
MOTORBOATING
MOTORCYCLING
MOUNTAIN CLIMBING

MOUNTAINS	POLO	SAND DUNES	ST. LUCIA	URBAN RENEWAL
MOUTH TO MOUTH RESUSCITATION	POLYNESIA	SANIBEL ISLAND	ST. MARTIN	URUGUAY
	PONDS	SAN MARINO	STORMS	UTAH
MULTIPLE SCLEROSIS	PORTUGAL	SARDINIA	STREAMS	VACCINATION
MUSEUMS	POST OFFICE	SCHOOLS	STRESS TESTS	VARICOSE VEINS
MUSIC	POWER LINES	SCOTLAND	STROKE VICTIM REHABILITATION	VATICAN CITY
NASA	PREGNANCY	SEASCAPES		VEGETABLES
NASSAU	PREMATURE BABIES	SEASONS	ST. THOMAS	VENEREAL DISEASE
NATIONAL PARKS	PRINCE EDWARD ISLAND	SECRETARIES	STUDENTS	VENEZUELA
NATIONAL MONUMENTS	PRISONS	SEYCHELLES	ST. VINCENT	VERMONT
NATIVES	PROVIDENCE	SHOPS	STRAITS OF MAGELLAN	VETERINARY MEDICINE
NEBRASKA	PSORIASIS	SHOPPING	SUBWAYS	VIEQUES
NEONATAL INTENSIVE CARE	PSYCHOLOGICAL TESTING	SHOWGIRLS	SUDAN	VIETNAM
		SICILY	SURGERY	VINEYARDS
NEPAL	PSYCHOTHERAPY	SIDS	SUMMER	VIRGIN GORDA
NETHERLAND ANTILLES	PUERTO RICO	SIGNS	SUNRISES	VIRGINIA
NEURONS	PULMONARY FUNCTION TESTS	SINGAPORE	SUNSETS	VIRGIN ISLANDS
NEVADA		SITKA	SUPERMARKETS	VOLCANOS
NEWBORNS	PUMPKINS	SKATEBOARDS	SURF	VOLUNTEER HOSPITAL WORKERS
NEWFOUNDLAND	RADIAL KERATOTOMY	SKIING	SURFING	
NEW GUINEA	RADIATION TREATMENT	SKIN GRAFTS	SWEDEN	WALES
NEW HAMPSHIRE	RAFTING	SKY	SWIMMING	WASHINGTON
NEW JERSEY	RAILROADS	SKY DIVING	SWIMMING POOLS	WATERFALLS
NEW MEXICO	RAIN	SKYLINES	SWITZERLAND	WATERSKIING
NEW YORK	RAINBOWS	SLEDDING	SYRIA	WATER WHEELS
NEW ZEALAND	RANCHES	SLEEP	TAHITI	WEATHER
NIGERIA	RAROTONGA	SMOKING	TAIWAN	WEDDING
NMR	RECONSTRUCTIVE SURGERY	SNOW	TANZANIA	WEIGHT LIFTING
NORTH CAROLINA		SNOWMOBILING	TENNESSEE	WEST GERMANY
NORTH DAKOTA	RECREATION	SOCCER	TENNIS	WEST INDIES
NORTH KOREA	RESORTS	SOMALIA	TEST TUBE BABIES	WEST VIRGINIA
NORWAY	RESPIRATORS	SOUTH AFRICA	TEST TUBES	WHEELCHAIRS
NOVA SCOTIA	RESPIRATORY TREATMENT	SOUTH CAROLINA	TEXAS	WHITE BLOOD CELLS
NUCLEI	RESTAURANTS	SOUTH DAKOTA	THAILAND	WILDLIFE
NUDES	RHODE ISLAND	SOUTH KOREA	THANKSGIVING	WINDMILLS
NURSES STATIONS	RHODES	SPAIN	THERMOGRAPHY	WINDWARD ISLANDS
NURSING	RIBOSOMES	SPEECH THERAPY	THERMOMETERS	WINTER
NURSING HOMES	RIVERS	SPINA BIFIDA	THOUSAND ISLANDS	WISCONSIN
NUTRITION	ROADS	SPORTS	TOGO	WOMEN
OBESITY	ROCK CONCERTS	SPORTS MEDICINE	TONGA	WORMS
OCCUPATIONS	ROCKS	SPRING	TORTOLA	WOUNDS
OCEANS	RODEO	SRI LANKA	TRAFFIC	WYOMING
OCEAN LINES	RUMANIA	STADIUMS	TRAUMA CENTERS	X-RAYS
OIL RIGS	RUNNING	STAINED GLASS	TREES	YACHTING
OHIO	RUSSIA	STATUES	TRINIDAD	YEAST
OKINAWA	SABA	ST. BARTHELEMY	TRUCKING	YOGA
OKLAHOMA	SAFARI	ST. CROIX	TUNISIA	YUGOSLAVIA
OLYMPICS	SAILBOATS	STITCHES	TURKEY	ZAMBIA
OLD AGE	SAILING	STILL LIFE	UGANDA	ZAIRE
OPERATING ROOMS	SAN ANDRES	ST. JOHN	ULTRASOUND	ZOOS
OP-SAIL	SAN BLAS ISLANDS	ST. KITTS	UNDERWATER	ZOSTERS
OREGON				
ORGAN TRANSPLANTS				
PACEMAKERS				
PAKISTAN				
PALM TREES				
PANAMA				
PANAMA CANAL ZONE				
PARACHUTING				
PARADES				
PARAGUAY				
PARAMEDICS				
PARKS				
PATIENTS IN HOSPITAL				
PATTERNS				
PEACOCKS				
PEDIATRICS				
PENNSYLVANIA				
PERIODONTAL TREATMENT				
PERSONALITIES				
PERU				
PETRI DISHES				
PET SCANS				
PHARMACISTS				
PHILIPPINES				
PHONIATRICS				
PHYSICAL CHECK UPS				
PICNICS				
PLASTIC SURGERY				
PLATELETS				
PODIATRY				
POLAND				
POLICE				
POLLUTION				

...ALL AT THE STOCK SHOP AND MEDICHROME, TOO!

The Stock Shop *Inc.*

MediChrome

232 Madison Avenue.
New York, N.Y. 10016
212/679-8480
Fax 212/532-1934

TOO BEAUTIFUL TO BE STOCK?

© John M. Russell

© Glen R. Steiner

© Ed Simpson

© Clark M. Dunbar

© David Cornwell

© Stephen Frink

© Ed Simpson

© Edward G. Young

© Simpson/Flint

CALL JOAN KRAMER AND ASSOCIATES
Thousands of photographs—all model released.
If you're in the market, we've got the stock.

(212) 567-5545 or (516) 466-5582
stock photography-photo assignments

© 1989 Joan Kramer & Associates, Inc.

THE STOCK BROKER

We Can Take You Anywhere

450 Lincoln St. • Suite 110 • Denver, CO 80203 • (303) 698-1734

Credits: Jeff Cook, Michael Weeks, Jeff Uhrlaub, Mark Heifner, Keith Brofsky, Kevin Saehlenou, Bruce Benedict, Kimball Hall

© The Stock Broker 1989

PRINT

RETOUCHERS
PRINTERS
LOCATIONS
CASTING
BACKDROPS
PROPS

NO OTHER COMPUTER RETOUCHER OFFERS THIS KIND OF SOFTWARE.

There are two things that separate Spano/Roccanova from all other computer retouchers: Spano and Roccanova. For information, call (212) 840-7450 and ask for Ralph (as in Spano) or Frank (as in Roccanova). You'll find them very user-friendly.

SPANO / ROCCANOVA • DIGITAL RETOUCHING • 16 W. 46TH ST. NYC 10036
The quality of our work is retouching other studios out of the picture.

FRED GRELLER.

★

RETOUCHER TO THE STARS.

THE A.D. SHOW, THE ONE SHOW, GOLD MEDALS AND ANDY AWARDS.

YEAR	ART DIRECTOR	YEAR	ART DIRECTOR
1956	Hal Davis	1971	Ralph Ammirati
1957	Herschel Bramson	1971	Bob Kuperman
1959	Hal Davis	1972	Lee Epstein
1961	Bert Steinhauser	1973	Mike Uris
1962	Ken Duskin	1974	George Euringer
1962	William Taubin	1974	Jim Burton
1963	Ken Duskin	1974	Mike Tesch
1964	William Taubin	1974	Stan Kovics
1964	Len Sirowitz	1975	Bob Reitzfeld
1964	Bert Steinhauser	1975	Joe Gregorace
1965	William Taubin	1975	Mike Tesch
1965	Len Sirowitz	1976	Amil Gargano
1965	Bert Steinhauser	1976	Joe Gregorace
1966	Rick Levine	1977	Lee Epstein
1966	Bert Steinhauser	1978	Michael Winslow
1967	Al Scully	1978	Jack Mariucci
1967	Amil Gargano	1979	Michael Winslow
1967	Phil Parker	1979	Stan Block
1968	Bert Steinhauser	1980	Stan Block
1968	Vince Dadiego	1981	Tony Angotti
1968	John Register	1982	Gordon Bennett
1969	Vince Dadiego	1983	Gordon Bennett
1969	Sam Scali	1983	Tony Angotti
1969	Bert Steinhauser	1983	Gary Johns
1970	Lee Epstein	1983	Len Fink
1970	John Register	1984	Gary Johns
1970	Charles Piccarillo	1985	Gary Johns
1970	Sal Auditori	1986	Mike Moser

Fred Greller

ASSOCIATES, INC.
325 EAST 64th STREET
NEW YORK, N.Y. 10021
(212) 535-6240

REPRESENTED BY ANDREA WARSHAW

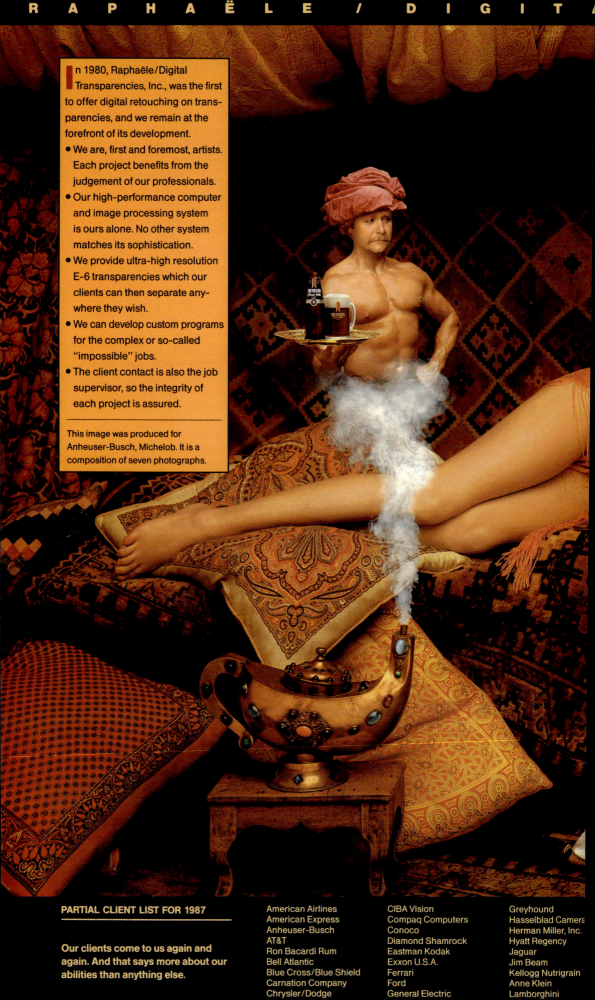

Creatively Solving Photographic

Dye Transfers C Prints Duplicate Transparencie

Problems For Over 20 Years.

Let Us Solve Your Problem.
212 683-6100

COLOR LABS, INC.

Display Transparencies   Black & White
37 West 26th Street   New York, NY 10010   212 683-6100

When your artwork looks this good, *you* look good.

We invite you to discover how the McWilliams/Welbeck Studio can make you and your work look better than ever. Our award winning retouchers can provide you with the finest black-and-white, dye-transfer and transparency retouching. We also offer you stunning composite work.

Creative problem-solving is another of our strong points. We'll help you realize your original vision *on time and within budget*.

Give us a call.

McWilliams/Welbeck Studio
(212) 725-0050

31 East 28th Street
New York, New York 10016
Outside New York 1-800 632-2336

NEIGHBORS REUNITED BY COMPUTER AFTER 14 YEAR SILENCE.

ZAZULA RETOUCHES THEM BY HAND.
1974

ZAZULA RETOUCHES THEM BY COMPUTER.
1988

They hadn't spoken for years, let alone visited.

So what did it take when Smith/Greenland's Glenn Scheuer asked if we could get Johnnie Walker Black Label's neighbors back together again?

It took the touch of an artist. *And* our unique computer system.

But that's just what Zazula Electronic Retouching is becoming known for. The best combination of retouching artistry and state-of-the-art technology there is.

So next time you're not on speaking terms with your art, call ZER.

And get the kind of retouching no one can remain silent about.

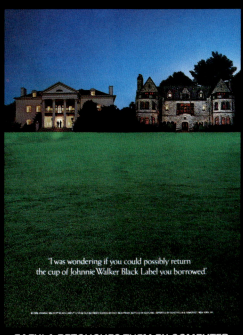

ZAZULA ELECTRONIC RETOUCHING, INC., 212-819-0444
508 West 26th Street, New York, N.Y. 10001   **212-463-0494**

WE'RE WELL

EATON & IWEN, INC.
70 East Lake Street, Chicago, Illinois
312/332-3256

24 HOUR FAX: 312/332-4605

Represented in Boston, Detroit and St. Louis

CONNECTED...

Creatives keep coming back to Eaton & Iwen for their electronic retouching. In fact, we're known for the companies we keep.

After 20 years in the business of traditional retouching we understand that knowing how to work "the system" is not the same as *making "the system" work*. The most sophisticated technology in the hands of our talented and experienced retouchers offers you creative potential as limitless as your imagination, delivered to you as an 8x10 E6 transparency.

PLUG INTO EATON & IWEN'S ELECTRONIC STUDIO

JOCKEY INTERNATIONAL   XEROX

Image Markets

BRITISH AIRWAYS   LINCOLN CONTINENTAL

The character of a company

INLAND STEEL   McDONALD'S

projected by its products or services

AUDI   CNA INSURANCE   FLORSHEIM

is a priceless performing asset.

CHAMPION INTERNATIONAL   LAND'S END   WALT DISNEY WORLD

Its results are not achieved

ARTHUR ANDERSEN & CO.   SEARLE   GEORGIA-PACIFIC

by accident.

FORD   HILTON

Image is a created business value.

SUNBEAM   VICOM ASSOCIATES

BORG-WARNER

QUAKER OATS COMPANY   UNITED AIRLINES

SPIEGEL   MACY'S

SAKS FIFTH AVENUE

TRIBUNE COMPANY　　　　　　　　HALO LIGHTING　　　　　　　　EVANS FURS

Image is a kinetic communication,

SAFETY-KLEEN　　　　　　　　DMB & B　　　　　　　　BERGDORF GOODMAN

transcending symbol or metaphor.

KOBS AND BRADY　　　　　　　　AMERICAN EXPRESS　　　　　　　　FIRESTONE

FEDERAL SIGNAL　　　　　　　　HILL & KNOWLTON

CAMPBELL SOUP COMPANY　　　　　　　　MAYTAG

FOOTE CONE & BELDING　　　　　　　　VOLVO

　　　　　　　　BBDO　　　　　　　　MERCEDES-BENZ

　　　　　　　　　　　　　　　　YMCA OF AMERICA

CUNARD LINES

LEO BURNETT　　　　　　　　SERVICE MASTER

JMB REALTY　　　　　　　　BELL & HOWELL

HARTER　　　　　　　　NEIMAN-MARCUS　　　　　　　　AMERITECH

FRANKLIN MINT MARSHALL FIELD TIFFANY & CO.

STERLING SILVER
FLATWARE

Mercedes-Benz is more than an automobile.

BONWIT TELLER KEMPER

Tiffany is more than a jeweler.

CORPORATE ANNUAL REPORTS KEWAUNEE SCIENTIFIC

TIFFANY & CO.

Neiman-Marcus is more than a department store.

MAGNAVOX SPERRY & HUTCHINSON QUAKER OATS COMPANY

Bradley embraces image markets

POLO STONE CONTAINER TRAILER TRAIN

with dynamic print reproduction

CADILLAC BEST PRODUCTS DINER'S CLUB

that becomes part of the value

BLUE CROSS & BLUE SHIELD VOLKSWAGEN POLO

you create.

BMW MEREDITH CORPORATION

Imagine

THE PRINCIPAL FINANCIAL GROUP DEAN FOODS

RALPH LAUREN

WICKES BRITISH AIRWAYS

Marshall Field

CHEVROLET TRANSAMERICA CHAMPION INTERNATIONAL

BRADLEY.

SEARLE

BRADLEY.
A Graphisphere Company

CHRYSLER

BELLSOUTH   BURSON-MARSTELLER   UARCO

Home Office and Plant:

SEARS   AMERICAN EXPRESS

2170 South Mannheim Road

YAMAHA   HILL & KNOWLTON

Des Plaines, Illinois 60018

CARMICHAEL LYNCH   DEAN FOODS

312.635.8000

WILSON   MATERIAL SERVICE CORPORATION   **BALLY**

McDONALD'S   FMC

Bradley is a premier quality,

STANDARD RATE AND DATA   J. WALTER THOMPSON

full-service printer producing

PLAYBOY   CPC INTERNATIONAL

materials for some of the

KEROFF ROSENBERG   MOTOROLA

most prestigious companies

Top Quality Printing for Top Creative Talent

DAI NIPPON

DAI NIPPON PRINTING CO., LTD.
1-1-1 Ichigaya-Kagacho,
Shinjuku-ku, Tokyo 162, Japan.
Telephone: 81.03.266.3307
Telex: J22737 DNPRINT TOKYO

DNP *AMERICA,* **INC.**
New York City 212.686.1919
Chicago 312.571.0150
San Francisco 415.788.1618
Santa Clara 408.988.2582
Los Angeles 213.540.5123

Hong Kong 852.0.4991031

Singapore 65.4697611

Jakarta 4881310

Sydney 61.02.27.1531

Düsseldorf 0211.320206

London 01.734.6621

ARNOLDO MONDADORI EDITORE

HEADQUARTERS
Officine Grafiche Arnoldo Mondadori
Via Mondadori
37121 Verona, Italy

Phone: 011-39-45-93-4111
Telex: 480071
Telefax: 011-39-45-93-4697

PRINTERS OF THE CREATIVE BLACK BOOK

PRINTERS OF EXCELLENCE

NORTH AMERICAN REPRESENTATIVE:
A.M.E. Publishing Ltd.
740 Broadway
New York, NY 10003

Phone: 212-505-7900
Telex: 422218
Telefax: 212-420-9721

PRINTING IS...

Howard Berman ©1985

FINE COLOR LITHOGRAPHY:

POSTERS/CALENDARS
The ability to make your work look as good as it is and result in a finished product that faithfully reproduces the original artwork.

BOOKS/ANNUAL REPORTS
Besides an unsurpassed attention to detail, there is a total understanding of artist and artwork, and an ability to communicate effectively with production personnel.

BROCHURES/DIRECT MAILERS/ INSERTS/COUPONS
Backed by 60 years worth of creative ideas and production methods that assist in achieving client goals while keeping costs down.

© Philip Morris Inc. 1986

DISPLAYS/PROMOTIONAL PACKAGES
Helping the client get full value and by developing a close client relationship we give true meaning to "a custom job." A craft which demands professional pride, excellence and quality.

UNITED LITHOGRAPHING CORPORATION

New Address: 47-47 32nd Place Long Island City, N.Y. 11101

Design by Lynn Mandeau
©ULC 1986

Contact: Steve Bernstein
718-786-8100

LOCATIONS & CASTING

FLORIDA'S THREE STARS ★★★

TODD WARREN
P R O D U C T I O N S

**COMPLETE PRODUCTION COORDINATION
CALIFORNIA • NEW YORK • FLORIDA**

725 MAJORCA AVENUE • CORAL GABLES, FL 33134
TEL. (305) 444-4430 • FAX: (305) 444-1546

★ ★ ★

Locations Extrordinaire
too extrordinary to only be in the background

boca raton, florida   (407) 487-5050

★ ★ ★

PICTURE PERFECT
TRANSPORTATION SERVICES

LOCATION MASTERS, INC. • 1107 HARRISON STREET • HOLLYWOOD, FL 33019

- MOTOR HOME RENTALS
- AIRPORT PICK-UPS AND DROP OFFS
- TRANSPORTATION COORDINATORS
  CAPTAINS AND CO-CAPTAINS
- PROFESSIONAL DRIVERS

TEL 305•920-5042   FAX 305•920-2084

BACKDROPS

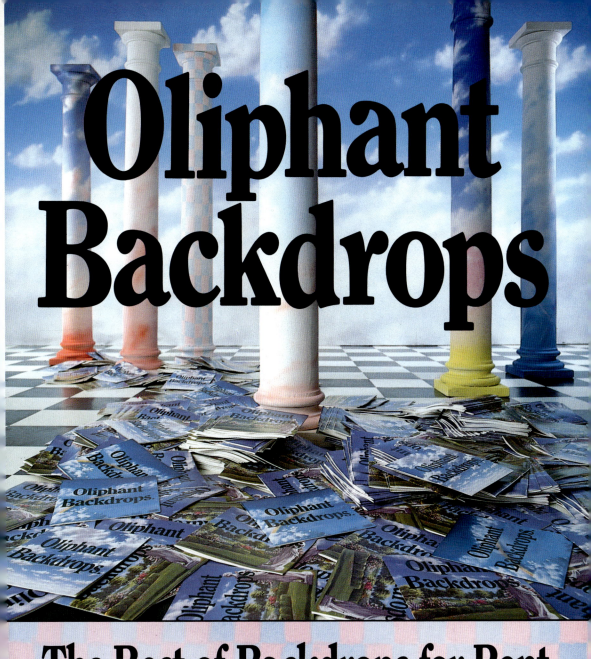

The Best of Backdrops for Rent
212·741·1233

We have a rental stock of over 800 backdrops. Call us for custom-made drops to rent or own.
Slides and 30 page color catalog available on request.

NEW YORK	CHICAGO	LOS ANGELES	BOSTON
212-741-1233	312-421-1212	213-938-2011	617-536-2277

JOHN FORTUNATO

NANCY BROWN

JANET BELLER

KIT DE FEVER

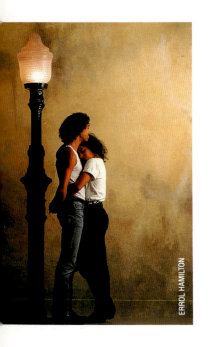
ERROL HAMILTON

HORST

CHARLES BRODERSON INC
873 BROADWAY SUITE 612
NEW YORK CITY 10003
212 - 925 - 9392
REPRESENTED BY CYNTHIA ALTORISO
COLOR CATALOG $5.00

DEBORAH FEINGOLD

DESIGNER/IRENE KUFMAN COSTUME/SUE ABLE

NANCY DE PRA

GREG STEPHENS FOR NEIMAN MARCUS

BORIS/PITTMAN PHOTOGRAPHY

NANCY BROWN

BRODERSON BACKDROPS EST. 1974

A.D. Kevin Creighton

James BRIGHT BACKGROUNDS

FAVORITE BACKGROUNDS OF THE FAMOUS!

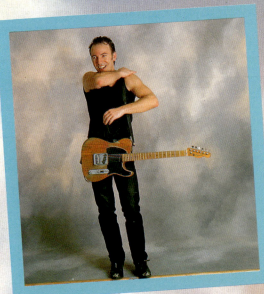

Call for our Color brochure

800-821-5796 Outside CA
213-973-8488 In CA

13535 Crenshaw Blvd., Hawthorne, Ca 90250

Photos by Neal Preston and Merrett Smith

1008

Sandro La Ferla Backdrops

92 Vandam Street   New York, New York 10013   (212) 620-0693

116   10' x 20'   Kiki Bridges

130   10' x 20'   Studio

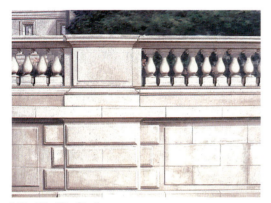

148   10' x 12'   Studio

181   10' x 16'   Dustin Pittman

5   9' x 12'   Bill King

179   12' x 18'   Michel Tcherevkoff

1009

PROPS

BRENT CARPENTER
PROPS FOR PRINT AND FILM · PORTFOLIO AND REEL AVAILABLE
REPRESENTED BY GERI LUKMANN · 314 WEST INSTITUTE PLACE · CHICAGO, IL. 60610 · 312 787 1774

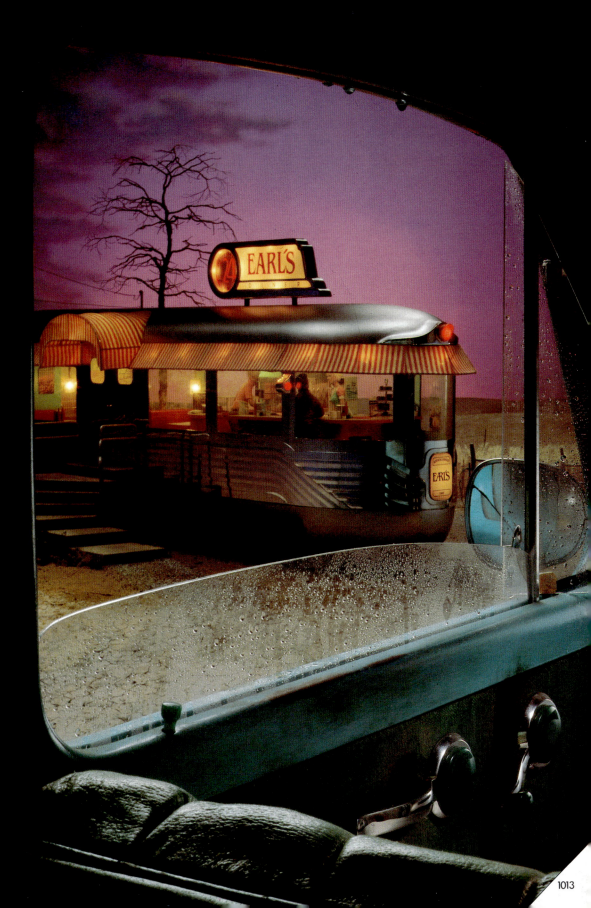

1013

Finneran's Model Shop

Film

FAX 212-979-9841
40 Great Jones Street New York, N.Y. 10012
212-473-6312

Video Reel & Portfolio Available

1015

"I have worked with many expert professionals... Peter Kuhn is by far the best."

JØRN WINTHER, PRODUCER

Your Best Choice For:

- Driving/Stunt Coordination
- Precision Driving
- Stunt Driving
- Racing & High Performance Driving
- Automobile & Race Car Acquisition
- Driving Instruction: Actors

DRIVING INCORPORATED USA

Television ■ Film ■ Print ■ Commercials

Peter Kuhn   201 579 6188

TOM KLEM

The Modelmaker

Scott Clifford Siken, Associate.

85 Leonard Street
NYC 212 431 4059

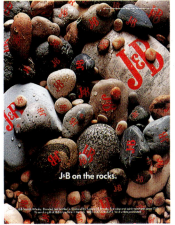
ROY GRACE GRACE & ROTHSCHILD

DAVID RENNING DCA

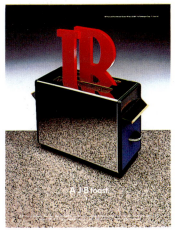
ROY GRACE GRACE & ROTHSCHILD

SUSAN LIPSCHUTZ YOUNG & RUBICAM

CAROL FRANKLIN DDB NEEDHAM WORLDWIDE

RAUL PINA DELLA FEMINA TRAVISANO & PARTNERS

ALL ADVERTISEMENTS PHOTOGRAPHED BY BRUNO PHOTOGRAPHY, INC.

1017

WHAT'S SO SPECIAL AB

He's the best problem-solver in print and film

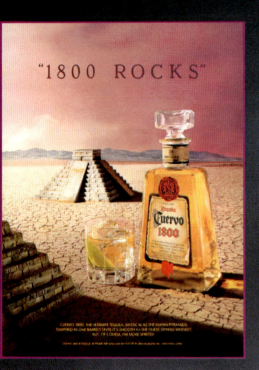

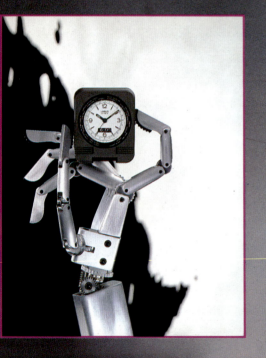

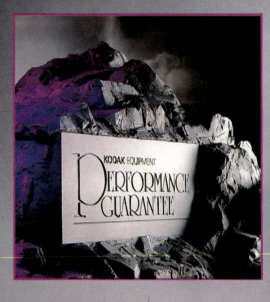

FAX: (212) 620-4281

UT MICHAEL MANIATIS?
(212) 620-0398 Call for samples.

48 West 22nd Street, New York City 10010

Fax or fiction

What *we* see is what *you* get when you fax a layout to The Prop Shop

You get a reliable estimate — not a guesstimate.

We can see exactly what prop, large-scale or mini model or special effect you need to have created, with no misunderstandings — and no messengers.

The Prop Shop, Inc. 26 College Place, Brooklyn Heights, NY 11201

FOR PRINT PORTFOLIO OR REEL CONTACT: **JOHN KUNTZSCH**

718/834.1944

**FILM/VIDEO
PRINT
PROMOTION
CUSTOM PROPS
SPECIAL EFFECTS
RIGGING
CASTING & REPRODU
MECHANICAL EFFECTS**

BROOKLYN MODEL WORKS INC. 60 WASHINGTON AVENUE BROOKLYN, NEW YORK 11205   FAX: 718/596-8934

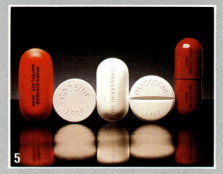
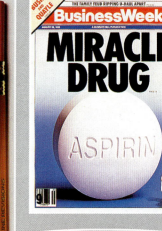

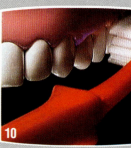

1 Open bottle is suspended in tank and rigged for repeated ejections of colored liquid.
Photographer: Kan
Client: Procter & Gamble
Agency: Saatchi Saatchi DFS Compton

2 Snow capped icicles for a very refreshing billboard.
Photographer: Gary Perweiller
Client: Anhauser Busch
Agency: Backer Spielvogel Bates

3 One of two oversized golf balls with debossed logo. Rotates on predetermined axes.
Production: Charlex*
Client: ESPN

4 Rows of chips rigged to sequentially flip at the wave of the master's hand. Live action. No optical effects. No strings.
Production: Murray Bruce Productions
Client: Milton Bradley

5 Pills, caplets and capsule enlarged.
Photographer: Russel Kirk
Client: Russ Pharmaceuticals
Agency: Brannigan-Demarco Communications

6 Brass pencil with etched type. One of a graduated series.
Photographer: Gary Perweiller
Client: Xerox
Agency: Lowe Marschalk

7 A visual metaphor for shrinking phone rates.
Photographer: Steve Prezant*
Client: SNET
Agency: Marquardt & Roche

8 Don't try to brush your teeth with this paste.
Photographer: Todd Haiman

9 Generic aspirin for cover story. Actual size 3" diameter.
Photographer: Ted Morrison
Client: Business Week Magazine

EXHIBITIONS & DISPLAYS
PROTOTYPES
ELECTRONIC EFFECTS
ARCHITECTURAL MODELS
MINIATURES
LOGO FORMATS
SETS
COSTUMES/PUPPETS

BROOKLYN MODEL WORKS

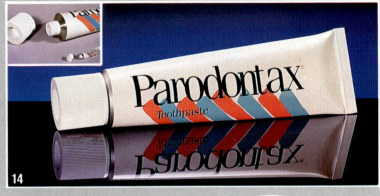

Lifesize model to show hard to "Reach" places.
Production: Exit Films
Client: Johnson & Johnson
Agency: Cadwell Davis Partners

Computer connector enlarged 1200%
Photographer: Joseph Mulligan/Philadelphia
Client: AMP
Agency: Lewis, Gilman & Kynett, Inc.

Tiny industrial baking equipment for "Time to Make the Donuts . . . *Cereal*" spot.
Production: Ulick Mayo Productions
Client: Ralston Purrina/Dunkin Donuts

13 Lift-off to a Rock Video.
Production: Eyeballs, Inc./California
Client: The Cars

14 Squeeze this! Big tube with threaded cap. Inset shows scale.
Photographer: Gordon Myhre/Florida
Agency: Altman & Co.

15 Big vacuformed capsule.
Photographer: Dennis Blachert*
Client: Time Magazine
Agency: Y&R

16 Breaking the ice with a Frosty.
Photographer: Lyn St. John
Client: Wendy's International
Agency: Backer Spielvogel Bates/Ohio

17 Translucent hemisphere.
Photographer: Cailor Resnick Studio
Client: IBM
Agency: Lord, Geller, Federico, Einstein

18 Tablets with logo relief.
Photographer: Cailor Resnick Studio
Client: Mellon Bank

All of the above are unretouched photos.

*The photo used here was shot in our studio by Sarah Van Ouwerkerk

❹ ❿ Image reproduced directly from video tape.

1023

LIVE ACTION

The only stock worth watching.

THE IMAGE BANK®

HEADQUARTERS
111 Fifth Avenue, New York City 10003
(212) 529-6700 Telex: 429380 IMAGE
Fax: (212) 529-8886

FILM SEARCH®
AN **IMAGE BANK** COMPANY
REPRESENTING
CINEMATOGRAPHERS & FILM COLLECTIONS

232 Madison Avenue, New York City 10016
(212) 532-0600 Telex: 4973657 FILMS Fax: (212) 779-9732

8228 Sunset Boulevard, #310, Los Angeles, CA 90046
(213) 656-9003

Scene from the Motion Picture *Koyaanisqatsi*

TIB, THE IMAGE BANK, TIB THE IMAGE BANK and FILM SEARCH
are Trademarks of THE IMAGE BANK, INC.   © 1988 The Image Bank, Inc.

CALL DIRECTING ARTISTS IN NEW YORK AT 212-995-0550,

S ANGELES AT 213-828-2332, AND IN CHICAGO AT 312-527-0888.

CALL DIRECTING ARTISTS IN NEW YORK AT 212-995-0550,

BILL WHITE
PRODUCTIONS

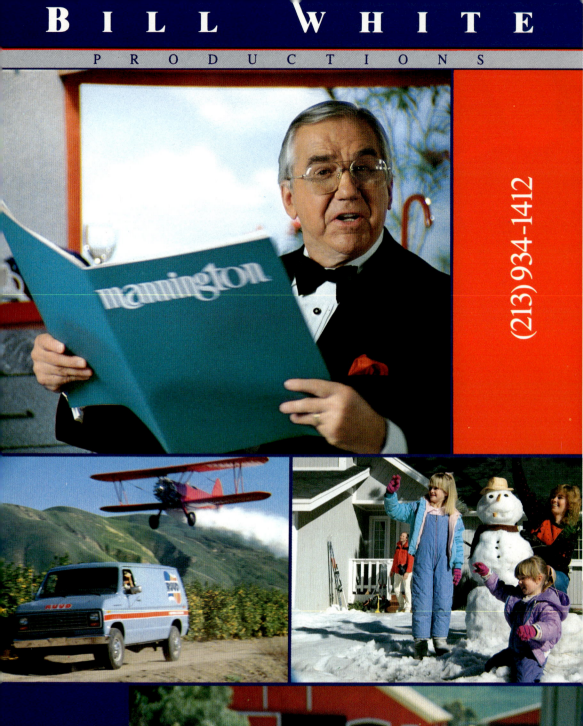

(213) 934-1412

5907 West Pico Boulevard
Los Angeles, California 90035

Get rid of unsightly, embarrassing spots in just ten minutes.

Okay, let's face it. Everybody knows
the awful feeling of showing a commercial
that hasn't turned out quite right.
But it's a feeling nobody should have to experience.
Just call for our reel. And in the short time
it takes to watch it, you'll see that we definitely
know how to keep a good idea
from becoming a blemish on your career.

TORONTO	NEW YORK	CHICAGO	DALLAS
593·5969	691·7711	372·6633	559·3640

BILL HUDSON + ASSOCIATES N.Y. (212) 679-7199 & L.A. (213) 467-7379 PRESIDENT: Roberto Cecchini

People you'd like t

Innovative Graphi

And food you can

Or any combinatio

know...

s.

ste.

WE LOVE OUR WORK...
AND IT SHOWS

RICHARD FOSTER
SHOOTS FILM AT 157 WEST ONTARIO, CHICAGO, ILLINOIS 60610.
CALL DEBORAH McMASTERS, EXECUTIVE PRODUCER AT (312) 943-9005.

© Copyright 1988, RICHARD FOSTER STUDIOS.

OH, HI! — WE'RE STILL RUNNING THE CARTOONS IN BACKSTAGE & SCREEN, BUT HERE WE THOUGHT YOU'D LIKE TO CONCRETELY SEE A LITTLE OF WHAT WE DO — GREAT FOOD & PEOPLE. IN FACT — IF YOU WANT THAT UNIQUE LOOK, AND YOU'VE GOT A FOOD & PEOPLE BOARD WHERE BOTH HAVE TO LOOK GREAT — CALL US.

BIG CITY PRODUCTION QUALITY, SMALL TOWN COSTS.

106 E. Cary Street, Richmond, Virginia 23219
(just south of New York and east of L.A.)
804-343-1934
Donald Silverman, Director
Television Commercials & Corporate Videos.
1988 *Silver Awards*, Houston Int'l Film Festival & Telly Awards.

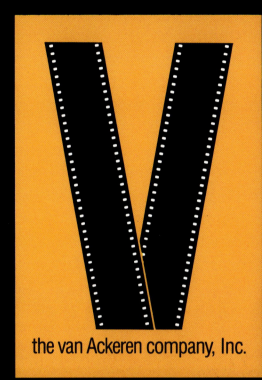

the van Ackeren company, Inc.
220 Minor Avenue North
Seattle, WA 98109
(206) 625-1000

Chicago Rep:
Jim Hill
(312) 866-6440

Directors:
Michael van Ackeren
Chuck Kuhn
Cliff Bole

In dialogue, visual storytelling, tabletop/food and special effects, we have players with impressive personal stats. And strong individual reels.

And the ability to collaborate.

Not only with agency art directors, copywriters and producers, but sometimes with each other. Because sometimes a spot with particularly sensitive dialogue also needs mouth-watering food. Sometimes the state-of-the-art special effect buttons a series of people-driven vignettes.

Sometimes, one director isn't enough.

We have four heavy hitters, an executive producer with a pragmatic view of today's business climate, and an approach to production that can be summed up in one word:

TEAMWORK

REID PAUL
Director, Special Effects

CURTIS KULP
Director, Tabletop/Food

GARY FLEDER
Director, Live Action

BRAD BATE
Director, Live Action

Productions, Inc.

111 E. Chestnut Street ▪ Suite 42B ▪ Chicago, Illinois 60611 ▪ (312) 440-1430

DIRECTORS

SCOTT MILLER   JIM GIDDENS   DAN HAINEY
COLIN CHILVERS   PETER HEATH

NEW YORK EXECUTIVE PRODUCER—*JEFF DEVLIN* SALES REPRESENTATIVE—*KATHY RUBIN*
130 EAST 62ND ST. NYC, NY. 10021. (212) 832-2288

LOS ANGELES EXECUTIVE PRODUCER—*SKIP SHORT* EXECUTIVE PRODUCER—*ROBIN BENSON*
7025 SANTA MONICA BLVD. HOLLYWOOD CA. (213) 856-4848

CHICAGO *JACK GUNNE*

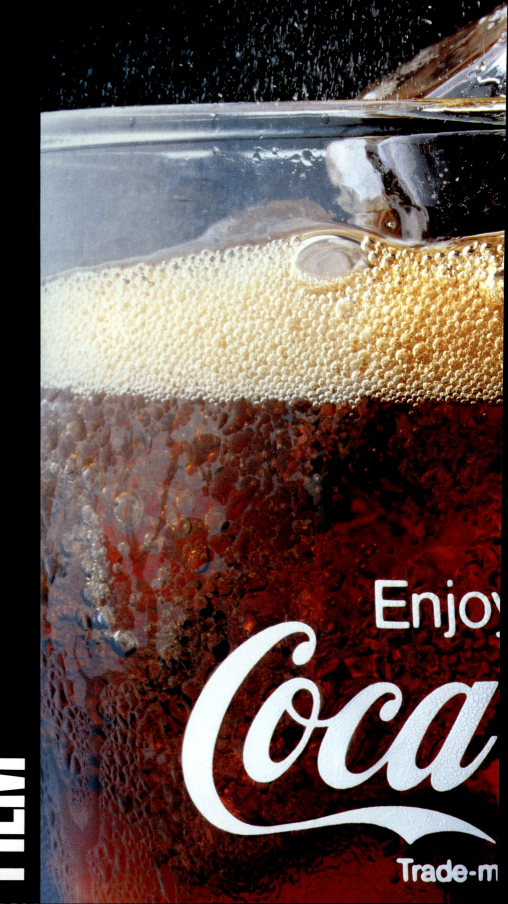

HEFFERNAN

415.626.1999

PRINT

HEFFERNAN

415.626.1999

WHY MADISON AVE. IS MOVING TO MAIN STREET.

To find a multi-faceted Director with a cinematographer's eye, a composer's ear and a gift for working with people. A relaxed atmosphere. Skilled support crews and fresh talent. Every imaginable location — mountains, beaches, urban, rural, historic — within a 90-mile radius. Cost-effectiveness. And a refreshing change of pace. From L.A. to the Big Apple, it's all happening on Main Street.

Continental Cablevision
Richmond: Still Making History

Lewis Advertising
Hardee's Food System

The Martin Agency
SCAN

Sentara Health Services
Norfolk General Hospital

Main Street Productions
Corporate and Broadcast Production
1300 West Main Street
Richmond, Virginia 23220
804-359-3937

SHOOT FOR THE STARS.

WE HAVE MORE THAN 50 STARS FROM ALL OVER THE WORLD. DIRECTORS AND CINEMATOGRAPHERS WHO HAVE WON EVERYTHING FROM CLIOS TO EMMYS TO ACADEMY AWARDS.

OFFICES AND AFFILIATES IN: NEW YORK, TORONTO, BALTIMORE, AUSTRALIA, LOS ANGELES AND LONDON.

CONTACT: DENNIS LOONAN
KAREN DOUGLASS

9 EAST 47TH STREET, N.Y., N.Y. 10017 (212) 888-8999 FAX (212) 888-9161

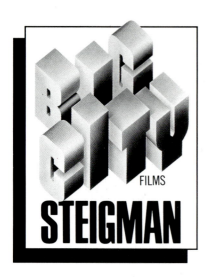

DRISTAN "HOW FAST IT IS"/MCCANN-ERICKSON

ROY ROGERS "LUNCHEON LADIES"/EARLE PALMER BROWN

**HUMOR,
PEOPLE,
SPECIAL EFFECTS**

STEVE STEIGMAN
435 W. 19TH ST. NYC 10011
(212) 627-3400
(212) 633-1228 FAX
REPRESENTED BY
EAST
CHARLES BYRNES
ELEANOR ZIMMER
WEST
COBB & FRIEND

**FOR REEL CALL
(212) 627-3400**

FLORIDA POWER & LIGHT "GUMSHOE"/HUME & SINDELAR ASSOCIATES

PACE FOODS "DRIVE IN" /BJK&E DALLAS

ROY ROGERS "DINGHY"/EARLE PALMER BROWN

TOTAL "DINER"/SAATCHI SAATCHI/DFS/COMPTON

WORLD GOLD COUNCIL "LOFT"/GEER, DUBOIS

MANDEE "BEHIND THE SCENES"/BERENTER, GREENHOUSE & WEBSTER

**CONTEMPORARY,
FASHION/STYLE,
DIALOGUE**

RON LEYSER
435 W. 19TH ST. NYC 10011
(212) 627-3400
(212) 633-1228 FAX
REPRESENTED BY
EAST
CHARLES BYRNES
ELEANOR ZIMMER
WEST
COBB & FRIEND

**FOR REEL CALL
(212) 627-3400**

MANDEE "OH, MANDEE!"/BERENTER, GREENHOUSE & WEBSTER

LIGHT-N-LIVELY "SKI TEAM"/GEERS GROSS

WORLD GOLD COUNCIL "INITIAL IMPRESSIONS"/GEER, DUBOIS

AMSOUTH BANCOR CORP "HEALTH CLUB"/LAWLER BALLARD

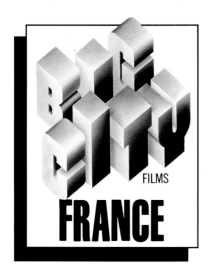

VIRGINIA LITTER CONTROL/"LITTER IN THE AISLES"

SOVRAN BANK/"ENTREPRENEUR"

**SUBTLE HUMOR,
SITUATION DIALOGUE**

JEFF FRANCE
435 W. 19TH ST. NYC 10011
(212) 627-3400
(212) 633-1228 FAX
REPRESENTED BY
EAST
CHARLES BYRNES
ELEANOR ZIMMER
WEST
COBB & FRIEND

**FOR REEL CALL
(212) 627-3400**

ALCOHOLIC BEVERAGE CONTROL/"VIRGINIA '21"

SOVRAN BANK/"RETIREMENT"

SOVRAN BANK/"PARTY"

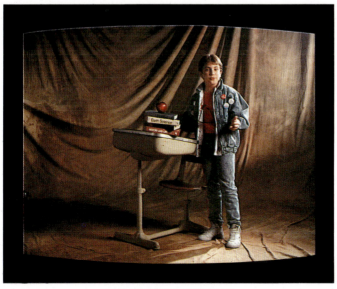

BUSCH GARDENS/"BIG 8'S OR BACON"

ANIMATION

:30 animated spot
**Prospect Associates
The National Cancer Institute**

:10 animated spot
**MTV
Station ID**

:30 animated spot
**JWT/Chicago
Northern Trust Banks**

For our latest sample reel call J. J. Sedelmaier at (212) 869-1630

Kurtz and Friends
A N I M A T I O N

L. A. • 2312 W. OLIVE AVE. • BURBANK, CA • 91506 • (818) 841-8188

NEW YORK • (212) 989-3535 • THE BLOCK FILM GROUP

CHICAGO • (312) 951-7404 • AIKO

CALL US, NOW!

OR THE PUPPY GETS IT!

Please, call or write for the demo reel. Don't make us do anything drastic.

RYAN & FRIENDS Animation
4740 'A' McPherson Ave.
St. Louis, Mo. 63108   (314) 361-2526

—DISCLAIMER—

Ryan & Friends Animation does not advocate gratuitous cartoon violence except when it is done tastefully, or in order to advance the plot, or in cases where the character's head is clobbered by a frying pan and he runs around with a pan-shaped head, or when a character is given a "hot foot" and burns to a crisp, then comes back later like nothing happened, or...

WHAT'S HOT & SWEET AND WEARS YELLOW & WHITE STRIPES?

AMERICAN AIRLINES

XEROX CORP.

MTV NETWORKS

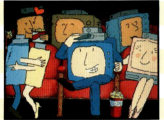
THE MOVIE CHANNEL

MTV NETWORKS

NATIONAL SCIENCE FOUNDATION

DIAPERENE BABY WASHCLOTHS

CTW/SESAME STREET

USA NETWORK

HANES HOSIERY

THE BUDGET GOURMET

CBS/TEEN WOLF

BUZZCO ASSOCIATES
110 West 40th Street, New York, NY 10018

Candy Kugel   (212) 840-0411   Vincent Cafarelli

ASK TO SEE OUR SHORT FILM—
"A WARM RECEPTION IN L.A."
ASIFA-East WINNER—BEST DESIGN (1988)
ACQUIRED BY THE MUSEUM OF MODERN ART FILM ARCHIVE

© 1987 BUZZCO ASSOCIATES, INC.

Presenting His
Dazzling Array
of Visual Feats!

His Award-Winning
**CEL & CLAY ANIMATION,
MOTION GRAPHICS &
COMBINED LIVE-ACTION/ANIMATION**
Have Captivated Audiences
Worldwide.

Call for a Sample Reel.
THE GREAT LIEBERMAN
Will Amaze You!

JERRY LIEBERMAN

PRODUCTIONS INC.

76 Laight Street
New York, NY 10013
212.431.3452
Fax: 212.941.8976

Kinetics

444 N. Wabash Ave., Chicago, Illinois 60611   312-644-2767

THE POST MODERN NEO-TRADITIONALISTS!

CREATING ANIMATION AND SPECIAL EFFECTS ON FILM FOR PEOPLE WHO APPRECIATE THE DIFFERENCE.

SEE THE REEL... GET THE PICTURE!

HURRY!

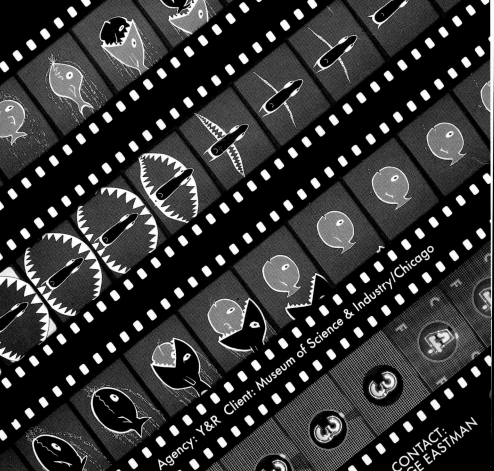

Agency: Y&R Client: Museum of Science & Industry/Chicago

CONTACT: GEORGE EASTMAN

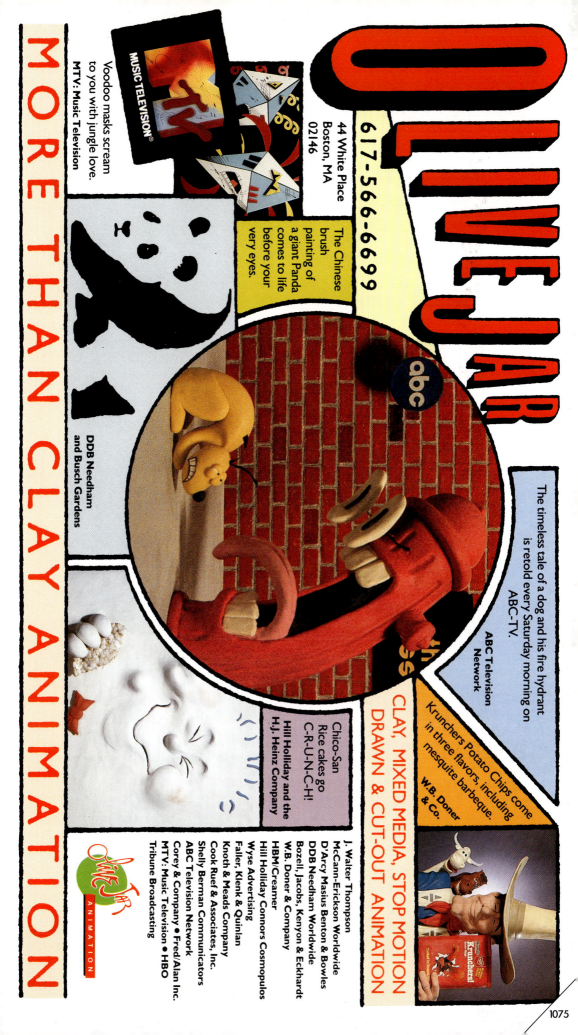

R&H presents

ABC MOVIE OF THE WEEK/GEM/F&C

SUNBEAM EXPRESSMeals/Chiat Day

7-UP/Leo Burnett

PAINE WEBBER/SSDFSC

KWHY LOGO/Telezign

R&H INC.

SPECIAL EFFECTS
COMPUTER ANIMATION
LIVE ACTION INTEGRATION

East Coast/ANN WARREN 212•877•5403
Midwest/CHET NICHOLS 312•527•4440
West Coast/SHIRLEY SCHACKMANN 213•938•3645
Canada/CYNTHIA TAYLOR 416•966•3500

KATHRYN RICCIO/EXECUTIVE PRODUCER
213•851•6500   910 N. SYCAMORE DR., HOLLYWOOD, CA 90038

Rhythm & Hues INC.

Vice Versa—Columbia Pictures

ENERGY PRODUCTIONS

SIGHTS UNSEEN

Baskin-Robbins—J. Walter Thompson

Commodore Amiga 500—Griffin Bacal

ENERGY PRODUCTIONS
2690 Beachwood Drive
Los Angeles, California 90068
213 462-3310   FAX 213 871-2763
Director Louis Schwartzberg

New York
Chicago
Atlanta
Tokyo

KIMMELMAN ANIMATION

MEMBER AICP

A DIVISION OF KCMP PRODUCTIONS

BURGER KING—N.W. AYER INC.

NEW YORK TELEPHONE—YOUNG & RUBICAM

MULTI-CAT—MONTGOMERY & ASSOC.

CALGON—GREY ADVERTISING

KCMP PRODUCTIONS, 50 W. 40TH ST., NEW YORK, NY 10011 (212) 944-7766
PHIL KIMMELMAN, ANIMATION DIRECTOR
CONTACT: JORDAN CALDWELL, DOTTY KIMMELMAN

KCMP PRODUCTIONS LTD.
LIVE & ANIMATION

Ovation Films, Inc., 15 West 26th Street, New York City 10010
To see Ovation's latest reel, call 212-686-4540
Art Petricone

Harold Friedman Consortium

**Designers/Directors
Full Production/Live Action
Cel/Clay/Computer Animation
Video Graphics/Special Effects
Stop Motion - Models - Motion Control**

John Allison
Ken Brown
Peter Conn
Fred Crippen
Sally Cruikshank
Gabor Csupo
David Denneen
Terry Gilliam
Milton Glaser
Bill Groshelle

David Jackson
Arlene Klasky
Steve Levitt
Bernard Lodge
Tony McVey
Keith Robinson
Lee Savage
Jill Taffet
Fred Vanderpoel

Harold Friedman Consortium Ltd.
420 Lexington Ave. New York, NY 10017
Tel. 212-697-0858
FAX. 212-983-5466
Producers: Harold Friedman, Kurt Teske

West Coast: 1350 West Washington Blvd.
Venice, CA 90291 Tel. 213-821-0100
FAX. 213-396-9720
Producer: D. Rufus Friedman

Another fine job Buzz… how do the words "vice-president" grab you?

"Just think, three months ago I was in the mailroom."

Go ahead, take all the credit. We don't mind. Even if the biggest contribution you made was what to order for lunch.

Because at No Soap, we have all the experience you'll ever need. For 19 years we've been creating and directing radio commercials and music tracks that have helped our clients win just about every creative award in the business.

More recently, our expertise in sound design has made television a medium worth listening to. And our newest venture, Voicecasting, will help you pull in the perfect voice every time.

So take a few moments and call (212) 581-5572 for a copy of No Soap's reel.

With a little luck your boss will think you're a genius.

NO SOAP PRODUCTIONS

161 WEST 54TH STREET, NEW YORK CITY, NY 10019 • (212) 581-5572

CLIENTS INCLUDE: AT&T, BURGER KING, BANK OF BOSTON, BRITISH STERLING, CHASE MANHATTAN, DIET PEPSI, GOODYEAR, KODAK, MIDAS, PAN AM, PIZZA HUT, POLAROID, OCEAN SPRAY, SUNOCO, TETLEY TEA.

TULLIO & RANS
THE REAL STUFF

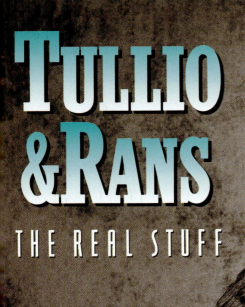

OLD **S**TYLE
HEARTLAND
CAMPAIGN

LOWENBRAU
LION'S BREW
CAMPAIGN

NO **N**ONSENSE
THE ATTITUDE FITS
CAMPAIGN

LONG **J**OHN **S**ILVER'S
WE WANT TO SEA YOU HAPPY
CAMPAIGN

DESIGN ROBERT HORN DESIGN ENSEMBLE PHOTOGRAPHY MARC HAUSER

TULLIO
& RANS
TWO MUSIC
GUYS

405 NORTH WABASH AVENUE
CHICAGO ILLINOIS 6 0 6 1 1
312 744 0197

1086

Buick, Cadillac, Chevrolet, Coca-Cola,
Coke International, Coors, Coors Light, Dodge,
Eveready, Emerson, Fanta, Ford Dealers, GTE, General Foods,
Goodyear, Hasbro, Kelloggs, Milton Bradley,
Pabst Blue Ribbon, Playschool, Procter & Gamble, Pontiac,
RC Cola, Southwestern Bell, Stride Rite, Zest, . . .

EASY-WRITER MUSIC INC.

433 EAST 51ST STREET
NEW YORK, NEW YORK 10022
212 · 758 · 6555

RICK BRENCKMAN   RED NIENKIRCHEN   LORI BETHE   RICHARD GREEN

Make the world whistle your tune.

Here are a few of the tunes we've produced in the past few years.

Original Vocals

Gotta Jump to The Trump Plaza
You Deserve a Break Today. At McDonald's.
The Bahamas
Like a Good Neighbor, State Farm is There
Head for the Mountains. Head for Busch Beer.
Mutual of Omaha is People
Take Life a Little Easier. At Jack-In-The-Box.
Kinney, the Great American Shoe Store
Bally's
Nobody Cares for Eyes More Than Pearle
There's a Difference at McDonald's
Miller Lite. Everything You Always Wanted in a Beer. And Less.
Crystal Light. Because I Believe in Me.
Texaco. Star Power for Car Power
What Keeps Amnerica Coming Back. Eagle Snacks.
For Once in a Lifetime, Get into this World. With Pan Am.
At McDonald's, We've Got Time for You.
Kentucky Fried Chicken. We Do Chicken Right.
Home Cookin', a Taste So Close To Home. From Campbell's Soup.

Original Instrumentals

Siemens
The Marines Are Looking For A Few Good Men
Emery Air Freight
The Secret of a Partagas Cigar
Come to Think of It, I'll Have a Heineken
Post Raisin Bran
Macanudo, the Ultimate Cigar
Rolls-Royce, the Heart and Soul of a Masterpiece
Blue Diamond Almonds

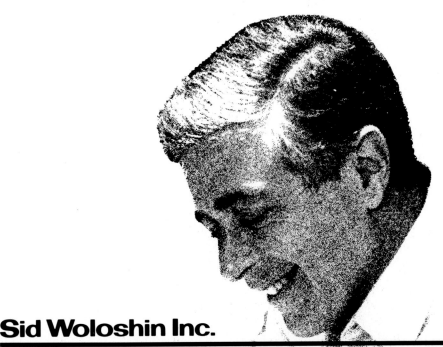

Sid Woloshin Inc.

95 Madison Avenue, New York, NY 10016
(212) 684-7222

MZH&F

Miller Lite
Phillips 66
Sunkist
ABC Sports
Duncan Hines
Maybelline
Stouffers
USA Today
L'air du Temps
N.Y. Post

THE NEW MUSIC COMPANY

WITH 28 YEARS OF EXPERIENCE

David Forrest
Billy Seidman & Co.

12 West 37th Street
New York City 10018
Tel. 212-594-2600

Represented By Patty Forbes

Home of MARATHON Recording Studios

WHEN THE MUSIC REALLY MATTERS

joy art

A MUSIC PRODUCTION COMPANY

CONTACT VICTORIA MARÍ 312 / 944-2310
299 EAST ONTARIO STREET / CHICAGO, IL 60611

CLIENTS INCLUDE: McDONALDS · COCA-COLA · SPUDS MACKENZIE · FORD · STROH BREWERY · ENERGIZER · FISHER PRICE · COORS · KRAFT · TENNIS OLYMPICS-CANADA · NCAA BASKETBALL PLAYOFF THEME · NFL FOOTBALL & TENNIS OPEN THEME · HYUNDAI · CALIFORNIA STATE LOTTERY · SPRITE · SHOWTIME CABLE · CBN

HONOR ROLL: CLIO/CEBA/US TELEVISION COMMERCIALS FESTIVAL · INTERNATIONAL RADIO AWARDS OF NEW YORK · INTERNATIONAL TELEVISION & FILM FESTIVAL OF NEW YORK · HOLLYWOOD RADIO AND TELEVISION AWARDS · INTERNATIONAL BROADCASTING AWARDS · WINDY AWARDS

CELEBRITIES: ASHFORD & SIMPSON · ARETHA FRANKLIN · JANIE FRICKE · RICHIE HAVENS · LENA HORNE · AL JARREAU · RAMSEY LEWIS · NEW EDITION · KENNY ROGERS · GRACE SLICK · MAURICE WHITE · NANCY WILSON · EARTH, WIND & FIRE · AND MANY MORE

ARMY   KODAK   TEXACO   NOXZEMA   ARMSTRONG   DOG CHOW   BUTTERFINGER

Look & Co.

170 FIFTH AVENUE NEW YORK 10010   ☎ 212.627.3500   JEANNE NEARY

TOO MANY NOTES

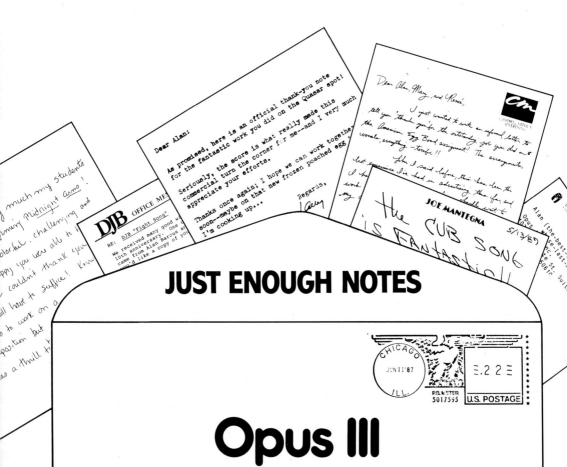

JUST ENOUGH NOTES

Opus III

1030 N. STATE ST. 60610   312-664-7334
PRODUCERS OF CELEBRATED MUSIC